ENTERPRISING AGRICULTURE

AF795599

NIPA® GENX ELECTRONIC RESOURCES & SOLUTIONS P. LTD.
New Delhi-110 034

About the Editors

Dr. Sharmistha Banerjee is a Professor of Business Management at the University of Calcutta. Her research areas include Small Business Management, Microfinance and Entrepreneurship, Human Resource Management, OB, Public Policy. She has been engaged in several US fellowships and US India and UK India collaborative interdisciplinary research projects. Dr. Banerjee has taught across the globe in, Bangladesh, South Korea and Japan and has travelled extensively for short academic interactions. She has used her global learnings on entrepreneurship and business education for initiating the seeds of entrepreneurship in different fields, agriculture being one of them. Additionally her interest in social entrepreneurship makes valuable contribution to this book.

Dr. Mohua Banerjee is a Professor of Marketing & Dean Placements, Corporate &Alumni Relations at International Management Institute Kolkata. She teaches courses in marketing specialization in Kolkata over the last twelve years, and has taught courses on digital marketing and consumer behaviour in Universities in France. Mohua has consulted in the telecom sector and has conducted practice-oriented retail research with Oxford Institute of Retail Management, University of Oxford. Her research work includes mapping the retail supply chain management practices from a business intelligence perspective, and scale development and validation for measuring non-coercive influence on upstream channel partners in the retail supply chain management context. Her current

Dr. Suneel Kunamaneni stands at the forefront of sustainability and inclusivity trend: packaging, agri-food and social care. He has spent the past five years evangelizing social and eco innovation and entrepreneurship through his various teaching, mentoring, research and consultancy activities. Suneel drives innovation ecosystems for developing and diffusing ideas and solutions to address pressing socio-environmental problems. A calculated risk taker with deep technical knowledge of materials, Suneel has championed commercialisation of eco materials and technologies with both MNCs and startups, and has built a reputation for developing new business strategies and incubating new business models that minimise the impact on the environment. In his current role as an academic, Suneel has also fed his insatiable interest in sustainable innovation in emerging countries and inclusive growth. His interest in emerging countries is rooted in his concerns that current western growth based business models cannot solve issues surrounding the environment, and affordable access to food and well-being. Suneel also advises social enterprises in the UK working on refugee entrepreneurship and mental health for the BAME community, thus facilitating the inclusion of marginalised communities. Suneel holds a bachelors in Chemical Engineering from Bangalore University, a masters in Chemical engineering from Indian Institute of Science, a PhD in Polymer physics from University of Leeds, and an MBA from Alliance Manchester Business School.

Dr. Alfred Chinta is a Course Director of MBA Apprenticeship Programmes at Leeds Business School, UK. He has worked with automobile industry in India and Aerospace industry in UK in areas of production and supply chain management. His work spans the role of technology usage in supply chains to enhance the effectiveness of organisations. He has deep knowledge of productions hubs in South-east Asia and Sub-Saharan Africa where he has taught over the last 15 years. His current work looks at Green Supply chains, the role of new technology to enhance environmental performance, socially inclusive supply chains and usage

www.nipaers.com
Browse, Search, Read & Buy...
Print Books
eChapters
eBooks
Publishers
Forthcoming
Subject Catalogues
New Titles
Online Resources on:
✓ Current Affairs
✓ Reasoning, Logic & Aptitude
✓ Competitive Examinations
✓ English Language Lab
✓ Writing & Pronunciation Tools
✓ Personality Development
✓ Online Programmes for Professionals
✓ Interview Preparation
Pay Using
PhonePe
Google Pay
paytm
PayPal
UPI
CCAvenue

ENTERPRISING AGRICULTURE

Market Awareness, Farm Innovation & Value Addition

Editors

Sharmistha Banerjee

Professor, Department of Business Management
University of Calcutta, West Bengal, India

Mohua Banerjee

Professor - Marketing
Dean - Placements, Corporate & Alumni Relations
International Management Institute, Kolkata, West Bengal, India

Suneel Kunamaneni

Senior Lecturer in Innovation Management
Senior Consultant, The Retail Institute
Course Leader, M.Sc. Entrepreneurship and Business Development
Leeds Beckett University, United Kingdom (UK)

Alfred Chinta

Course Director - MBA Programmes
Leeds Business School
Leeds Beckett University, United Kingdom (UK)

nipa®

NIPA® GENX ELECTRONIC RESOURCES & SOLUTIONS P. LTD.

NIPA® GENX ELECTRONIC
RESOURCES & SOLUTIONS P. LTD.

101,103, Vikas Surya Plaza, CU Block
L.S.C. Market, Pitam Pura, New Delhi-110 034
Ph : +91 11 27341616, 27341717, 27341718
E-mail: newindiapublishingagency@gmail.com
www: www.nipabooks.com

For customer assistance, please contact
Phone: + 91-11-27 34 17 17
Fax: + 91-11- 27 34 16 16
E-Mail: feedbacks@nipabooks.com

© 2023, Publisher

ISBN: 978-81-19103-48-5

All rights reserved. No part of this publication may be reproduced, stored in a retrieval system or transmitted in any form or by any means, including electronic, mechanical, photocopying recording or otherwise without the prior written permission of the publisher or the copyright holder.

This book contains information obtained from authentic and highly reliable sources. Reasonable efforts have been made to publish reliable data and information, but the author/s, editor/s and publisher cannot assume responsibility for the validity, accuracy or completeness of all materials or information published herein or the consequences of their use. The work is published with the understanding that the publisher and author/s are not attempting to render any professional services. The author/s, editor/s and publisher have attempted to trace and acknowledge the copyright holders of all material reproduced in this publication and apologize to copyright holders if permission and/or acknowledgements to publish in this form have not been taken. If any copyrighted material has not been acknowledged, please write to us and let us know so that we may rectify the error, in subsequent reprints.

Trademark Notice: NIPA®, the NIPA® logos and their presentations (the way they are written/presented) in this book are the trademarks of the publisher and hence may not be used without written permission, if copied or used without authorization, the infringer will be prosecuted as per law.

NIPA® also publishes books in a variety of electronic formats. Some content that appears in print may not be available in electronic books, and vice versa.

Foreword

Agriculture is a state subject, i.e. it forms a part of the state list of Indian Constitution, which essentially means that the State Governments are supposed to address all the issues related to agriculture. This is based on the fact that the local knowledge of each agro-climatic zones and cropping patterns, and regional uniqueness give rise to various geography-specific agricultural issues, which are best addressed by the State Governments. However, over the years, Indian agriculture scenario has definitely evolved and demands more attention from the State as well as the Central government.

The modern day challenges relating to farmers in each region move beyond extreme weather conditions like too much rain or no rain, drought, vagaries of nature, and include ever-increasing price of fertilizers and pesticides, exorbitant interest rates of moneylenders, the pressure from the banks to repay the loan, global food crop and dietary changes. On the other hand, trade and commerce, import and export and banking are in the union list. So the Union and the State Governments have passed several laws relating to agriculture and allied areas like export of agricultural produce, import of seeds, fertilisers, etc. Over the years, agriculture has been influenced by international agreements and legal regulations.

Considering India is also a signatory to several international treaties and the division of power between the Centre and the State is not likely to stand in the way while implementing such commitments. As agriculture has been debated in the trade talks (WTO and in many other multilateral forums) where the Union Government participates, it may be considered that the country as a whole may be represented and the diversity be included in the comprehensive decisions.

Agriculture is no more a simple way of life, employing more than 30% of the country's workforce; contributing about 15 % to India's GDP and it also brings in foreign exchange of 35 Billion USD. Thus engagement of farmers cannot be comparative analysis of India and UK", and I applaud UGC and BCL for supporting this joint research project under the aegis of UK-India Education and Research Initiative (UKIERI). The encouragement of the farming community into entrepreneurial business is one of the most important ways of developing the rural youth of India. The Government has been reorienting the agriculture sector by focusing on an income-centeredness which goes beyond achieving merely the targeted production. The income approach focuses on achieving high productivity, reduced cost of cultivation and remunerative price on the produce, with a view to earn higher profits from farming.

Keeping this in mind, the States are encouraged to participate in an Index i.e. Ease of Doing Agri-Business. The concept is to consider farming not solely as a production-oriented activity carried out to achieve food security for the country, but as a business activity carried out by the farmer as an entrepreneur. The proposed index has taken the aspects of increasing production/productivity, increasing price realisation of agri produce and decreasing input costs of production, risk mitigation and investment related attributes. Apart from this, Agrinnovate India Limited, a Government of India Enterprise is making efforts on "Agriprenuership - making business easy". The various issues related to technology acquisition, IP management, fund raising and attracting the enthusiastic entrepreneurs and start-ups for providing the panorama of technology-based opportunities existing in the agricultural sector, panning crops, horticulture, dairy, fisheries, animal husbandry, agricultural engineering and biotechnology are also the focus of the Central Government. In an attempt to promote innovation and entrepreneurship in agriculture, the Government is launching a new AGRI-UDAAN programme that will mentor start-ups and help them connect with potential investors. Managed by India's premier farm research body, the Indian Council of Agricultural Research (ICAR), the food and agri-business accelerator programme is being launched to convert innovative ideas from India's rural youth into viable businesses.

Indian entrepreneurs are developing new technologies and business models to meet this challenge. In 2018, the country had nearly 500 agricultural start-ups. In the past five years alone, these start-ups raised nearly $130 million from investors in about 70 deals. But they need much more investment and support to fulfil their potential. Supply chains for perishable commodities such as fruits and vegetables and non-perishables such as wheat and rice remain largely fragmented in India, with smallholder farmers earning low margins. Unpredictable demand, price volatility and post-harvest losses compound the

At this juncture I find this book to be a noble effort to bridge the gap between academic research on agriculture, and innovative practices that will attract the youth from agricultural communities and others with an interest in this high potential sector and train them so they can add value to the farmers' produce. Such a collection of articles which combines knowledge based pieces, innovative case studies and exploratory research will encourage start-up revolution in agriculture which so far has been limited to the services sector. The different articles in this book focus on modernising Indian agriculture which will require nothing less than a step change in key elements of the sector: supply chains and markets; production support; and credit and crop insurance.

-Sd-

10th July, 2019

Somesh Bhattacharya
(Department of Agriculture, West Bengal)

Contents

Part-II: Government Policies and Interventions in Entrepreneurship

Part-III: Farmers' Development and Welfare through Agriculture

List of Contributors

Abhik Mukherjee
Assistant Professor, University of Burdwan, India

Alokananda Bhattacharya
Independent Researcher, India

Alfred Chinta
Course Director- MBA Programs, Leeds Business School, UK

Amitava Roy
Assistant Professor, St. Xaviers College (Autonomous), Kolkata

Ananda Mohan Pal
Professor, University of Calcutta, India

Anisha Pandey
Research Scholar, University of Calcutta, India

Arindam Dutta
Faculty and Coordinator, Indian Institute of Social Welfare and Business Management, India

Arkadipta Roy
Research Scholar, University of Calcutta, India

Arundhati Ray
Assistant Professor, Institute of Engineering and Management, India

Ashish Kumar Sana
Professor, University of Calcutta, India

Ayesha Afreen
Research Scholar, University of Calcutta, India

Biswajit Paul

Debisree Banerjee
Assistant Professor, Naba Ballygunge Mahavidyalaya, India

Joydip Dasgupta
Associate Professor, Nabadwip Vidyasagar College, India

Karabi Bhattacharya Rao
Chief Manager, International Management Institute Kolkata, India

Kavitha Sundararajan
Assistant Professor, Shri Shikshayatan College, India

Manisha Dey
Assistant Professor, Amity University Kolkata, India

Pritha Adhikari
Research Scholar, University of Calcutta, India

Pritha Chanda
M.Phil Scholar, Indian Institute of Social Welfare and Business Management, India

Rupam Mukherjee
Barrackpore Rastraguru Surendranath College, India

Shaunak Roy
Assistant Professor, St. Xavier's College (Autonomous), Kolkata, India

Sneha Km Pandey
Research Scholar, University of Calcutta, India

Tanusree Das
Assistant Professor, Shri Shikshayatan College, India

Tuhin Narayan Roy
Department of Agricultural Economics, Uttar Banga Krishi Viswavidyalaya, India

Prelude

Enterprising Agriculture: Market Awareness, Farm Innovation and Value Addition

Sharmistha Banerjee, Mohua Banerjee, Suneel Kunamaneni and Alfred Chinta

Agriculture is the science and art of cultivating plants and livestock (ILO, 1999). It involves practices relating to production, processing, marketing, distribution, utilization, and trading of food, feed and fiber. This explanation to the term 'agriculture' indicates that agricultural development must address not only farmers but also those in processing, trading, marketing and overall agri-business. The word agriculture comes from the Latin words *ager*, which means the soil or land. Agriculture may be defined as *"the basic and applied sciences of the soil and water management, crop production including production of all garden crops, control of plants, pests and diseases, horticulture including floriculture, animal husbandry including veterinary and dairy science, fisheries, forestry including farm forestry, home science, agricultural engineering and technology, marketing and processing of agricultural and animal husbandry products, land use and management."* Agri-business for the purpose of sustainable and inclusive development may include agricultural functions like pre and post-harvest operations, assembling, grading, storage, transportation and distribution. The Indian Council of Agricultural Research (ICAR) has suggested involvement of three important functions, namely assembling (concentration), preparation for consumption (processing) and distribution as the core activities in agri-business.

Entrepreneurship is critical to addressing agri-business challenges. The goal of fostering entrepreneurship in agriculture is to apply new business models and technologies to improve food production. Developing countries and emerging markets, particularly those with large rural communities, suffer from inadequate

Comparative Analysis of India and UK" which has shaped the collection of articles in this book, aims to promote agriculture as a genuine enterprise, particularly for the young unemployed in semi-urban and rural areas, so that combined strategies can be developed for stimulating agri-entrepreneurship to meet global food challenges, namely health, well-being, sustainability and ethics.

A farmer is an agro-businessman and in most cases an entrepreneur. He procures the agricultural inputs that will be required in the fields, carries out the production process, cultivates the crops, manages the farms, engages in harvesting and post-harvesting activities, arranges for storage, processing of the produce, and the go-to-market strategies (Figure 1).

Fig. 1: The Agro Value Chain
Source: Author

Farmer-entrepreneurs operate in a complex and dynamic environment. They see their farms as a business proposition and are willing to take calculated risks to make their farms profitable and enable their businesses to grow. They are also a part of a larger ecosystem including other farmers, suppliers, traders, transporters, processors and many others. Each of these intermediaries has a role to play in adding value to the products and moving them to the market through the value chain. It is pertinent to keep in mind that each player in the value chain develops forward and backward linkages to extract value as a channel intermediary and simultaneously contribute to further value creation. In the farmers' scope of activities, his entrepreneurial initiatives start from taking decisions on each operational aspect of the value chain and the required investments to be made, enduring non-insurable risks such as fluctuations in demand and supply, or tremendous fluctuations in prices. His entrepreneurial nature of activity pushes innovation at each of the stages in this value chain. The concept of agro-entrepreneurship entails bringing about transformational change in the agribusiness sector to augment incomes, create more sub-industries within the agricultural sector and help the rural poor add to their agricultural resources. Small and medium enterprises that are set up at rural levels, supplement traditional farm income in a big way and create alternative sources of income.

Role of Innovation, Governmental Policies, and Farmers' Developmental Initiatives in Promotion of Agri-Entrepreneurship

Agriculture sector plays a significant role in the sustainable growth and development of the Indian economy. It is responsible for the food and nutrition requirements of 1.3 billion Indians and creates employment opportunities through forward and backward linkages to support 60% of the population. However, this sector is constrained by several factors such as small and fragmented land holdings, low productivity, low profitability, wastage of crops due to lack of storage and inadequacies in the supply chain management. These challenges are the store house of dormant opportunities for businesses which are referred as agro-enterprises. Agri-entrepreneurship can play a significant role in solving the challenges related to information dissemination, farm management, capital availability, mechanization of farm and the agriculture supply chain.

There is a connection between entrepreneurship and innovation. Entrepreneurs who innovate primarily display traits of entrepreneurs and secondarily the traits of innovators (Knudson et al., 2004). Innovative entrepreneurs improve products and various processes to make a niche in the market. However, entrepreneurial innovators are innovators first and entrepreneurs later. They identify market gaps and build business models, processes and products. The presence of entrepreneurial-innovation mix is necessary for innovation and entrepreneurship to occur. Lack of knowledge, inadequate access to venture capital, unimpressive business plan or credibility act as obstacles in the path of entrepreneurship and innovation. Innovators in the agricultural domain are mainly focused on raising production along with improving the quality of the produce and process of production (Van der Veen, 2010). Agricultural innovation usually affects crops, soil, animals as well as managerial practices. Even if innovations are not always radical, 'micro-inventions' like modifying means and ways of doing agriculture have meaningful and positive impact on the society and economy. Thus agro-innovation is more about adaptation of existing technologies rather than adoption of new technologies.

It is pertinent to think about reconsidering the role of the Government in upcoming agro-food systems. Farming as a business is not distinctive from other medium, small and large businesses. It is a commonly held belief that industrialization in agro-food business is guided by forces at the consumer level (Caswell, 1997). Government policies should address market failures, imperfections and other outcomes that are undesirable. Consumers should primarily be benefitted from on "peasant society" had been built up. The general view related to subsistence production, safety-first principle, and a steady village system with moral obligations that led to conservative behaviours towards change. A study on relevant institutional and organizational modifications, including materialization of formal credit system and growing land market, revealed that some peasants actively participated in the agricultural transformation and did not demonstrate a conservative attitude toward change (Svensson, 2006). Studies on Indian rural markets illustrate that in a chiefly agrarian economy, investments in non-farm business area for rural industrial development might come from landowning farmers (Dutta, 2007).

This book aims to consider this wide variety of issues. It focuses on the broad theme of agri-entrepreneurship and brings to the reader innovative ideas across the three specific subthemes. Starting from the illustrations of entrepreneurial innovations that impact agriculture, to the discussions on the governmental policies and interventions that have been undertaken in agro-entrepreneurship; the book finally deliberates on the initiatives that can create the farmers' overall development and welfare.

Entrepreneurial Innovations that Impact Agriculture

The second chapter of this book focuses on implementing low-cost technologies in the existing agricultural extension activities that help farmers enhance operational decisions (Chinta, 2019). Incorporating high technology-based data into simple to understand terminology will help reduce the burden on farmers and the valuable contribution of remote sensing data in farming has been identified, that ultimately impacts a farmer's profitability.

Innovative vertical farming practices are currently propounded for sustainable food production (Mukherjee and Roy, 2019). Through the case study of Urbagrow Aquaponics, the authors elucidate that vertical cultivation of plants as well as breeding of livestock on vertically inclined surfaces, such as skyscrapers and other high-rise buildings in urban regions, has gained prominence. The systems make use of less water, require less work in man-hours and can grow vegetables in greater density than a traditional soil-based food growing endeavour.

In the context of two innovative products, Dragon Fruit and Water Hyacinth, two dimensions of technology and market are used to explain four different kinds of innovation – incremental, architectural, radial and descriptive (Roy and

Innovative technology such as the Manual Axis Tracking Solar Pump can provide access to reliable and affordable irrigation facilities to increase agricultural productivity and income for the farmers (Dutta, 2019). This study deliberates upon the technical features that make the Manual Axis Tracking Solar Pump an advantage over its nearest competitor, the diesel pump.

Minimising harvest and post-harvest wastages, both in and beyond the fields, through innovative alternative solutions of waste reduction and waste management are depicted through process observation (Rao, 2019). The author recommends methods for decreasing the post-harvest losses (PHL) as a sustainable solution towards increasing food availability and improving farmers' livelihoods.

The following chapter highlights the need for new innovative ideas for food packaging (Das and Sundararajan, 2019). Customer awareness about safety of processed food has given rise to entrepreneurship opportunities in the area of safe and hygiene packaging. Market preferences, state reputations and cost benefit analysis play major roles in packaging decisions of processed food products.

Government Policies and Interventions in Entrepreneurship

The six chapters that follow cover the role of the Government in aiding agro-entrepreneurship. The performance of various agricultural insurance schemes in terms of coverage and the benefits being delivered in India and in West Bengal are analysed (Banerjee, 2019). Through a diffusion model the author explores whether the recipients consider the schemes as an effective risk mitigation tool or merely a habit of credit-dependence.

Though Minimum Support Price (MSP) is one of the mechanisms used by the Government to protect the producers from price fluctuations, MSP variation has been observed among states (Dey, 2019). Her study analyses the existence of deviation in *mandi* prices of staple food between two states from 2007 to 2018 to identify whether a centralized price system can reduce the cost of the Government and help the farmer to get fair valuation.

The Intellectual Property Rights (IPRs) affect the extensive and intensive margin in agricultural trade (Ray, 2019). This study focuses on identifying the micro-level dynamics of IPRs in agriculture and its effects on the rural enterprises in India, as it can lead to identification of policies that would help in harnessing IPRs for the growth of Indian agriculture.

improving CG practices and the need for a policy framework in supporting good CG, are important areas in the Indian context (Roy and Pal, 2019).

Organic farming can help India reverse the damage caused by Green Revolution by allowing for natural methods of agriculture rather than a severely mechanical form of farming (Afreen, 2019).The author identifies that the prospects of organic farming should be considered for its effectiveness from the perspectives of both consumer awareness and state initiatives.

The Government and voluntary agencies have recognised the need for women in the farming community to become self-reliant and active participants in the agricultural sector (Pandey et al., 2019). Highlighting the example of Anita Devi – the Mushroom Lady of Bihar, the study examines the several State initiatives that support women entrepreneurs and create a supportive ecosystem for women to become agricultural entrepreneurs.

Farmers' Development and Welfare through Agriculture

The relationship between infrastructure investment by the state and rural entrepreneurship in India, has established evidence in support of greater investment in infrastructures enhancing rural entrepreneurial opportunities (Paul and Sana, 2019). The authors elucidate that as 67% of the Indian population live in rural areas, it is apparent that the livelihood of this vast majority is closely related to rural enterprises.

Entrepreneurship in the Food Processing Industry is fuelled by a strong domestic demand, rising export opportunities, increasing global demand and strong policy support from the Government (Bhattacharya, 2019).Being the second largest producer of fruits and vegetables along with its strategic geographic location and proximity to food importing nations, the author elaborates that India is in an advantageous position for exporting processed food.

The role and status of Indian Agricultural Market Intelligence System(IAMIS) in improving the economic returns of agri-sector in India is significant, as marketing intelligence makes agricultural marketers, including agri-entrepreneurs, aware and updated and reduces risk in decision making (Roy, 2019).The author highlights that the essential pre-requisite of ensuring farmers' income is that they need credible information about the "likely price situation" and Agriculture Marketing Intelligence System has emerged with the aim to provide services in agriculture and allied sectors.

in terms of the area of land insured and the number of farmers covered. There are the problems of low risk awareness and lack of insurance culture among the farmers.

'Ecopreneurs' possess singular focus on the safe-keep of the ecology (Dasgupta, 2019). But, the author explains that, in order to sustain the efforts of businesses in ecology, it is imperative that they remain economically viable too. Thus ecopreneurial process is not only about fulfilling the businesses' responsibility towards ecology, but also about the marketability of the product or service. The author studies selected organic farms are analysed in an environment-market continuum.

This book is based on the premise that all farmers are entrepreneurs. Simply stating, a farmer procures land (owns or leases), provides labour (own, family and hired), provides inputs (seeds and fertilizers), equipment, capital and performs the entrepreneurial functions of coordinating and decision making. The primary decisions on which crop or combinations thereof (what to produce), what process to be undertaken, the method and mix (how to produce) and where to sell the produce (for whom to produce) are taken by the farmer himself. Thus the premise of agriculture as a business suggests that all farmers are entrepreneurs, *per se*. Farming is extremely complex since it is both a business and a way of life. The nature of the farm household, as both a producer and consumer with multiple goals, requires close attention and more in-depth investigation. The core idea offered by the book is agriculture is as much a business like any other; hence the functional areas of business, production, processing, marketing, distribution and insurance take up specific form for agricultural entrepreneurship. The essays in this book highlight the idea that agro-entrepreneurship uses entrepreneurial skills, models and innovative ideas to economically solve problems in the agriculture sector and increase the profitability of the farming business.

The fundamental questions that are emerging are: Is under-production an issue in Indian agriculture? Or is over-production and excess stock of produce creating bottlenecks in the value chain that is lowering the prices offered to the farmers? Is asymmetrical market information on what to produce and how much to produce, a cause of concern? Can a farmer with marginal share of landholding and minimal capital assume the role of an entrepreneur? Does opportunity exist for other entities with access to funds, concepts, skill sets and technology, to perform as entrepreneurs? Is it possible for agro-technology to create innovations in the ecosystem? Does the encompassing ecosystem enable the farmers, increasing an understanding of agro-entrepreneurship as an emerging phenomenon and stresses on the combined role of innovative practices, Governmental initiatives and farmers' development and welfare activities for building the ecosystem through a wide variety of approaches.

References

Caswell, J. A. (1997). Rethinking the role of government in agri-food markets. American Journal of Agricultural Economics, 79(2), 651-656.

Dutta, S. (2007). Non-Farm Entrepreneurship of Farmers in West Bengal: A LISREL/Logit Analysis. Indian Economic Review, 231-253.

Forastieri, V. (1999). The ILO programme on occupational safety and health in agriculture. International Labour Organization, Geneva, Switzerland.

Knudson, W., Wysocki, A., Champagne, J., & Peterson, H. C. (2004). Entrepreneurship and innovation in the agri-food system. American Journal of Agricultural Economics, 86(5), 1330-1336.

Mondal, P. (2010). Major Agricultural Problems of India and their Possible Solutions.

PAY-Shodhganga, W. T. Farmer Willingness to Pay for Seed-Related Information-CiteSeerX.

Svensson, P. (2006). Peasants and entrepreneurship in the nineteenth-century agricultural transformation of Sweden. Social Science History, 30(3), 387-429.

Van Der Veen, M. (2010). Agricultural innovation: invention and adoption or change and adaptation?. World Archaeology, 42(1), 1-12.

https://shodhganga.inflibnet.ac.in/bitstream/10603/206923/9/09_chart%201.pdf (Accessed on 10th June, 2019)

https://techstory.in/india-ready-for-full-scale-agri-entrepreneurship/ (Accessed on 12th June, 2019)

http://www.yourarticlelibrary.com/agriculture/10-major-agricultural-problems-of-india-and-their-possible-solutions/20988 (Accessed on 12th June, 2019)

Part-I: Entrepreneurial Innovations that Impact Agriculture

1

BOP Model for Satellite Data for Small and Marginal Farmers to Overcome the Waste of Inputs, Financial Difficulties and Sustainability

Alfred Chinta

Abstract

This chapter will look at the major reasons why farmers in India are unable to take advantage of Agricultural profession as a mode of generating income and suggest ways to change this by employing new technologies. Agriculture has basic processes which require identifying the season for planting the seeds at the right time, watering the plants to the required level, undertaking maintenance for the different plants and then finally harvesting at the right time to ensure that the effort that has been put into the agricultural process results in useful output. In business terms the output when it is valued in terms of money, should enable the farming business to sell their output at a certain price that will enable them to pay off the money that has been used for setting up the crop for that cycle. This chapter will underscore the valuable contribution of remote sensing data in farming to enhance operational decisions. We will look at how low-cost technologies can be implemented into the existing agricultural extension activities and help farmers make better decisions that will enable them to be more business oriented. It is envisaged that incorporating high technology-based data into simple to understand terminology will help reduce the burden on farmers. This is due to the lack of knowledge but also due to the low volume of information that is possible to be fed to the farmers through the agriculture extension network in the country. However, due to the varied nature of farming in India it is difficult for extension officers to specialise but

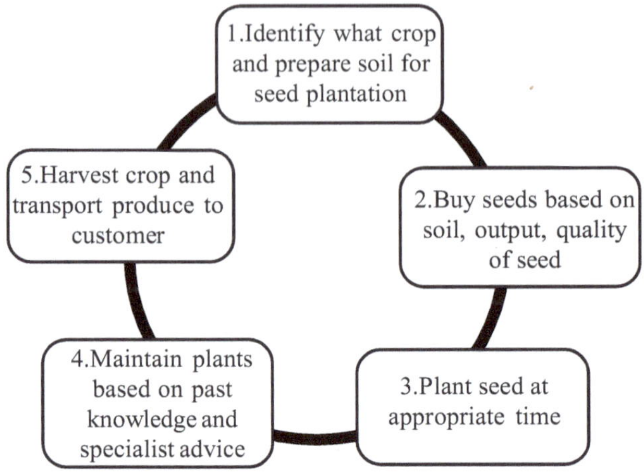

Farmers cycle of activities

Fig. 1: Agricultural Statistics in India

The data from the Ministry of Agriculture (2017) shows that agricultural output has been falling in comparison to other areas such as industry and services. A big reason can be that the low value of reward from farming not only reduced the attractiveness of the industry, but also encourages wastefulness in the overall supply chain. These effects are compounded in developing countries where farming is affected on the input side due to lack of road infrastructure for procuring fertiliser. Further the harvest from farming is also impeded from being transferred to the markets and customers in time due to lack of refrigerated storage, transport systems and lack on investment in this area.

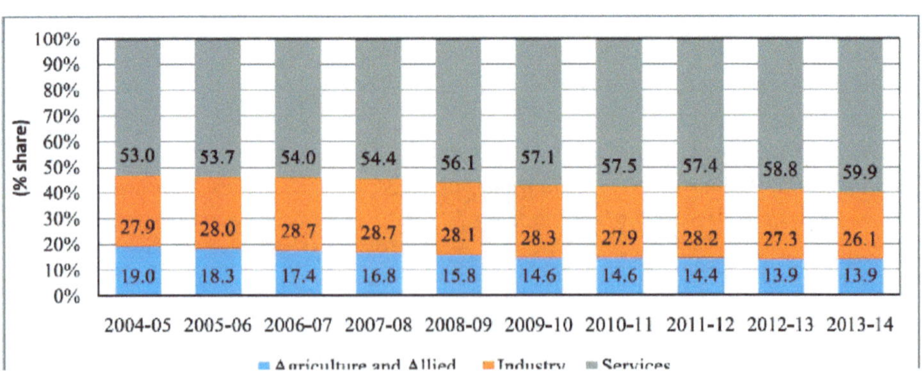

It can be evidenced that there is an increase in cropped area, and thereis a shift from staple cereals like rice, wheat, maize and millets to crops such as cotton and sugarcane. Cotton and sugarcane have replaced the traditional areas which produce cereals which indicates that there is a change in the production for the farming businesses to be more effective, they need to be able to change from one type of product to the other very quickly. One of the key factors has been the changes to the dietary patterns which has impacted on what crops have been produced.What is also evidenced is the growth in horticulture has outstripped the growth in food grains, similarly the livestock sector has emerged as a key area toensure agricultural sector is able to increase overall incomes.The production of milk is already an area where India has fared better and has been able to increase the availability of milk above the average for the world. However, the government realises that food security is an important factor for the Indian economy and therefore soil fertility has to be maintained and further the impact on the water table has to be reduced. This requires the farmers to be able to realise that aggressive cropping and cultivation of water intensive agricultural produce such as cotton can be harmful to the local arable farms and the water table. This requires understanding the farmers financial situation but also how these issues in the lower economic strata of the population in countries like India can benefit from improving the farm efficiency and reduce wastage (Narayanamoorthy, 2016).

Knowledge of Agriculture

Farmers gain the knowledge of Agriculture over their lifetime on a daily basis where they are from agricultural backgrounds, where farming is a way of life and this knowledge is passed on from generation to generation.This type of knowledge transfer can be useful when the conditions for farming do not change and the competition also adopts the same approach. However, modern agriculture has changed significantly where farmers in the West have been able to increase their productivity by the use of machines; typical machines which are used for harvesting demonstrate that an area of 5 acres can easily be harvested by using a combine harvester in a day. What we also see is that the average size of the farm is also increasing so that the overheads the average overheads for a given Farm have reduced.Further we also see that smaller farms are working in cooperatives to ensure that the risk is minimised. Due to the changes in weather patterns around the world, the timing of the rain, cold and heat around the year cannot be accurately predicted in the same way as it was in the past.

seen below that a comparison off productivity in agriculture in different countries and how the lack of investment and knowledge of farmers results in low productivity in the developing countries. The advances in the availability of mobile phones is one area where farmers can utilise the availability of up-to-date low-cost information that can be utilised to ensure that they're able to change their farming practices based on the input provided by these new Technologies in a simple format for e.g. Mittal et al (2010) suggest more use of mobile phones by farmers ti bridge their lack of appropriate information.

BOP Market

Prahlad (2005) identified to the world of the many opportunities that await the businesses who tackle the bottom of the consumer pyramid with new products and services. Hasan et al (2017) identify the role of visual cues in promoting products and services to the BOP segment where the customer is less literate. The success of Jio services on the mobile market in increasing the consumption of mobile data, Hindustan lever in leveraging small sachets in selling shampoo to BOP households, growth of Uber in major towns and cities, development of cars like Tata Nano and Renault Kwid are positive efforts to work towards introducing products and services aimed at the BOP market. The issues with most farmers making mistakes is due to the lack of information that is available to them which can help them realise the fertility of soil, whether fertilizer intervention will help correct these.

Choice of Crop

When the different groups are compared what we see is there are some crops which will give a higher yield in a particular location. We also see that lot of crops are over produced which is one of the main reasons why farmers fail to get adequate compensation for the efforts that they have put in into the farming. Therefore it is necessary that farmers have the knowledge that they have to follow the demand-supply patterns and insure that they minimise risk by using multi cropping or diversifying their business into the different products and possible services. These can be offered to increase this income from the farming activity. What we also see is that in the current climate the rural population has a wide choice of employment options which could be better positioned in comparison to the farming practices prevalent in that particular time in that particular region. Therefore it is necessary for the different policy makers to ensure that farming is an attractive employment proposition so that they continue

It was by making these interventions, these big businesses have not only been able to ensure that farmers get adequate compensation, but also ensure that there is a steady stream of farmers who know that there are supply chain partners who are willing to invest and then show a sustainable supply of agricultural produce is available.

Does the use of Pesticide and Fertiliser Improve Productivity?

Liu et al (2015) studied the long term effects of pesticide application in cereals over a 50 year period. The assumption made is that fertiliser helps improve yield of crops. However their impact on environment has been raised as an area of urgent attention by Popp et al 2013 and Pelosi et al 2014. Global distortions in nitrogen levels are noticeable from area to the other. Similarly phosphorus is deficient in South America and excessive in East Asia. Liu et al (2015) identify that lack of roads in Africa restrict the availability of fertiliser than can reduce the nutrient deficit and adversely impact the productivity. Ray et al (2012) have developed a method for classifying the fertiliser use into I,D,N

As per data collected by Liu et al 2015 the Cereal production per person in India has been in between 200 and 300 Kg per person and an average productivity of 2000 and 2600 Kg per hectare. They suggest use of changing crop variety, planting time, use of fertilise and irrigation to reduce losses in production of cereal.

Maredia and Pingali (2001) summarised the several research papers on overuse and misuse of fertiliser and concluded that this resulted in impact on rice and wheat production, and suggested the careful selection of inputs to reduce unintended outcomes such as salinity of water. They found several problems with yield enhancing and use of chemicals such as:

- Soil fertility problems
- Vulnerability of crops to pests and diseases
- Lowered water levels due to excessive irrigation
- Ground and surface water pollution
- Herbicide resistance
- Cultivation in environmental fragile areas

Jeyanthi and Kombairaju (2005)summarise that India is one of the major production, health issues for farmers, pollution of the environment. An important finding has been that excessive use of chemicals is due to risk averse behaviour and low levels of knowledge on the effectiveness of these chemicals.These point to the fact that timely relay of information will be helpful for farmers to make better choices, therefore a review of the agricultural extension services is necessary for us to identify how they can enable farmers to make accurate data based decisions for their farm.

Peskircioglu (2008) identifies how using the project-based productivity approach has been effectively employed in various parts of Turkey to bring in improvements to farm output. Zakaria and Nagata (2010) identify how agricultural extension officers were helpful in conveying knowledge useful for farmers and also convey their issues to research centres. They further make an important assertion that farmers have realised that agriculture is a risky business. Therefore they will need to make accurate decisions based on improved knowledge and to realise return returns without making any negative outcomes for their business. For this they depend on regular, specific, advice from the extension officers and also the farmers who have a better knowledge setup.

Use of Satellite Data

Several studies indicate the importance of using satellite data in improving the farming practices. Nutini et al (2018) identify that nitrogen fertilisation plays a key role in the productivity of flies and also on the environmental impact, farmers income. It was also used to identify if nitrogen use efficiency leads to contamination of the groundwater and increases in emission and losses to farmers by looking at the nitrogen nutritional index. By using satellite data farmers can be advised as to how they can improve their practices.Utilising the role of satellite data in this paper helps Identify that inexpensive and user-friendly applications. how positively impact on the sustainability of the Farmers they allow them to collect data that is reliable with very less technical knowledge this technique can also be utilised for monitoring of crops in Real-Time and Darius Anand agricultural project where the nitrogen deficiency is severe this enables the Farmer's to identify areas where fertiliser application has to be prioritised. Roth et al (2019) also identify the use of large scale remote sensing data to classify clove plantation in difficult to reach areas, especially farms in inaccessible regions can be monitored remotely using these advanced techniques making farmers labour to be reduced and increase other value adding activities or diversify incomes by reducing their non value added time.

realise the impact of water used on farms, and the additional need based on requirement for that crop. This was accomplished using satellite data from Sentinel-2 and Landsat satellites and processed using Google Earth Engine. These inputs will enable farmers to identify the crops suitable for certain sections of land and avoid the use of crops that can be damaging to the water table. Christian (2018) highlighted the role of spatial data from satellites to study the impact of other activities than farming resulting in change to the topography of a district in Rajasthan, this can drive strategy by local administrations to advise farmers as to how their surrounding landpatterns are being affected and encourage them to work together. This can also be useful in cultivating organic produce which require soil conditions to be monitored as per desired specifications.

Current application of remote sensing has also shown move away from high level data from satellites to use of drones to map soil topography and make decisions on farm inputs. These applications are in the early stage of adoption and show fewer avenues for profitable application in agriculture (Tenkorang and Lowenberg-DoBoer, 2008). Delince (2015) lists many sources of satellite data and use in agriculture quoting rates of \$3.50 per km^2, there are other cases where imagery is free however the costs of conversion and interpretation are expensive, which can be restrictive although they can offer vast benefits to groups of farmers, cooperatives or use by Govt agencies. Higher adoption will allow reduction of cost per km^2 of data. This will go together with increasing farmer incomes by making smarter decisions on farm inputs to reduce use of pesticides whose use has been rampant and unchecked with negative outcomes for farmer and their environments.

Conclusion

Charities, governmental agencies, groups of farmers and agri food companies can work towards adopting satellite data or drone based imagery to make better informed decisions on farm inputs. This requires education of farmer groups in interpreting this data and make informed choices. The combined benefits will not only help reduce financial hardship to farmers, but also contribute towards the sustainability agenda by taking water table into account. Further monitoring long term trends will enable shifting crops based on their impact to the local landscape and ensure farming as a source of livelihood will continue for generations to come. BOP model will ensurethat the use of imagery does not get limited to scientific community but ensure its permeation to the vast number

References

Christian ,B.A.,Dhinwa, P.S., and Ajai (2018) Long term monitoring and assessment of desertification processes usingmedium & high resolution satellite data, Applied Geography, vol 97, pp 10-24.

Delince,J. (2015) Cost – Effectiveness of Remote Sensing for Agricultural Statistics in Developing and Emerging Economies, FAO Technical Report Series GO-09-2015, Available at http://gsars.org/wp-content/uploads/2016/02/TR-on-Cost-Effectiveness-of-Remote-Sensing-100216-FINAL.pdf

Hasan, M.R.,Lowe,B. andRahman,M. (2017) "Visual cues and innovation adoption among bottom of the pyramid consumers", Qualitative Market Research: An International Journal, Vol. 20 Issue: 2, pp.147-157, https://doi.org/10.1108/QMR-04-2015-0032.

Jeyanthi, H. and Kombairaju, S. (2005)Pesticide Use in Vegetable Crops: Frequency,Intensity and Determinant Factors, Agricultural economics research review, Vol.18, pp.209-221.

Liu,Y., Pan, X., and Li,J.(2015) A 1961–2010 record of fertilizer use, pesticide application and cereal yields: a review. Agronomy for Sustainable Development, Springer Verlag/EDP Sciences/INRA, 2015, 35 (1), pp.83-93.

Maredia,M. and Pingali,P. (2001) Environmental impacts of productivity-enhancing crop research:A critical review, FAO, Technical Advisory report.

Mittal, S., Gandhi, S. and Tripathi, G. (2010) Socio-Economic impact of mobile phones on Indian Agriculture, working paper no.246. ICRIER, available at https://www.econstor.eu/bitstream/10419/176264/1/icrier-wp-246.pdf

Narayanamoorthy,A. (2016) Farm Income in India: Myths and Realities, Keynote, Indian society of Agricultural economics, available at http://www.isaeindia.org/wp-content/uploads/2016/11/Keynote_%20paper_%202016.pdf

Nutini,F., Confalonieri, R, Crema, A., Movedi,E., Paleari, L, Stavrakoudis ,D., Boschetti, M.(2018) An operational workflow to assess rice nutritional status based on satellite imagery and smartphone apps, Computers and Electronics in Agriculture, 154, 80-92.

Peþkircioðlu, (2008) "MPM's productivity improvement project approach in provinces", International Journal of Productivity and Performance Management, Vol. 57 Issue: 6, pp.440-448, https://doi.org/10.1108/17410400810893374

Prahalad, C. K. (2005). The fortune at the bottom of the pyramid: Eradicating poverty through profits. New Delhi: Pearson Education and Wharton School.

Raganathan, T, Tripathi,A and Rajoriya, B.D. (2016) Changing Sources of Income and Income Inequality among Indian Rural Households,

Roth, S.I.B, Leiterer, R. Volpi, M., Celio, E. Schaeepman, M.E, Joerg, P.C. (2019) Automated detection of individual clove trees for yield quantification in north-eastern Madagascar based on multi-spectral satellite data, Remote Sensing of Environment, 221, 144-156

Tenkorang,F. and Lowenberg-DoBoer,J. (2008) On-Farm Profitability of Remote Sensing in Agriculture, The journal of terrestrial observation, Vol1,1, pp 50-59.

Zakaria,S., and Nagata,H. (2010) "Knowledge creation and flow in agriculture: The experience and role of the Japanese extension advisors", Library Management, Vol. 31 Issue: 1/2, pp.27-35, https:// doi.org/10.1108/01435121011013377.

2

Implementing Vertical Farming for Sustainable Food Production in Urban India: A Case Study of Urbagrow Aquaponics, Kolkata

Abhik Kumar Mukherjee and Shaunak Roy

Abstract

The upsurge in global population rates has triggered a significant escalation in food demand across the world. This is accompanied by urbanisation and a pressing need for sustainable agriculture. In this context vertical cultivation of plants as well as breeding of livestock on vertically inclined surfaces, such as in skyscrapers and other high-rise buildings in urban regions has gained prominence. The dynamics of urban agriculture is captured through the case study of Urbagrow Aquaponics, an urban, aquaponic, soil-free, food garden based in Kolkata. The garden exhibits an assortment of aquaponic systems for growing a variety of vegetables as well as the tilapia and catfish. The systems make use of less water, require less work in man-hours and can grow vegetables in greater density than a traditional soil based food growing endeavour. A feasibility study has been conducted to explore the potential of scaling such a venture across myriad other high-rise buildings across Indian cities.

Keywords: Urban population; Land shortage; Vertical farming; Aquaponics; Hydroponics; Aeroponics; Urbagrow Aquaponics

Introduction

In an era marked by rampant change and fast-paced development, humankind nine billion people by 2050 (Cohen, 2001; Cleland, 2013). The problem of providing adequate food resources for the whole world in 2050 happens to be one of the primary challenges faced by humanity in present times. Hence, with food security becoming a pressing issue amidst skyrocketing rates of global population, environmentalists, researchers, practitioners, policy-makers, governments and communities have since been probing into alternative modes of food supply to such cities, without having to alter the existing paradigm of sustainable agricultural and horticultural practices. Beyond the risks of mounting global population, rampant urbanisation also plays a key role in aggravating the global supply of food, as it is predicted that an excess of 80 percent people shall be dwelling in urban spaces in the near future (Despommier, 2010; Islam and Siwar, 2012). This would be translated as greater land requirements for residential and occupational purposes and less farmland spaces. However, such urban sprawls continue to cast an excessive amount of pressure on the challenge at hand.

In this context, vertical farming offers a unique solution to the existing problem of depleting farmlands and growing urbanisation. It is harboured on the premise that, urban spaces need to be utilised for agricultural requirements on the vertical dimension, more than the horizontal dimension. Urban areas are encroached upon for not only for residential requirements, but also for professional and recreational needs. Given such inherent limitations in horizontal land expansion, there is not enough space for sustaining farmlands. Thus, if horizontal land expansion is rendered infeasible, the only space available is along the vertical scale. Vertical farming is a novel agricultural endeavour to generate opportunities for food production and supply in crowded cities in conjunction with contemporary agricultural practices in a sustainable manner. It involves the farming of fruits, vegetables and food grains within the confines of a city, such as the inside of a multi-storeyed building, where various floors have been utilised for different farming purposes, using the concept of hydroponics, aquaponics or aeroponics.

This is particularly important since vertical farming engages multiple disciplines of natural sciences, architecture, and engineering and affects both people and the environment (Despommier, 2014; Touliatos et al., 2016; Muller et al., 2017). In India, such systems are at a rudimentary stage and further research is crucial to fathom its profound environmental and economic impact. Nonetheless, as innovation continues to tackle the production obstacles, vertical farming in urban India is likely to become more conventional in urban settings. The current chapter is essentially a conceptual case-based inquest and primarily endeavours to

(i) To probe into the concept of vertical farming

(ii) To establish the key notions associated with vertical farming

(iii) To determine the principal driving forces responsible for developing vertical farming across the world

(iv) To assess the real-world application of aquaponics farming with reference to a mini- case on UrbaGrow Aquaponics, Kolkata

The current endeavour shall primarily serve as an illustrative case for aspiring entrepreneurs and farmers who are considering alternative farming techniques for sustainable food production, especially in the confines of congested cities and towns. It offers insights into not only the core fundamentals of vertical farming, but also sheds light on its pros and cons, its major driving forces and a real-life case study on UrbaGrow Aquaponics in Kolkata, which shall serve as an exemplar for potential agri-entrepreneurs in the future.

Industry Context of Vertical Farming

Over the last decade, the agenda of cultivating sustainable food in cities has garnered considerable attention among academic and practical circles alike (Despommier, 2013; Ackerman et al., 2014; Jamal and Mortez, 2014; Specht et al., 2014; Wiskerke, 2015). At present, nearly 1.98 billion acres of land across the world is allocated for soil-based farming, which roughly constitutes 38 percent of the aggregate global land area. Furthermore, around 80 percent of the entire arable land across the globe is being effectively utilised (Ellingsen and Despommier, 2008). The rising global demand for food has culminated in a critical need for utilising greater levels of arable land for farming, while escalating farming efforts that would have a profound influence on agriculture on the global scale. A new-fangled contemporary technique that offers significant potential to address this demand lies in conceiving and developing vertical farms (Glaser, 2012; Despommier, 2013). Notwithstanding, the concept of vertical farming is relatively new and only a few erstwhile studies have investigated its prospects in the context of urban integration.

Concept of Vertical Farming

Controlled environment agriculture (CEA), more popularly known as Vertical Farming, is essentially an agricultural technique encompassing comprehensive food production in high-rise buildings. It enables rapid development and planned applications for the society and the environment at large (Perez, 2014). It adopts a hands-on and proactive approach in warranting the sustainability of cities across the world by addressing food security to the world's mushrooming urban population.

The implementation of vertical farming presents its own range of technical and practical application issues. Yet, such farms have found immense success in their capacity to nurture different varieties of crops in several prominent cities within countries such as Canada, China, England, Italy, Japan, The Netherlands, Singapore, South Korea, The United Arab Emirates and The United States of America (Sivamani et al., 2013; Despommier, 2014).

Table 1 presents a snapshot of some of the prominent vertical farms across the world in various countries across the world.

Table 1: Prominent Vertical Farming Companies across the World

Name of Vertical Farming Company	City of Establishment	Founded in
CellGarden	Aalen, Germany	2016
Bright Agrotech	Ontario, Canada	2016
Wallfarm	Rome, Italy	2015
Plants & Machines	Weimar, Germany	2015
Lettus Grow	Bristol, England	2015
Infarm	Düsseldorf, Germany	2015
Here, There & Everywhere	De Lier, The Netherlands	2015
Visualnacert	Valencia, Spain	2014
Scriptr	New York, USA	2014
Less	Buenos Aires, Argentina	2014
Celotor	Cali, Colombia	2014
Plenty	San Francisco, California	2013
Metropolitan Farms	Chicago, Illinois	2013
Intelligent Growth Solutions	Dundee, Scotland	2013
GrowUp Urban Farms	London, England	2013
Green Spirit Farms	New Buffalo, Michigan	2013
Bov Control	São Paulo, Brazil	2013
Aponix: Vertical Barrel System	Heidelberg, Germany	2013
Agrilution	Munich, Germany	2013
Trifecta Ecosystems Inc.	Meriden, Connecticut	2012
Sky Greens Farm	Singapore	2012
Green Living Technologies	Rochester, New York	2012
Trusted Renewables	Ipswich, England	2008
Spread Company Ltd.	Kyoto, Japan	2006
Heliospectra	Gothenburg, Sweden	2006
Illumitex	Austin, Texas	2005

Although the concept of vertical farming is quite popular across several developed nations, it is beginning to find its approval in the Indian context. In fact, this form of farming is widely used in small residential houses in various urban areas of India, but its commercial acceptance is yet to be established.

Table 2 summarises four of the most popular start-ups that are responsible for promoting vertical farming in India.

Table 2: Prominent Vertical Farming Companies in India

Name of Vertical Farming Company	City	Brief Description
Letcetra Agritech	Mapusa, Goa	• Goa's first indoor hydroponics farm, growing good quality, pesticide-free vegetables • Produces 1.5 to 2 tons of different varieties ofleafy vegetables such as lettuce and herbs
BitMantis Innovations	Bengaluru, Karnataka	• Enables individuals and commercial growers to grow fresh herbs throughout the year • Uses hydroponics methods for efficient use of water and nutrients and is equipped with two traysto grow micro-greens at one's own convenience
Junga Freshn Green	Junga, Himachal Pradesh	• Create a hydroponics model of cultivating farm fresh vegetables having a predictable quality, little or no pesticides and unaffected by weather or soil conditions • Grown in a protected, greenhouse environment
Future Farms	Chennai, Tamil Nadu	• Focus on being environment-friendly through rooftop farming and precision agriculture • Development of efficient and affordable indigenous systems and solutions, made from premium, food grade materials

Source: Singh (2017)

Vertical farming has transpired into a major theme of deliberation in the context of food security as well as contemporary urban farming practices for generating sustainable food production. These farms are vastly technologised edifices that capitalise on the available resources in an efficient manner, while focussing on adequate food production in confined spaces. Unlike developed nations, India commencing a vertical farm, the cost of maintaining the day-to-day operations of such a facility is extremely sizeable as well.

From Table 1, it is evident that most of the world's popular vertical farms are prevalent in countries such as the USA, UK, Germany, Singapore etc. The relative gains of possessing such a unique food producing technology can be explained from an environmental and economical perspective. The geographic localisation of such vertical farms can be explicated in terms of the electricity prices, coupled with the availability of the vegetables in the said region. For instance, in the USA as well as Brazil, electricity is relatively cheaper in contrast to the United Kingdom or Germany, and hence, it is easier to maintain and operate vertical farms in such nations. Again, in manufacturing-dominant economies such as Japan, there is a dearth of fresh vegetables sourced from open field cultivation (Beghin, et al 2003). Yet, vertical farming continues to attract more attention due to the prospect of inclusive control and autonomy of climatic fluctuations.

Key Variants of Vertical Farming

The concepts 'hydroponics', 'aquaponics' and 'aeroponics' are variants of organic, ecologically sensitive and sustainable gardening. Since they do not utilise soil, they can be set up in an indoor environment, in settings that have cold and harsh climates, or in localities that have fragile, sandy soils. These three distinct systems are noteworthy techniques utilised by urban growers in the niche of alternative farming mechanisms.

The oldest among the three techniques is the principle of hydroponics, given the use of soil-less arrangements that have been in practice since the era of the Hanging Gardens of Babylon. A hydroponics system makes use of liquid, sand, gravel, and other materials to grow plants away from a soil environment. The plants' roots get nutrient ions from water, enriched with liquid plant food. It encompasses two critical constituents: the grow beds and the reservoir. The reservoir contains the nutrient solution or the water blended with anassortment of nutrients that plants require in order to grow successfully in the media bed. The grow beds, such as coconut coir, perlite, organic-polymer composites etc. contain the media and the 'cups' that secure the plants in their respective places.

Aquaponics is a hybrid system that amalgamates the best of aquaculture and hydroponics. Aquaculture is the farming of fish, crustaceans, molluscs, aquatic plants, algae, and other organisms. From a systems perspective, it is akin to a conception of a natural ecosystem, wherein fish, plants, and bacteria flourish off each other. The waste output from fish and the living bacteria in an aquaponics system deliver the requisite nutrients by the plants. The concoction of the fish and the bacteria create a cleaner, non-toxic environment for the fish to subsist, thereby eliminating the need for a nutrient solution blended with chemicals.

Aeroponics is a variant of hydroponics, with the exception that, instead of using a grow bed filled with media, the plants are suspended instead, with roots fronting a sprinkler system linked to the core nutrient reservoir. It is a technique of growing plants in a moist environment. These systems are frequently employed in an enclosed environment such as greenhouses such that the temperature and humidity can be precisely synchronised. Despite sunlight being the principal source of light, certain additional sources of lighting may also be injected.

The pros and cons of the three systems are discussed in Table 3, which helps bring out the more superior system among the three.

Table 3: Relative Merits and Demerits of Hydroponics, Aquaponics and Aeroponics

	Merits	Demerits
Hydroponics	• Designed for the long-term cultivation of any kind of crop • The system works simply and can be easily expanded if one wants to commercialise the system	• With the recent rise in interest levels towards hydroponics, the price of the chemical compounds to create a viable nutrient solution has been steadily rising due to the over-mining of such minerals • Need to regularly check the electrical conductivity of the water as fluctuations in the pHlevel of water can damage plants
Aquaponics	• Ability to raise fish and grow crops at the same time • Fish waste is a popular source of nutrition for the plants • Plants serve as an absolute ammonia control centre for the fish tank, reducing the ammonia load and preventing watertoxicity	• One would have to be specific with the design of the system so as to avoid shutting it down during winter seasons • Even if one only wants to grow crops for sale, the fish still have to be tended adequately such that they do not continually die off
Aeroponics	• Crops grow exceedingly quickly • Higher yields • Utilises the least amount of water over time and all the unused excess	• Humidity is not enough to sustain the roots of plants • Highly reliant on the misting system; if it fails then the plants

In conclusion, since hydroponics, aeroponics and aquaponics do not make use of soil, they can be established indoors in locations that have cold as well as severe climates. From a commercial grower's viewpoint, aquaponics has a definite edge over hydroponics. In this system, plants grow faster and with better crop yield, while producing fish that deliver a supplementary revenue stream. Moreover, there is a condensed negative impact on the environment, as aquaponics produces no nutrient-salt-filled wastewater and it saves water due to its circulatory nature.

Key Driving Forces of Vertical Farming

Interestingly, the model of vertical farming was propositioned with the aim of expanding the amount of agricultural land by adopting the mantra of 'building upwards'. Thus, the effective arable land area for crops can be augmented by constructing high-rise buildings with multiple levels on the same footprint of land (Despommier, 2010). Many a few aspiring farmers often contemplate on the factors that ensure the success of their farm. Despite an array of solid practices, economics continues to be a determining factor in establishing a successful vertical farm. Vertical farming also happens to be attractive in the context of India, where there is a high demand for green and nutritious food, coupled with the fact that it continually suffers from extreme pollution and soil depletion issues. The key driving forces for promoting vertical farming in the Indian context are deliberated upon in Table 4.

Table 4: Major Driving Forces of Vertical Farming

Driving Force	Explanation
Efficient and productive utilisation of space	• It maximises the entire volume of space, from the floor up • To maximise space use (i.e. density), growers must maximise the growing specific surface area within a volume
Reduced labour costs	• Farming on a vertical plane ensures that compliance processes and safety nets are relatively uncomplicated in their creation and maintenance, since all processes can be implemented in a targeted manner • Vertical farms are usually modular and lightweight, and hence, each component of the vertical farm can be moved and consolidated fortreatment, thereby making it better for compliance and food safety
Greater profitability	• Vertical farming establishes fewer limitations on the ability to occupy a volume of space, as a function of labour use • Capital and operational expenditures and usually do not

Savings on transportation	• Location of food production in urban areas in closer proximity to consumers is a major driving force for the growth of such firms, thereby resulting in the dramatic reductions in transportation costs • Eliminates greenhouse-gas emissions from several heavy carrier-vehicles, thereby supporting adaptation and mitigation withreference to climate change
Cultivation of green and nutritious food	• Round-the-year production of crops without any seasonal intervention, in a temperature-and-humidity-controlled environment shall help produce fresh produce on demand. • Utilising recycled water and nutrients in a confined, indoor, climate-controlled environment contributes to food security andmitigates the need for pesticides and herbicides
Better health of plants	• In a vertical space, the impact of heat is removed more easily, andlighting interacts with plane orientation thereby influencing airflow

Source: Vertical Farm Systems, Australia (2017)

Vertical farming has been successful at the introductory test levels as well as at the production levels. It has demonstrated prospective gains over rural farming, including the use of hydroponics, which contests the need for soil-based farming for a range of crops. In fact, productivity expands with the number of levels in the premises of a high-rise building or number of racks in a single high-rise enclosure. Many of the subsidiary technologies have been delved into in past variations of greenhouse farming, but these are now blending into commercially feasible mechanisms due to rapid contemporary advances in electronics, engineering, solar, wind and computing power.

About the Organisation

This section shall expound upon the concept of vertical farming with the aid of the central case study on UrbaGrow Aquaponics, based in Kolkata, India.

Company Background

Blueplanet Urban Agro Services Pvt Ltd (Urbagrow) is an urban-based, aquaponic, soil- free, food garden based in Kolkata. It is located in Survey Park, a neighbourhood in the suburban part of South-East Kolkata, atop a 1,000 square feet rooftop. Founded by Anirban Chanda, the company is an effective new age urban food gardener in the city of Kolkata, given that they aim to promote self-sustenance, with the production of organic fish and vegetables in an urban setting without the intervention of soil requirements and water

Company Objectives

UrbaGrow Aquaponics practices soil-free aquaponics and are taking massive strides in accomplishing self-sustainability. The founder, along with his members subscribe to a rising global community of *aquapons*, who pursue a mutual goal of nurturing an eco-friendly sustainable development endeavour. The company aims to grow large quantities of food in the rooftop garden, while exhibiting their research to all parties interested in experiencing the concept of aquaponics. Their aim is to promote a culture of aquaponics in the city. To this end, they follow an unassuming process, commencing with a visit by interested parties, who seek to join in for a learning session. This would help such individuals replicate the model by building or ordering seeds, seedlings and fish fingerlings etc. from the company. This binds the parties into a niche community of aquapons, who happen to be a rapidly expanding community, comprising of individuals, excited by the endless prospects from food exchanges to organic markets.

The aquaponic urban food garden in the city of Kolkata displays the fruits of approximately three years of concerted self-regulating research in aquaponics. The output was reflected in the shape of a contemporary variation to an age-old science, existent for centuries. UrbaGrow employs a method of growing vegetables and certain fruits, in cyclical, self-balancing natural structures that function without the inevitability of soil and any requirement for chemical-based additives, such as fertilizers or pesticides. Aquaponics is effectively amended to work with modern-day materials and the usage of electricity.

The proliferating use of unrestrained, misconstrued and unsustainable industrial processes in agriculture has substituted almost all traditional growing techniques and long- standing sustainable practices. Greater food miles, yield additives, pesticides and warehousing have amplified the price of most food products for all Indians. This has triggered the need for UrbaGrow to grow nutritious and healthy food in a clean and sustainable manner.

It started when the founder, Anirban Chanda, decided to examine the quantity of food that could actually be grown on a small roof in Kolkata of about 1,000 square feet, using the principle of aquaponics. Today, the company is engaged in the process of building aquaponic systems for other clients, with their Indian adaptations. The company is known to offer various urban aquaponic systems, all tried and tested in the company's own food garden and on display for all to see and be acquainted with. The systems are all developed from locally sourced materials by the team of aquapons. This makes them scalable and easy to

Process of Aquaponics used by UrbaGrow

The rooftop garden demonstrates an assortment of aquaponic mechanisms for growing a range of vegetables and Tilapia as well as catfish. The symbiotic liaison between the fish and plants coupled with the temperate climate of Kolkata enables the company to grow a wide range of seasonal vegetables and edible fish. The garden serves as an exhibition for systems of diverse sizes and escalating techniques, all designed to occupy open spaces in urban environments such as penthouses, rooftops and balconies, where there is adequate availability of electricity, and which receives sufficient amount of sunlight to nurture green, healthy and nutritious plants. The systems designed by UrbaGrow consume less water in contrast to archetypal land gardening, while necessitating reduced work in man-hours and facilitating the process of growing vegetables in greater density, i.e. more vegetables per square feet, as opposed to a traditional soil-based food sprouting undertaking. All the systems are appropriately *Indianised* in that they are suited to the temperature, humidity and other climatic conditions of the country. Furthermore, they are handmade and cost less to build and maintain than most other aquaponic systems available across the world.

The company designs, builds and installs aquaponic systems of different dimensions on the rooftops and ground floor spaces in and around high-rise buildings and other residential or commercial buildings in and around the city of Kolkata. The pricing structure adopted by the company for installing such a system is captured below:

- Simple rudimentary single barrel mechanism: INR 12,000
- Six bed mechanisms (approximately 75 square feet): INR 72,000
- Ten bed mechanisms (approximately 100 square feet): INR 1,20,000

The company has been able to grow a variety of vegetables such as tomato, cucumber, bitter gourd, bottle gourd, kohlrabi, cauliflower, cabbage, red and green spinach, chilly, capsicum, cherry tomato, basil, green bean, brinjal, ridge gourd, pumpkin, lettuce, turnip, papaya, and an entire range of distinct herbs and seasonal flowers. They have also ensured the growth and harvest of the *tilapia* and catfish.

Central Questions

The current endeavour is an attempt to deliberate on the effectiveness of vertical farming as a novel agricultural practice in congested urban settings. The key

1. To what extent can aquaponics farming be considered as a feasible alternate farming practice in the Indian context?
2. How does UrbaGrow Aquaponics, Kolkata utilise vertical farming (aquaponics) for developing sustainable food production in the urban context?

Implications for Future Research

The worldwide megatrends of declining water supply, ever-increasing population, reckless urbanisation, and unabated climate change have triggered a global decline in the availability of arable land per individual. Under such harsh surroundings, the sustainability of the traditional farming model pillared on large-scale rural farms is likely to be threatened in the near future. The paper has established a definite approach for confronting this challenging problem through the practice of vertical farming, which is grounded on the presence of a controlled-environment agriculture and greenhouse designs that are apt for urban settings.

The current undertaking further defines the inherent concept of vertical farming and its constituents, while highlighting the implications for future food production. Vertical farming, in essence, has provided novel opportunities for architecture as well as urban designing. Urban designers have demonstrated the relevance of making cities green, healthy and secure. By concocting food production and architecture, vertical farming, through hydroponics, aquaponics or aeroponics, helps in the production of buildings that are capable of yielding multiple functions.

The case study of UrbaGrow Aquaponics, based in Kolkata, India is testimony to the fact that vertical farming is highly feasible in the densely populated city. Their handmade designs and systems, customised to suit the Indian context, would not only be effective in the context of sustainable food-production with round-the-year crop production, but would also provide independence from droughts, floods, and pests as well. The approach adopted is indeed compatible with water recycling, ecosystem restoration, reduction of pathogens, and more importantly, generation of new jobs as novel start-ups. In future, as horizontal spaces for farming start to dwindle, farmers and growers shall be perusing more sustainable techniques of growing food in vertical spaces, rather than on shrinking level spaces. The case shall serve as a success story, thereby furnishing multiple entrepreneurial opportunities for future agri-entrepreneurs who are contemplating on germinating sustainable food production techniques.

even space exploration, where food production may be indispensable (Giroux et al. 2006). In light of such circumstances, several recommendations have been outlined for future research in this novel domain. Preliminarily, a more precise quantification of the economics of vertical farming and its derivatives is warranted using computer simulation and detailed analysis of new commercial installations. There is also a requirement to compare the return on investment with respect to that of a traditional firm as compared to the vertical firm. This should be backed by a transactional study on the principal cost-drivers including land, plant depreciation, market demand, and moderated transportation costs. Second, future researches are required to concentrate on the examination of vertical farming constituents, in novel urban arrangements, not only on rooftops, but also underground, or in derelict warehouses. Such studies should examine the economic implications of the alternatives. Third, policy-makers could consider the development of change-management strategies such as the education of farm workers with newly-developed business and management skill sets, to empower them to be more suited to regulated-environment agriculture. This would help in determining the success rate of transitioning from traditional modes of agriculture to the urban farming context. Fourth, it is critical to identify employment opportunities in technology, monitoring, maintenance, customer service, and research and development related to vertical farming activities. Finally, there is a pressing need for augmented funding in light of research in plant genetics for yield optimisation, extending the range of crop types, and fine-tuning for optimal response to controlled variables such as impact of LED lighting, temperature, humidity, and carbon dioxide levels.

There are still multiple unanswered questions, such as whether farm output would be able to keep pace with the skyrocketing demands of the global population. Other major questions also persist, such as whether the requisite quality for healthy living would be delivered by the farm produce in future. The key lies in the effective utilisation of scarce and depleting resources by agricultural entrepreneurs. Vertical farming is one such implement used by contemporary agri-entrepreneurs in the quest to establish sustainable production of food products. Das (2019) affirms that the last decade has witnessed considerable attention from entrepreneurs in terms of using innovative farming techniques such as vertical farming. This is complementary to the emergent practices of cultivating food in the confines of a greenhouse, on the rooftop, in the basement of an apartment or inside shipping containers. Notwithstanding, most of such growers have adopted soil-based organic farming practices. A

References

Ackerman, K.; Culligan, P.; Plunz, R.; Sutto, M.P. and Whittinghill, L. (2014). Sustainable Food Systems for Future Cities: The Potential of Urban Agriculture. The Economic and Social Review. Vol. 45; pp. 189-206.

Calderone, L. (2018, December 26). Growing with Hydroponics, Aeroponics and Aquaponics. Retrieved January 02, 2019, from https://www.agritechtomorrow.com/article/2018/05/growing-with-hydroponics- aeroponics-and-aquaponics/10733

Cleland, J. (2013). World Population Growth: Past, Present and Future. Environmental and Resource Economics. Vol. 55; doi: 10.1007/s13278-012-0079- 3

Cohen, J. E. (2001). World population in 2050: Assessing the Projections. In Conference Series-Federal Reserve Bank of Boston. Vol. 46, pp. 83-113.

Corvalan, C.; Hales, S.; McMichael, A.J. (2005). Ecosystems and Human Well- Being: Health Synthesis; World Health Organisation: Geneva, Switzerland.

Das, A. (2019, February 21). Evolution of Commercial Aquaponics in India. Retrieved April 20, 2019, from https://www.entrepreneur.com/article/328679

Despommier, D. (2010). The Vertical Farm: Feeding the World in the 21st Century; Thomas Dunne Books: New York, USA.

Despommier, D. (2013). Farming up the city: The rise of urban vertical farms. Trends Biotechnol. Vol. 31; pp. 388–389.

Despommier, D. (2014). Encyclopedia of Food and Agricultural Ethics (Vertical Farms in Horticulture); Springer: Dordrecht, The Netherlands.

Healy, R.G.; Rosenberg, J.S. (2013). Land Use and the States; Routledge: New York, New York, USA.

Muller, A.; Ferré, M.; Engel, S.; Gattinger, A.; Holzkämper, A.; Huber, R.; Müller, M. and Six, J. (2017). Can soil-less crop production be a sustainable option for soil conservation and future agriculture? Land Use Policy. Vol. 69; pp. 102–105.

Singh, N. (2017, June 8). These #4 Start-ups Are Promoting Hydroponics in India. Retrieved January 2, 2019, from https://www.entrepreneur.com/article/295531

Thomaier, S.; Specht, K.; Henckel, D.; Dierich, A.; Siebert, R. and Freisinger, U.B.; Sawicka, M. (2015). Farming in and on Urban Buildings: Present Practice and Specific Novelties of Zero-Acreage Farming (Z-Farming). Renewable Agriculture and Food Systems. Vol. 30; pp. 43–54.

Touliatos, D.; Dodd, I.C. and McAinsh, M. (2016). Vertical farming increases lettuce yield per unit area compared to conventional horizontal hydroponics. Food Energy Security. Vol. 5; pp. 184–191.

VentureRadar. (2018). Top Vertical Farming Companies. Retrieved January 02, 2019, from https://www.ventureradar.com/keyword/Vertical Farming

Vertical Farm Systems, Australia. (2017). Advantages of Vertical Farming. Retrieved January 2, 2019, from http://www.verticalfarms.com.au/advantages- vertical-farming

Wiskerke, J. S. (2015). Urban Food Systems. In H. D. Zeeuw and P. Drechsel (Eds.), Cities and Agriculture: Developing Resilient Urban Food Systems (pp. 1- 25). New York and London: Routledge.

3

Innovation in Agriculture: Case of Dragon Fruit and Water Hyacinth

Arkadipta Roy and Pritha Adhikari

Abstract

Sustainable development and success in any field, agriculture being one of them, goes hand in hand with Innovation. To tackle the current growing problems in the agricultural sector, and long-term sustainability of the agri-ecosystem, agricultural innovations are needed that might bring new products or processes or open up new markets, thereby optimising the use of the limited resources to attain maximum benefits. The authors discuss innovation from the perspective of two dimensions: Technology and Market to illustrate four different kinds of innovation - incremental, architectural, radial and descriptive. This paper deals with the concept of innovation in agricultural field [referred to as agri-innovation] using illustrations of two innovative products namely Dragon Fruit and Water Hyacinth, both of which have significant role in the agri-ecosystem of India. The introduction of Dragon Fruit in a new market is illustrated as an agri-innovation. Efforts by state and private sector of introducing Dragon Fruit, a popular production in South & South East Asia to Indian markets are an example of Architectural Innovation. Also the most common weed Water Hyacinth is considered to be used in news forms so that it can be modified as a new product for a new market. The paper thus documents the suitability of these innovative agri-products in the current Indian market scenario.

Keywords: Innovation, Agri-Innovation, Dragon Fruit, Water Hyacinth.

Introduction

Innovation is the increase in value by implementation of something new or improved (whether technology or otherwise) in products (goods or services), processes, marketing and organisational methods. In other words, it means application of ideas, knowledge or practices that are new to a particular context with the purpose of creating positive change that will provide a way to meet needs take on challenges and seize opportunities [*OECD (2005)*]. Thus innovation is said to be an assimilation of multiple cumulative small changes or a few larger ones by discovering or rediscovering new ways to do things that brings about changes in the current norms. It is the use of relevant knowledge, practices, technologies and ideas, transforming them into a change that proves to be beneficial for the productive or organisational life as well as the society as a whole. In business as well as in economics, innovation can become a catalyst for growth by creating bigger opportunities and is critical for the sustainability, survival, long-term growth, and success of any organisation in any given field (*Gertner, 2004*).

Agricultural Innovation

Innovation, as applied to agriculture may be a product or a service which results in improvement in productivity, competitiveness in the agri-sector and economic growth of the economies, to make agriculture sustainable and profitable through processes like farm mechanisation, value addition, optimum utilisation of resources, energy management etc. Despite India being primarily an agrarian economy, innovative products and processes is grossly far and few, with respect to what are being complied with globally. The agricultural processes are still traditional in most parts of the country, resulting in lower yields, lower profitability thus leading to underdevelopment in the sector, making it a non-lucrative occupation for the present generation. Moreover the new challenges of climate change, strain of increasing population, energy crises etc. adds to the ever growing list of problems faced by the farmers and the agricultural sector as a whole. These problems can be effectively dealt with the implementation of newer and innovative technologies and processes.

Objective of the Study

The broad objective of the study is to analyse the theoretical understanding about innovation and thereafter use specific cases of agri-innovative products which have potential for economic growth, specifically the paper discusses the

Research Methodology

The case study method is a very popular form of qualitative analysis and involves a careful and complete observation of a social unit, be that unit a person, a family, an institution, a cultural group or even the entire community. The object of the case study method is to locate the factors that account for the behavioural patterns of the given unit as an integrated totality.

This research study focuses on two of the most recent innovations in the field of agriculture namely Dragon Fruit and Water Hyacinth, both of which have immense potentialities yet hardly received much recognition for the same. Thus, in this paper, with the help of *Case Study* methodology, the authors make an in depth and exhaustive study of these two prospective value additive products. The problems encountered in commercial success of these two products and their probable solutions and their future prospects are included in the paper.

Innovation

The concept of innovation dates back to Rogers' definition of innovation as 'an idea, practice or object that is perceived as new by an individual or other unit of adoption' [*Everett M. Rogers, 2003*]. Hence it is an invention, a product that is new to the market or produces a change in a social process. Innovation in the context of agriculture can be explained in terms of the following matrix by breaking down innovation into two dimensions: Technology and Market, which gives us the following 4 combination types of innovation:

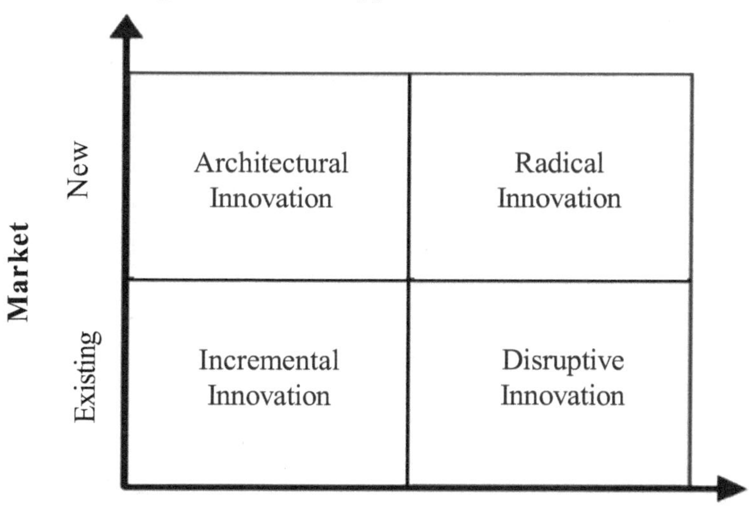

Incremental Innovation

Incremental innovation, the most common form of innovation, deals with the utilisation of the existing technology and increases value of the product to the customer (by incorporating changes in features, design changes, etc.) within the existing market. Thus in simpler words it is said to be adding or sustaining value to existing product, services or processes that almost all organisations need to delve into time and again for better chances of survival in the market.

Seedless grapes which are greatly popular in places like California, Italy, Greece, Spain and other parts of the globe may be an example of incremental innovation. The technology of hybridisation makes seedless grapes as a product with an added feature in existing. By introducing the techniques of hybridisation to create seedless grapes, a new incremental product was invented which was introduced into the existing markets, thereby adding value to the existing product for the consumers. [*eurofresh-distribution.com, farmprogress.com*]

Architectural Innovation

Architectural innovation is the introduction of existing technologies or products into a new market, to further increase the reach and coverage of the product base. This innovation is good for increasing new customers as long as the new market is receptive. It involves less risk due to their reliance and reintroduction of proven technology, though most of the time finer improvements and adjustments to the system are required in order to match the requirements of the new market.

Cultivation and commercialisation of Dragon Fruit falls under this very category of architectural innovation. Dragon Fruit, a major product of Central and South America, South East Asia, Australia, Cambodia, China, United States, Cyprus, Canary Islands and Vietnam, is an already existing product with wide global presence. The introduction of this fruit in India is considered to be an architectural innovation. This case study has been discussed in details later in the study.

Radical Innovation

Radical innovation can be considered to be the true definition of an innovation as it results in the origin of new industries (or swallows existing ones) and creates revolutionary technologies in relevant fields. Over the recent past, the world has witnessed the emergence of numerous exciting breakthroughs in agriculture, like indoor farming techniques that are able to leverage refined towards the integration of these techniques at crucial points in our agricultural production framework. In this context, Water Hyacinth is also said to be a product of radical innovation, and the same notion is justified and discussed in details later in the study. Water Hyacinth is a common product mostly considered a water weed in tropical water bodies. This paper unearths the modified uses of byproducts of Water Hyacinth and suggests how they can enter new market.

Disruptive Innovation

Disruptive innovation, also known as stealth innovation, involves the application of newer technologies, product types and processes in an already existing market. It is termed as disruptive as the product/ process is not an iteration of any existing product, but rather an entirely new one with new and unique prospects that never existed before. Such innovation creates a new market and a value network that eventually disrupts the existing one by displacing the previously established market-leading firms, products, and alliances.

Examples of disruptive innovations in the field of agriculture ranges from the replacement of the ploughing bulls with tractors (a change that took 40 years for full adoption and adaption), to inorganic fertilizers, hybridisation, GMOs, no-till, GPS and auto steer, fancy and sophisticated farm equipments (self-propelled sprayers) to name a few. [*www.omafra.gov.on.ca*]

Regardless of the type, innovations in agriculture is becoming increasingly important to make agriculture a sustainable, profitable and competitive enterprise through engineering interventions of farm mechanisation, value addition and energy management in production and post-harvest operations. In this paper the two cases, namely Dragon Fruit and Water Hyacinth, have been used to illustrate the Architectural and Radical innovation with reference to the Indian agri-ecosystem.

Case Study I - Dragon Fruit

The Product

Pitaya or Pitahaya or more commonly known as Dragon Fruit, is an exotic tropical fruit that has become increasingly popular off late across the globe. People enjoy it for its unique look, taste and more importantly for its high medicinal and nutritional values. The plant is native to southern Mexico and Central America but today, it is grown all over the world with Vietnam being the largest producer and exporter.

of the Night") as well as is very popular for the curative benefits it offers. There are bracts or scales on the Dragon Fruit skin and hence it is named as pitaya meaning "the scaly fruit". Worldwide currently it is being cultivated in at least 22 countries in the tropics including Australia, Cambodia, China, Malaysia, Thailand, Sri Lanka, Mexico, Central America, Taiwan, South East Asia, United States, Cyprus, Canary Islands and Vietnam. The crop is a cactus and thus can be grown abundantly in tropical and sub-tropical countries with arid soil, thereby providing great scope for cultivation and farming all over India.

India being a tropical country with moderate climate all-round the year is suitable for Dragon Fruit cultivation, as it adapts well to tropical and sub-tropical climatic conditions. Thus the fruit can suitably be grown in tropical and sub-tropical climatic conditions along with availability of adequate sunlight and can even survive with minimal average annual rainfall. It can further be cultivated in a wide range of soils namely red soils, sandy soils mixed with black soil and well drained soils, clay loamy soils or sandy loamy soils that should be rich in organic matter.

The New Market

Several enterprising farmers have already ventured into Dragon Fruit cultivation, and are known to take the first-mover advantage since the Indian market is grossly undersupplied and untapped at the moment. If the market is developed properly, Dragon Fruits hold immense potential since the awareness and acceptance regarding the same is gradually increasing, with evident increase in imports along with increased local production initiatives. But the local markets are still latent and can be expanded not only domestically but vastly internationally for its well recognition, acceptance and popularity outside India's geographical borders.

The demand for Dragon Fruit is increasing steadily in the *Indian markets* with consumers getting more aware of this exotic fruit, along with its various health benefits. The potential for this fruit is exponential as we see a gradual life style shift in today's society towards natural and healthy living, opening up a wide market for such health conscious people who opt to consume this food for its taste, nutritional and medicinal properties. Thus we see that in recent times, Dragon Fruit cultivation has become quite a lucrative venture for farmers ready to invest in this up and coming new age fruit.

Nowadays, these fruits are also cultivated in many regions in India, like Pune, with irrigation facilities. ATMA (Agriculture Technology Management Agency) introduced plantation of Dragon Fruit as an alternative crop for 125 drought prone villages of Sangli district in Maharashtra. Small marginalised farmers, women and disabled farmers have successively adopted the crop as an alternative livelihood source for income augmentation. Suitability of this fruit in that region and high market demand led him to buy plants from a nursery in Kolkata, which soon inspired others. This was the first instance where farmers in the state had planted Dragon Fruit on a commercial basis. South Gujarat is gradually gaining popularity in Dragon Fruit cultivation like in Surat, Tapi and Baruch districts, sites near Rajkot, Junagadh and Porbandar districts to name a few. Nagaland is another hub for nutritious fruits like Dragon Fruit cultivation, which is not only a source of income in the state, but also a way for women empowerment and entrepreneurship.

In India, commercial cultivation of this fruit is picking up and market price of this fruit ranges between Rs.150-250, and can even be as high as Rs.400 per kg based on the region it is cultivated in, market, demand etc. Thus steady growing demand coupled with market expansion opportunities is increasingly pushing Dragon Fruit as mainstream commercial product in the Indian market.

The Architectural Innovation: Dragon Fruit as an Existing Product in New Market

Dragon Fruit is thus deemed as an architectural innovation in the Indian agricultural sector, as it is the introduction of an existing product in an entirely new market. The cultivation of Dragon Fruit is an architectural innovation where old technology and processes are being utilised to expand the known products into unknown markets. Dragon Fruit cultivation is not a new concept globally, but its introduction in the Indian market is an innovative leap for the Indian agri-businesses and the sector as a whole. Not only the farming is profitable, it also has multi-various uses, and is quite suitable for the Indian climatic and soil composition. Thus Case study is deemed as an example of architectural innovation as it applies the lessons of the global market in a new market i.e. the Indian agricultural sector.

Dragon Fruit cultivation is hardly a new one in the global scenario with large producers and exporters like Vietnam, Mexico and other countries beyond India's geographical boundaries, catering to the huge international demands for this miracle fruit. But it can be seen that this concept is still quite a new one when hoped. This is an entirely new market for this fruit and if marketed properly, will take the market by storm. The technology and skills used for Dragon Fruit farming requires special training, and though it is a little unconventional, it cannot be deemed as new. Thus all the above issues justify the use of Dragon Fruit as an illustration for architectural innovation, with widespread social and economic impact on the country's agri-market.

Case Study II – Water Hyacinth

The Product

Water Hyacinth, a free floating perennial herb of fresh water ecosystems, is one of the most noxious weeds in the tropical and sub-tropical regions. It is a fast growing perennial aquatic macrophyte. It is a South American plant growing worldwide between 40 degree North and South latitude. Water Hyacinth is aquatic vascular plant with rounded, upright and shiny green leaves and lavender flowers similar to orchids. Each one carries six to eight spirally arranged succulent leaves that are produced sequentially on a short vertical stem. Petioles are bulbous and spongy with many air spaces which allow plants to float on a water surface.

It is well known for its reproductive potential and as a plant that can double its population in twelve days which is the secret behind its massive growth. Growth of this plant is primarily dependent on two things: ability of the plant to use solar energy, nutrient composition and -environmental factors. It has a well-known ability to grow even in polluted waters.

Conventionally, it is considered as a waste product which is of not much value to the eco-system rather detrimental to it. The fast growth and rapid spread of this plant are often consequences of large quantities of nutrients and other pollutants present in the contaminated water with effluents from agriculture industry, municipality and other sources. In India it has started eating into a number of lakes like the Katraj Lake in Pune, Picholalake in Udaipur and UlsooruLake in Bangalore. In many settlements Water Hyacinth has destroyed economy (fishing, river transport).

It also displaces native vegetation communities and adversely affects the fish population. Due to the decomposition of the Water Hyacinth mats sedimentation increases and the dissolved oxygen levels are reduced thus affecting the quality of water. Water intake points become blocked; the screens and filters of water

Water Hyacinth can be severely detrimental to the water as it interferes with the navigation of both recreational and commercial craft. In addition to this it also interferes with the boating by fisherman and water skiers in recreational waters, with swimming.

This has driven the rural communities where Water Hyacinth is prevalent to think about alternative use of the product, so that the product which was considered to be a waste previously can put to some product that can add some value to the ecosystem.

Innovative Uses of the Product

It has been proved that Water Hyacinth, an environmental waste can be converted into renewable energy thereby meeting both the challenges at the same time and thereby helping in maintaining the ecological balance. The biogas plant uses Water Hyacinth in order to produce energy. Hence utilising it to the possible use can convert Water Hyacinth from an environmental 'bane' to an environmental 'boon'.

The Water Hyacinth can be used as a substrate for compost or biogas production. The sludge from the biogas process contains almost all of the nutrients of the substrate and can be used as a fertilizer. The use of Water Hyacinth compost on different crops has resulted in improved yields. The high protein content makes the Water Hyacinth possible to use as fodder for cows, goats, sheep and chickens. In Africa the nutrient deficit soils are regenerated by using Water Hyacinth as a potential fertilizer, due to its abundant growth and high concentrations of nutrients. Applying the Water Hyacinths directly without any other processing than sun drying, seems to be the best alternative in small-scale use due to the relatively small losses of nutrients and workload required. Degraded soils can be regenerated by utilizing it as a green fertilizer or compost and ash. It has an ability to remove different pollutants from water hence this ability can be taken as a positive influence on the fish population in natural water or fish growing in artificial accumulation. Interesting fact about this plant is that it can be used for energy production in the sense that using it as briquettes or biogas for lighting furnaces or cooking purposes.

The characteristic of Water Hyacinth that it is capable of growing in nutrient rich water and accumulating very high concentration of Nitrogen, Phosphorus and Potassium and upon decomposition it releases accumulated nutrients rapidly qualifies Water Hyacinth as a potential mulching material in soil nutrient

Innovating Uses of the Product in New Market

It produces large quantity of seeds which are viable for up to thirty years. It has been researched that this weed can be blended with polyester to make clothing and domestic textiles and its fibres can be used as a raw material for the manufacture of clothing and home fabrics. Hence it has a positive impact on the textile industry. In India, Water Hyacinth is also used to produce similar goods for the tourist industry using traditional basket making and weaving skills are used.

The weaving industry is positively dependent on Water Hyacinth in the sense that in settlements where Water Hyacinth has destroyed the economy (fishing, river transport, etc.) population can be reoriented to manufacturing of art paper, crafts, ropes, furniture and other things from Water Hyacinth which will lead to reduction of unemployment and increase of income. The fibre from the stems of the Water Hyacinth plant can be used to make ropes. They can also be dried and used to make baskets and matting for domestic use.

In Bangladesh an attempt was made to produce paper from Water Hyacinth. In Bangladesh handmade paper from Water Hyacinth is already a modest source of income to the poor. Several experiments on how to use the Water Hyacinth to produce fibre board had been conducted after which they developed a locally manufactured production plant for producing fibre board for general-purpose use. This is because the two most important ingredients to make paper that is water and soluble fibre is present in this herb.

The fibre from the stems of the plant can be used to make ropes. The finished rope is used by local furniture manufacturers who wind the rope around a cane frame to produce an elegant finished product which is then is sold in the market. In settlements where Water Hyacinth has destroyed economy (fishing, river transport) people can reorient to manufacturing of art paper, crafts, ropes, furniture and other things from Water Hyacinth which will positively influence to reduction of unemployment and increase of income.

The Radical Innovation: Water Hyacinth, the New use of Product in a New Market

Use of Water Hyacinth in a new innovative way may be used as an example of Radical Innovation, which is modification of the product with organisational capabilities; individual and organisational human capital for a new market. This type of innovation blows up the existing system or process and replaces it with

In Cambodia the fibres of Water Hyacinth are also put to use and they do so by plaiting the ropes from the fibres and even sacks are produced from the Water Hyacinth. In Thailand, the dried plant material is soaked in glycerin to make the fibres more pliable and more receptive to dyes for making hard-wearing sandals. Napkin-rings, chair seats and placemats made out of this weed have in the meantime appeared on the market. Most of the products come from non-governmental organisations (NGOs) in Kenya, Bangladesh, Thailand and the Philippines. In Luzira Maximum Security Prison in Kampala the prison Water Hyacinth is collected carefully from the lake by boat, and laid to dry in the sun for a few days, before being treated with a preservative. They make bags, tables, sleeping mats, and hospital screens. Easy chairs are made with wooden frames, and dining chairs using metal frames.

Recommendation: Way Forward

From this research it is concluded that commercially, Dragon Fruit appears to have numerous selling points; they are attractive in shape and colour, and possess high nutritional values which attract growers from all over India. The crop is hardy and can survive in any type of climatic condition favourable for flowering and fruiting and soil condition provided with good drainage. In general, they produce fruits quickly and few diseases and pests are encountered at the present time. It also has high industrial and marketing potential which can be processed in numerous ways like ice-creams, jams, jelly, desserts, fruit juice, wine to name a few, not to mention its various nutritional and medicinal benefits.

Both the farmers, as well as scientists agree to the beneficial properties of the plant, but they are also wary of the future market prospects. Despite its exotic and beautiful outward appearances, many people do not consider Dragon Fruit as tasty, often deeming it bland. Currently, it is preferred only by certain segments of people- those who are health conscious and prefer low-sugar fruits. Clear requirements of the market are lacking too. So, until the stabilisation of the market, many farmers are hesitant to go all out, and often avoid large-scale production. To make the market sustainable, the product should be demand driven, keeping future prospects in mind. Customers demand may be created so that the fruit is well marketed, because it is highly nutritive, and efforts should be made to tap it. Also, proper research in terms of cultivation practices and value addition would go a long way in establishing the fruit as a crop. To do so, the Government and private sector marketers plays a vital part in raising awareness and supporting budding farmers so that they can sustain in local renewable resources are already in a decreasing spree. There has been a sporadic expansion of Water Hyacinth which is considered to be a not so useful plant rather a burden to the nature. But this plant has some specific characteristics which make it a perennial herb of multiple uses. Making most of the innovative use of this particular natural resource can save the environment by introducing a new market for the products made from Water Hyacinth. To counter the negative aspects of this weed, numerous villagers and artisans from different parts of India have come together to make this weed into a source of income by weaving it into a natural fibre and further weaving it into various utility products thereby creating a new market for the same. Different handcrafted products from Water Hyacinth are sold in the handicrafts market. The government and private markets as well as NGOs have made several attempts to use the Water Hyacinth based new products and thus create a new market to generate income.

Agricultural innovation is the solution to the growing food crises in the world. Sustainable developments in this field are the only way that can support the ever growing world population and reduce the strains on the limited resources of the earth. Since agriculture is one of the primary economic and social activities that cannot be substituted, hence there is ever growing need to better utilise the available resources and make these activities more productive with the help of innovative ventures. Innovation in this field leads to overall sustainability, and will also help combat major issues life resource management and sustainability, climate change, global food crises, energy crises, optimum land and water usage etc. Various new agri-innovations like vertical farming use of Artificial Intelligence and Internet of Things, drones and bees in the farming techniques, Genetic modification and upgradation are some of the innovations which are helping develop the global agricultural sector by leaps and bounds. Thus agricultural innovation is one of the solutions that should be encouraged and developed by all, to lead us towards a brighter and sustainable future.

References

Agengo, George (2013). Effects of Water Hyacinth on economic activities of the community around lake Victoria: A case of Dunga Beach in Kisumu-Kenya.

BinhThuan Dragon Fruit promoted in India. https://vietnamnews.vn/economy/466575/binh-thuan-dragon-fruit-promoted-in-india.html#4clWK0EKYlWrQwAt.97

Current status of Dragon Fruit and its prospects in Philippines .http://ap.fftc.agnet.org/ap_db.php?id=876

Disruptive Technologies are Nothing New In Agriculture - But What's Around the Corner? 2018. http://www.omafra.gov.on.ca/english/crops/field/news/croptalk/2018/ct-0318a3.htm

Dragon Fruit farming.https://www.asiafarming.com/dragon-fruit-farming

Dragon Fruit Suppliers in India. https://www.exportersindia.com/indian-suppliers/dragon-fruit.htm

Dragon Fruit takes off in India. http://www.fruitnet.com/asiafruit/article/163468/dragon-fruit-takes-off-in-india

Dragon Fruit, the new favourite. https://www.deccanherald.com/spectrum/statescan/dragon-fruit-new-favourite-678086.html

Dragon Fruit. https://en.wikipedia.org/wiki/Pitaya

Dragon Fruit. https://www.agmrc.org/commodities-products/fruits/dragon-fruit

Eusebio, Jocelyn E.; Alaban, Ma. Cecilia S. (2018). Current Status of Dragon Fruit and its Prospects in the Philippines, Country Report for the Dragon Fruit Regional Network Initiation Workshop, April 23-24, 2018, Taipei, Taiwan.

Farmers take up Dragon Fruit cultivation to juice up profits. https://timesofindia.indiatimes.com/city/rajkot/farmers-take-up-dragon-fruit-cultivation-to-juice-up-profits/articleshow/65789604.cms

Feedipedia, Water Hyacinth. https://www.feedipedia.org/node/160

Gibbons, M., Gibbons Jr. H. & Sytsma M. (1994) First Edition, Washington Department of Ecology, A Citizen's Manual for Developing Integrated Aquatic Vegetation Management Plans, in Water Environmental Services. Available Water Environmental Services.https://fortress.wa.gov/ecy/publications/documents/93093.pdf

Goel, Sapna (2018) Researchers innovate their way to make money out of Water Hyacinth. https://india.mongabay.com/2018/01/23/researchers-innovate-to-generate-money-out-of-water-hyacinth/

India gets a taste of exotic Dragon Fruit, at lower rate; imports up 20 times.https://economictimes.indiatimes.com/news/economy/foreign-trade/india-gets-a-taste-of-exotic-dragon-fruit-at-lower-rate-imports-up-20-imes/articleshow/45302184.cms

Nesic, N &Jovanovic, Ljubinko. (1996). Institute of Forestry, Center for multidisciplinary studies, University of Belgrade, Serbia and Montenegro Potential Use of Water Hyacinth (E. crassipes) for Wastewater Treatment in Serbia

Patwary , M. M. Alam; Rahman ,M. H.; Barua , H.; Sarkar ,S.; Alam , Md. Shamsul (2013). Study on the Growth and Development of two Dragon Fruit (Hylocereusundatus) Genotypes, The Agriculturists: A Scientific Journal of Krishi Foundation, Volume 11, Issue 2, pp. 52-57.

Penfound, W. T. and T. T. Earle. (1948). The biology of the Water Hyacinth. Ecological Monographs vol-18, pp. 447- 472.

Perween ,Tamanna; Mandal,KK ; Hasan ,MA (2018). Dragon Fruit: An exotic super future fruit of India, Journal of Pharmacognosy and Phytochemistry, Volume 7,Issue 2, pp. 1022-1026.

Plans To Commercialise Dragon Fruit. http://fijisun.com.fj/2018/09/10/plans-to-commercialise-dragon-fruit/

Rajasthan plans Dragon Fruit, Cassia tora cultivations. https://www.indiatoday.in/pti-feed/story/rajasthan-plans-dragon-fruit-cassia-tora-cultivations-545927-2016-01-29

Rao, C.Chandrasekhara; Sasanka,V.Mrunalini (2015). Dragon Fruit – "The Wondrous Fruit" – for the 21st century, Global Journal For Research Analysis, Volume 4, Issue 10, pp. 261-262.

Rao, VS (1988). Oxford and IBH Publishing Co. Pvt. Ltd., New Delhi (India), Principles of

Table Grape. https://en.wikipedia.org/wiki/Table_grape.
Teygeler, R. (2000) Water Hyacinth paper. Contribution to a sustainable future
Types of Innovation. June 2015. https://techblog.constantcontact.com/software-development/types-of-innovation/
Use of Water Hyacinth in a Sustainable Fashion, May 2010 https://www.textiletoday.com.bd/use-of-water-hyacinth-in-sustainable-fashion/
Variety innovation driving table grape industry forward, May 2019. https://www. farmprogress.com/orchard-crops/variety-innovation-driving-table-grape-industry-forward
What Is Dragon Fruit and Does It Have HealthBenefits?https://www.healthline.com/nutrition/dragon-fruit
Woman entrepreneur promotes Dragon Fruit cultivation in Nagaland. https://timesofindia.indiatimes.com/city/kohima/woman-entrepreneur-promotes-dragon-fruit-cultivation-in-nagaland/articleshow/65652710.cms

4

Innovative Model of Solar Water Pump Penetration in India

Arindam Dutta

Abstract

Access to reliable and affordable irrigation is one of the most important enablers to increase agricultural productivity and income for farmers. An innovative Manual Axis Tracking Solar Pump model and its utility in providing affordable irrigation has been discussed in this paper. The proposed Manual Axis Tracking Solar Pump can increase output on an average 8%-12% more than fixed panel and is much cheaper than automated tracking. This paper deliberates upon the technical features that make the Manual Axis Tracking Solar Pump an advantage over its nearest competitor, the diesel pump. Government of India has already introduced various subsidy-based solar pump schemes and most of them are not popular because of low discharge issue. The low discharge issue can be solved by this proposed optimum tilt-based Manual Tracking Solar Pump, whose sustainable market penetration is suggested through various strategies in the paper, supported by case studies. The proposed entrepreneurship model not only opens a new era of agricultural business but also helps to reduce the GHG emissions.

Keywords: Solar Pump, Innovative Manual Axis Tracking, Entrepreneurship Model

Introduction

In India more than half of the country's total workforce is employed in the agricultural sector. The cost of irrigation can be up to 30% of the total expenses for farmers. So switching to solar pump is more economical to the farmers there are 19 million electrical pumps and about 9 million diesel pumps, till date 55% of India's net sown area remains un-irrigated as per the Agriculture Census 2010–11 (MoAFW, 2015). Government of India provides huge subsidy to electrical pumps but power supply in rural areas is unreliable. Also the cross-subsidy for the rural consumers creates a burden to urban electricity consumers. On the other hand, there is an undue economic pressure on farmers when they use diesel pump and additionally it creates an adverse ecological impact on the environment. In this situation, solar pumps are the most reliable solution for irrigation. As solar PV price is reducing day by day, academic policy- makers try to find the life cycle cost of solar pump in India.

Some of them found that in India, electricity from solar panels now costs only half as much as that from diesel generators, even when diesel is subsidised (Pearson, Natalie O, 2012). Campana et al. (2013) studied water demand for crops and requirement of solar power through dynamic modelling of solar water pump. Tomas et al. (2012) suggest a solution on efficiency optimization through MPPT (Maximum Power Point Tracking) and MLPT (Minimum Loss Point Tracking) method. Deveci et al. (2015) worked on Drip Irrigation and found that direct coupled MPPT can increase the flow rate of solar water pump. To promote solar pump a 'credit-linked capital subsidy' scheme had been launched through the National Bank for Agricultural and Rural Development (NABARD) in 2014. As per this scheme, the Government of India (GOI) will provide financial assistance of 60% to farmers to buy solar pumps which would be equally shared by the Centre and State governments. Recently, Government of India introduced KUSUM (Kisan Urja Suraksha Utthaan Mahaabhiyan) Scheme which has proposed Rs. 14 million worth of investment. But the question of free money not generating wealth for farmers will remain. In maximum cases the questions of maintenance of solar pump, insurance, getting the money from Distribution Companies in India (Discoms) for on-grid solar power, sustainability and job creation in villages come along with free or subsidised solar pump installation. It was also found that in most of the states solar pump subsidy is not economical for more than 5 H.P. whereas with 5 H.P only hectare land irrigation can be done. Other drawbacks include the pressure of boring that has to be done by farmer. In the entire subsidy-based schemes it was found that up to 5H.P solar pumps are economically viable but to get the subsidy the marginal farmers have to invest money to construct Diggi/pond. It is not expected that a small farmer can take the advantage of Government Initiative after investing huge money. The solar pump has low discharge and it is totally dependent on climatic condition

- Are the small and marginal farmers getting the benefit of subsidy?
- Can any efficient measure be adopted to overcome the low discharge challenge of solar pump?
- Is there any way out for small and marginal farmers who are interested to use solar pump?

All these questions raised above lead to the objectives.

Objective

1) To study the technical benefits of the Manual Axis Tracking Solar Pumps (MATS Pumps) and their utility for the farming community.
2) To establish the entrepreneurial model of improving the MATS Pumps through case studies.

Methodology

Model for High Discharge of Solar Water Pump

Solar PV panels collect the maximum solar radiation when the sun's rays are perpendicular to the surface of the panel. However, the earth's diurnal and seasonal motions affect declination angle of the sun making it dependent on the latitude of the site and the month of the year. Therefore, the optimal tilt angle for a PV panel varies with latitude on a monthly basis and can play a significant role in determining its optimum performance. For big solar power plants, automatic solar tracking is used. But for a solar pump where 15KW is the highest rating, an automatic solar tracking is not economically viable. Normally the solar PV angle is tilted to the south in the Northern Hemisphere but its output highly depends on the tilt of the angle. In that case the author draws upon a manual axis solar tracking method through an experimentally validated solar tracking system (Dutta et al 2016). In this paper, we have proposed 12 equations which are valid for a wide range of latitude, from 13° to 39° in Northern Hemisphere which covered all part of India and other countries. The equations are listed below:

January	$1.28\varphi + 11.04$	February	$1.36\varphi + 0.22$	March	$1.22\varphi - 7.15$
April	$0.71\varphi - 5.099$	May	$0.28\varphi - 2.8$	June	$0.03\varphi + 0.2$
July	$0.03\varphi - .098$	August	$0.63\varphi - 6.21$	September	$1.04\varphi - 6.57$
October	$1.28\varphi - 0.66$	November	$1.28\varphi + 8.61$	December	$1.37\varphi + 9.67$

All the equations for optimum tilt are dependent on latitude and tested for five climatic zones of India. Based on monthly optimum tilt angle, a manual solar tracking system has been commissioned at the rooftop of the Indian Institute of Social Welfare & Business Management (IISWBM), Kolkata. There is 640Wp solar system comprising of eight 80Wp solar module. Out of them four solar PV panels (module C&D) are fixed at Kolkata's latitude angle (i.e. 22.57° N) and another four solar panels (module A&B) have a manual solar tracking mechanism. The tilt position of solar PV modules can be changed from 0° to 90° manually. The overall positions of the eight solar panels including the solar panels having manual tracking facility and the connection diagram of overall rooftop solar system of IISWBM is shown in the Figure 1 and Figure 2 respectively.

Fig. 1: Snapshot of solar module with manual tracking system
Source: Photograph by Author

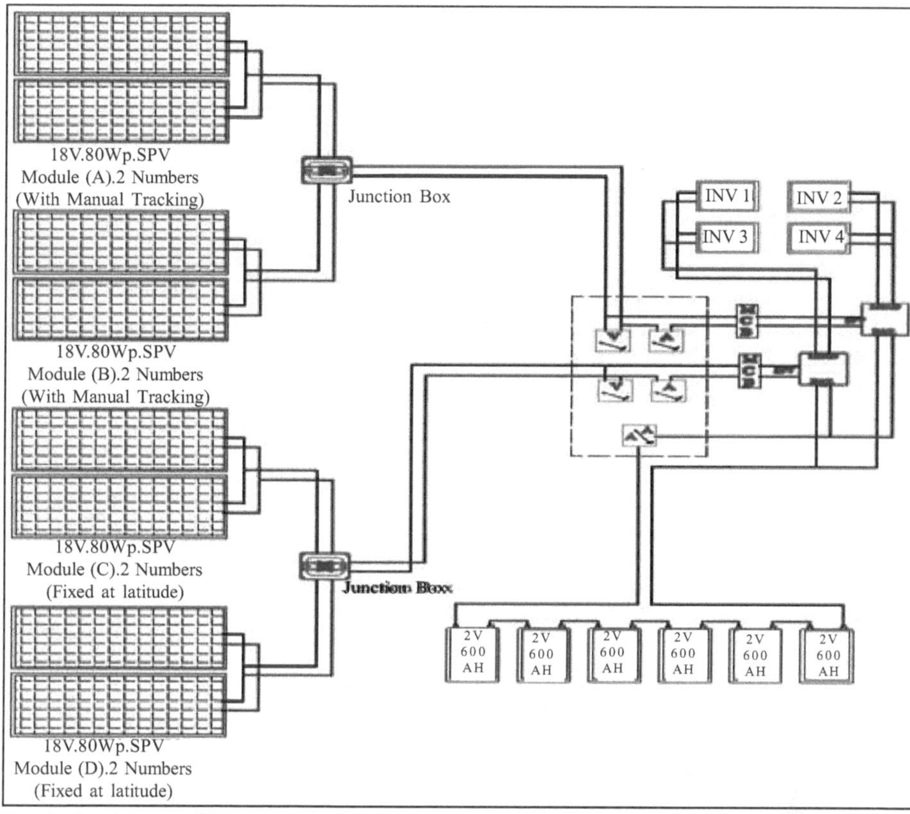

Fig. 2: Positions of SPV and the connection diagram of IISWBM rooftop solar system
Source: Optimum Tilt Angles for Manual Tracking of Photovoltaic Modules (2016)

Entrepreneurship Model for Manual Axis Tracked Solar Pumps Deployment

Instead of providing huge subsidy, the government can promote MATS Pumps through entrepreneurship models. On one hand, solar pumps with manual tracking should be mandated as it will increase the water discharge to 8-12% and cost is only 2% of total system cost. Other than targeting the small capacity pump the government should make an arrangement to promote the entrepreneurship model (MATS Pumps) for farmers who rent its usage as a service to small farmers at a cheap rate. They may be supported to procure large solar water pump i.e. more than 10 H.P. All sorts of advertisement, awareness and training to the marginal farmers and the entrepreneurs of water may be undertaken by the GOI. In every village if such type of water service entrepreneurs when there is any surplus generation if they are connected to the grid and give an opportunity to them to supply to other households as power backup when there is power failure.

Findings and Analysis

Learning from Technical Model

In manual solar tracking the modules (A&B) in Figure 2 are positioned at optimum tilt angle at the starting of every month as per angle stated in equation 1 for Kolkata, by manual solar tracking mechanism. A compass, as shown in Figure1, has been connected also to set the angle on monthly basis. The actual output from the fixed and tracked panel has been shown in Table 1.

Table 1: Energy Gain through Manual Axis Solar Tracking

Month	Fixed panel (at Latitude), kWh	Tracked Panel (As per proposed Equation), kWh	Energy Gain, kWh	Energy Gain%
January	113.7	124.5	10.8	9.5
February	113.9	125.5	11.6	10.2
March	126.3	138.3	12	9.5
April	121.4	132.5	11.1	9.1
May	122.6	134.4	11.8	9.6
June	105.1	117.1	12	11.4
July	101.9	114.3	12.4	12.2
August	106.7	118.7	12	11.2
September	93.1	101.4	8.3	8.9
October	99.5	107.8	8.5	8.3
November	90.2	99.6	9.4	10.4
December	107.8	117.8	10	9.2
Total Generation	1302.2	1431.9	129.7	10

(Source: Optimum Tilt Angles for Manual Tracking of Photovoltaic Modules, 2016)

From Table 1, it is depicted through the experimentally validated model that the manual tracking based on monthly optimal tilts from our proposed set of equations, yields an annual increase in electric power over fixed panel. In our paper we have shown that for manual axis tracking, the output of solar PV will increase

In case of pump the efficiency depends on the following equation:

$\eta = [(\rho*Q*g*h)*100] /Pa$... (2)

Where η = Efficiency in water pumping

Q= Discharge of water (m^3)

h = pumping height (m)

Pa = Active power supplied by motor pump set (w)

ρ = Density of water (kg/m^3)

g = Gravitational Constant

Discharge of water (Q) is dependent on solar radiation. If the output through manual axis solar model is more, the discharge of solar water pump will definitely increase. So, if by the manual axis tracking the solar output can increase 8% to 12% (Dutta et al. 2016) then the discharge of water will also be increased. The payback period for manual axis tracked solar water pump is more or less five months (Dutta and Neogi,2016). For the cost calculation, the price mentioned by MNRE (Edelweiss, 2015) has been considered and there will be maximum 2% additional system cost escalation for optimum angle tracking. It was pointed out that discharge of normal solar water pump is 16% less than the diesel pump (Sombodhi, 2015). In that case the manual tracked solar water pump is only the cheapest solution which can increase the water discharge 8% -12%.

Learning from Entrepreneurship Model

To support the proposed entrepreneurship model some successful case studies have been presented below-

Case I: Research carried out by the IWMI Tata Water Policy Program (Shah, 2016) showed that promoting bigger solar pump is better than small solar pumps because small solar pumps only act as a standby of electric pump. They support six young farmers in Chakhaji village of Bihar, India by offering 60% capital cost subsidy on 5 kWp solar pumps. The farmers who take the note of service providers have to pay 40% of the cost in four instalments, so that they create a water market aggressively to pay the instalments. Before the pilot, diesel pump owners sold water at INR 120/hour; now solar pump suppliers sell water at INR 90/hour and finish watering a field in much shorter time. Earlier, only tube well owners sowed rice pre-monsoon while others waited for rains; tube well owners grew maize when buyers grew fodder. Now, the buyers of water source

Case II: Researchers showed (Kishore and Shah, 2014) that a farmer would be more willing to invest borrowed funds in a solar pump if he was offered a guarantee of buyback of surplus power at a remunerative price. The Government of Gujarat has offered guaranteed buy-back of solar power at Rs 15/kWh for the first 13 years. A 5,000 Wp solar panel can produce about 8,400 kWh electricity, in a year in the Indian plains, enough to run a 5 hp pump set for more than 2,100 hours. A guarantee to purchase surplus solar power at say Rs 10/ kWh would assure maximum revenue of Rs 84,000/- year, if the solar pump owner sells all the electricity generated to the utility. This guarantee will create a high opportunity cost of using electricity for irrigation. Every unit of electricity that owner uses for irrigating his fields will cost the owner Rs10/- in lost revenue. Such high incentive would lead to significant energy and water savings in agriculture.

Case III: The Infrastructure Development Company Ltd. (IDCOL)in Bangladesh has reached almost 3,500 people by deploying 277 solar pump sets through water service entrepreneurship model in 2015. The farmers may select to have the pump on their own land and sell water to nearby farmers. In Bangladesh's fragmented land ownership situation, a group of 20-25 farmers are able to form an association to buy water from one irrigation pump. The scheme is very popular now in Bangladesh and they are trying to install 50,000 solar pumps through the water service entrepreneurship model within 2025.

Policy Implication

Already huge subsidies have been provided by Government to promote the adoption of solar pumps for irrigation. But the problem is a majority of these programmes reflect a top- down, supply-side push with limited consideration of farmers' perspectives. India has deployed 142,000 pumps till November 2017(Jain and Sahadi, 2018) against a target of one million pumps by 2021. Most of the marginal farmers depend on buying water, the costliest option for irrigation or simply renting pumps to meet their needs. The estimate for the number of irrigation diesel pumps in the country is around nine million whereas it has found that 30 million farmers reported using them for irrigation, as of 2012 (Kishore and Shah, 2014). This indicates that pumps are shared by farmers. In many states like Punjab and Rajasthan, the government gives subsidy to farmers for solar pump only when they built Diggi (water body) costing around 0.2-0.4 million (Kishore and Shah, 2014). The farmers also have to deposit a reasonable portion of solar pump base price at first before its installation. It has in monthly/daily payment scheme. The newly proposed KUSUM scheme by the GOI is to give benefits to the marginal farmers. But it has been seen that the marginal farmer's awareness level and the ability to take the subsidy after performing lots of paper work is not satisfactory. So again through the KUSUM Scheme, the chances of the marginal farmers gaining a benefit are less. The authors point that subsidy is not always the only solution for farmer's financial improvement as it benefits only the large farmers. The marginal farmers most of the time do not get any benefit as most of them have no proper bank account and proper support system to avail the benefit. It has also been observed that a 2 HP pump can cater to about two acres of land and a 7.5 HP is said to cater to 10 acres of land depending on water level. From here also it is can be clearly concluded that rather that subsidy for solar pump, if the proposed "Entrepreneurship Model of Manual Tracked Solar pumps" is adopted, then it will add a new vertical of agri-based business.

Conclusion

With rapidly falling price of PV cell, rising diesel prices and interrupted power supply in villages, the solar pump is going to open a new era of India's irrigation system. An appropriate techno-commercial approach can create a sustainable economical solution for India's farmland irrigation and change it for the better. All the main obstacles like low discharge of solar water pump unutilised, subsidy benefit to marginal farmers etc. can be solved by the innovative Manual Tracked Solar Pump Entrepreneurship Model as described in the paper. The Manual Tracked Solar Panel can increase the water discharge up to 8-12%. The current model in India is offering 80-95% capital subsidy on small 1-2 kWp solar pumps that imposes restrictions on expansion of the market and removes incentives to enhance product quality and lower product costs. With high capital subsidies and unit costs determined through a competitive bidding process, solar pump manufacturers have little or no incentive to innovate on product design. This approach often results in low consumer awareness, high consumer apathy and poor after-sales service. The proposed entrepreneurship model can create more business opportunity for the youth of villages. The solar water pump can be used as a water service model for all the farmers including marginal farmers at a cheap rate than diesel pump water service. The manual tracked solar pump is so easy to operate that one semi-skilled person who has been trained once with the details provided in a user- friendly document can also handle that. They have to change the angle once a month only. The maintenance of solar pump is

If the proposed entrepreneurship model gets technical support by the government, the entrepreneurs have to put effort for marketing and awareness-building among users. The entrepreneurs may enjoy a guarantee of buyback power from government when the MATS Pump system is on-grid; they also get the opportunity to supply power to other households if the MATS Pump system is off-grid. Such model may attract a loan with lowest rate. Therefore in a nutshell, the proposed manual tracked solar pump water service entrepreneurship model is a profitable business plan. Increasing productivity in the agriculture sector is widely recognised as one of the most effective ways to fight poverty and stimulate socio-economic development. In order to make solar irrigation systems accessible to farmers, instruments are needed to either improve access to credit and/or bring down the capital cost of systems to affordable levels. All the entrepreneurship case studies described here support the proposed "Entrepreneurship Model of Manual Tracked Solar pumps" that will improve more generating prospects of farmers and other youth in the community who may not be involved in farming. On the other hand, if the GOI takes the initiative to implement the proposed entrepreneurship Model, it will not only save huge money of subsidy but can transfer the benefit to the marginal farmers directly. If the GOI promotes such MATS Pumps, it will not only popularise the solar pump system but also enable itself to fulfil its ambitious target of 100GW solar within 2022 as committed before the United Nations Framework Convention on Climate Change (UNFCC).

References

Agrawal. S. & Jain. A, (2015). Solar Pumps for Sustainable Irrigation: A Budget Neutral Opportunity.New Delhi: Council on Energy, Environment and Water.

Campana. Pietro Elia, Li. H, Yan. J. Jinyue, (2013).Dynamic modelling of a PV pumping system with special consideration on water demand. Applied Energy, p. 11.

Deveci. Onur, Onkol.M, Unver. Hakki Ozgur, Ozturk. Zafer, (2015). Performance Assessment of Solar Agricultural Water Pumping System.Elsevier Ltd.1-32.

Dutta. Arindam & Neogi. Subhasis, (2016).Reassessment of the Indian Renewable Energy Policy through Technology Implementation. International Conference on 21st Century Energy Needs – Materials, Systems and Applications at IIT Kharagpur.

Dutta. Arindam, Biswas. J, Roychowdhury. S, Neogi. S, (2016).Optimum Tilt Angles for Manual Tracking of Photovoltaic Modules. Distributed Generation and Alternative Energy Journal,7-35.

Edelweiss Research, MNRE (As at June30, 2015). [Online]. Available: www. mnre.gov.in/file-manager/UserFiles

IDCOL (Infrastructure Development Company Ltd.) (2015). IDCOL Solar Irrigation Projects. Presentation by Farzana Rahman, at Kathmandu, Nepal, source: www.icimod.org/resource/

Kishore. A.K., Shah. T., Tiwari. N.P, (2014). Solar Irrigation Pumps- Farmers' Experience and State Policy. Economics & Politics Weekly.54-62.

MoAFW, GoI. (2016), All India Report on Input Survey 2011–12. From http://agcensus.nic.in/document/is2011/reports/all_india_report_2011_12.pdf.Accesse d on June16, 2019.

Shah. Tushaar et. al. (2018), Promoting Solar Irrigation Service Providers in Ganga Basin: Jobs, Affordable Irrigation and Accelerated Green Revolution. Science Forum.

Sombodhi (2015),Impact assessment of the National Solar Pumps Programme Through a survey based approach Evolving Broad Policy Recommendations.

Tomas Perpetuo Correa, Seleme Issac, Seleme Jr.Selenio, Rocha Silva., J, (2012), Efficiency optimization in stand-alone photovoltaic pumping system. Renewable Energy, v41, 220-226.

5

Harvest and Post-Harvest Wastages A Farm Level Study of Modern Trade Value Chain in West Bengal

Karabi Bhattacharya Rao

Abstract

More than one-third of food is lost or wasted in post-harvest operations in India. Decreasing the post-harvest losses (PHL) may be a sustainable solution to increasing food availability and improving farmers' livelihoods. As per Associated Chambers of Commerce of India, India loses approximately US$ 14.33 billion annually on account of PHL (ASSOCHAM, 2017). The objective of this study is to analyse the agricultural wastes that are produced in the value chain for a modern trade retailer, identify their causes, and discuss methods for minimising field wastages. A case study approach has been used to depict the agricultural value chain (vegetable segment). A field visit was conducted to a farmland and a privately operated Collection Center in Barasat area of West Bengal. The author discusses solutions towards minimising harvest wastages in the farm by focusing on waste reduction. Post-harvest wastages beyond the farm can be reduced by undertaking measures that focus on waste management. Going forward, adoption of technologies by farmers may lessen inefficiencies such as wastages and improve their income. Further scope for research lies in exploring joint interventions by private players, government agencies, non-profit organisations and entrepreneurs through public-private partnership models or through development of clusters for creating sustainable value chains and achieving greater profitability.

Keywords: Agricultural Waste, Post-Harvest Losses (PHL), Modern Trade,

Introduction

India is the second largest producer of food, next to China, with estimated food processing industry size at US$ 70 billion. Agriculture sector which employs more than 50 percent of the total workforce in India contributes only 17-18 percent to the country's GDP[1].To fulfil the food demand of the increasing population remains a major global concern. According to Alexandratos and Bruinsma (2012), food supplies would need to increase by 60 percent (estimated at 2005 food production levels) in order to meet the food demand in 2050. Food availability and accessibility can be increased by increasing production, improving distribution, and reducing the losses. Reduction of post-harvest food losses is a critical component of ensuring future global food security. More than one-third of food is lost or wasted in post-harvest operations. Both the qualitative and the quantitative losses occur from the pre-harvest to post-harvest stages – through handling, storage, transportation, to the delivery to the consumer. The major operational issues that cause post-harvest losses include lack of demand forecasting, inadequate harvest preparation, inefficient transportation, fragmented logistics management and improper inventory control (Shukla and Jharkharia, 2013).

Harvest and Post-Harvest Losses

When the time comes to harvest, it is important to choose a suitable method to maximise the yield and minimise crop losses and quality deterioration. Many farmers have difficulties in harvesting and handling their crops. They have to know the exact time for harvest, because harvesting period and its duration affect the quality, durability, transportation and storage of harvested crops. Harvesting can be done manually, mechanically, or through a combination of both. Regardless of the method the farmers use, good practices should be followed to ensure that harvest losses are minimised and crop quality is preserved during harvest operations. Agricultural farm-wastes produced after harvest of every crop are of great concern because of the problems of environmental pollution, rural sanitation, recycling and utilisation. Agricultural wastes are generated from a number of sources, notably from cultivation, livestock and aquaculture. Decreasing the post-harvest losses (PHL), especially in developing countries, may be a sustainable solution to increase food availability, reduce pressure on natural resources, eliminate hunger and improve farmers' livelihoods.

As per latest estimates by the Associated Chambers of Commerce of India, India loses approximately INR 926 billion (US$ 14.33 billion) annually on account

- 6 percent cereals, 4.3 percent -6.1 percent pulses, 2.8 percent -10.1 percent oilseeds, 5.8 percent -18.1 percent fruits, and 6.9 percent -13 percent vegetables were lost during harvesting, post-harvest activities, handling and storage[3]. PHL in India stems from a range of factors including lack of post-harvest infrastructure, limited technical know-how on good agricultural practices, imperfect market knowledge, and inadequate market access. About 30 percent to 40 percent of the fruits and vegetables grown in India (40 million tonnes amounting to US$ 13 billion) get lost annually due to poor infrastructure, insufficient cold storage capacity, unavailability of cold storages in close proximity to farms, poor transportation infrastructure, etc. This results in uncertainty in prices and farmers cannot get remunerative prices for their produce that further adds to their frustrations (Rajasri et al., 2010; Maheshwar and Chanakwa, 2006; Rolle, 2006; Ali, 2004).

Fragmentation of agricultural landholdings and a post-harvest value chain that is marked with inadequacies, cause PHL to stack up increasingly throughout the value chain. Small-Holder Farmers (SHFs)in India, comprising 80 percent of India's farming community[4], are affected by the challenges of fragmentation and value chain inefficiencies in the form of weak access to markets, low investment in agriculture, low productivity and low income.

Literature Review

Through the literature review, the paper focuses on identifying the agricultural wastes that are produced in the harvest and post-harvest stages by farmers, their causes and modes of prevention. The papers are mainly related to perishable produce like horticultural crops, vegetables and fruits. The results have been studied to identify the causes of post-harvest and storage losses in developing countries.

Post-harvest loss can be defined as the degradation in both quantity and quality of a food product at any stage from harvest to consumption (Kiaya, 2014). Factors affecting the post-harvest losses include poor logistics set-up from farm to the marketplace (Kereth et al., 2013), inaccessibility of appropriate storage and transport facilities (Fehr and Romão, 2001; Aujla et al., 2011; Musasa et al., 2013), inappropriate packaging (Fehr and Romão, 2001; Aujla et al., 2011), shortages in the post-harvest management and processing (Choudhury, 2006), insufficiency of information management (Kader, 2004) and poor marketing systems (Kereth et al., 2013; Kader, 2004). Among other fruits and vegetables, and control the losses, in terms of waste, proper management among the stakeholders is an important aspect (Gustavsson et al., 2011; Kosseva and Webb, 2013; Oelofse and Nahman, 2013; Parfitt et al., 2010).

Primarily the agri-food products can be categorised in two groups based on their duration for freshness, short-term and long-term. The agri-food products which remain fresh for a shorter duration come under the category of perishable products, whereas the agri-food products which can survive for longer durations come under the category of non-perishable products (FAO, 2016; Kosseva and Webb, 2013; Lipinski et al., 2013). Improved forward and backward linkages between producers and other actors in the value chain will decrease transaction costs and increase involvement of service providers like input dealers, commercial and cooperative banks, private firms and NGOs (Huilgol et al., 2004). Keeping in view the approach of sustainability (Elkington, 2004; Henriques and Richardson, 2013), there are a few factors which play an important role in addressing the issue of agri-food waste management such as, training and awareness programs for farmers, disaster management planning, storage infrastructure, storage technology, supply chain management, demand forecasting, information dissemination, direct approachability to markets, and use of information technology.

Objective

The broad objective of this study is to analyse the agricultural wastes that are produced in the value chain for a modern trade (MT) retailer, and identify their causes. The study also proposes to discuss methods for minimising field wastages through waste reduction, channelising surplus produce through processing units, and mitigating PHL through waste management measures for enhancing productivity in the agricultural produce value chain.

Methodology

This study uses a case study approach to analyse the creation of agricultural wastages in the value chain. McCutcheon and Meredith (1993) recommend use of case study research for exploratory studies to close the gap "between operations management research's prescriptive advice and workable answers for managers". The case study method is widely accepted as a popular form of qualitative analysis and requires a detailed and exhaustive observation of the operational unit.

interviewed to identify existing practices/bottlenecks in the farm-to-fork value chain. The study makes use of the SWOT Analysis (Hill, 1997) for studying the strengths, weaknesses, opportunities and threats in the Indian agriculture. Secondary data has been accumulated from a variety of sources including government resolutions, annual ministry reports, and statistical data from books, newspapers and internet.

Swot Analysis of Indian Agriculture (Vegetable Segment)

SWOT Analysis is a strategic planning method to evaluate the strengths, weaknesses, opportunities and threats involved in a sector. The present paper uses the SWOT Analysis for analysing the challenges that exist in the vegetable segment of the Indian agriculture.

Strength

Contribution to GDP - Agriculture sector has a high contribution of 14 percent to the country's Gross Domestic Product.

Source of employment - Agriculture employs over 52 percent of the labour force of the country and over 70 percent of the Indian rural work force (Singh, 2011).

Area under agriculture - The country has the second largest area under agriculture and is first in production of Pulses (Masood et al, 2009). It was based on the strength of Indian agriculture that the country was not affected by the global recession in 2008-2009 when many economies of the world were greatly impacted.

Weakness

Low income - Farmers in India are marked by the low remunerative prices that they receive for their agricultural produce. Due to this, children of the farming community hesitate to pursue agriculture as a profession.

Post-harvest losses (PHL) - Due to low processing levels in the country, there is a substantial amount of wastage of agricultural produce. As mentioned earlier in this study, India loses approximately INR 926 billion (US$ 14.33 billion) annually on account of PHL.

Food wastage -There have been instances when large stocks of harvested food grains that were stored in the open due to lack of storage infrastructure,

No access to modern technology - To improve a small land-holding farmer's involvement in high value and emerging markets requires upgrading the farmer's technical ability. The possibility for rural economic progress would remain very limited if the production and marketing strategies continue to remain based on traditional agricultural production that focus on selling total amount produced (supply driven) rather than producing amounts required for consumption (demand driven).

Opportunity

Developing technologies in agriculture -As an example, about 60 percent of agricultural land is currently rain-fed. So, emphasis should be laid on strengthening Research and Development in dry land areas for developing technologies like drip irrigation, etc. to enhance the productivity of the land.

Organic farming - It avoids the large scale use of artificial fertilizers, pesticides, growth regulators and solely depends upon the use of on-farm and off-farm use of crop deposits, animal wastes, green fertilisers and biological pest control to maintain soil efficiency.

Food processing sector -It has an enormous potential. Provision of well-organised supply chains and processing infrastructure may be helpful in generating employment and making of value added products in rural areas.

Agri-business scheme - The Government of India has launched several such schemes in the past decade with an aim to provide self-employment opportunities to jobless agriculture graduates, thereby converting them into job providers instead of job seekers.

Threat

Size of farm holdings -Most of the farmers are marginal farmers with small landholdings. Such small holdings create scalability issues in carrying out farm automation initiatives.

Decreasing importance of agriculture - A survey by National Sample Survey Organization (2005) had revealed that 41 percent of farmers wanted to leave agriculture, if any other income option was available to them. The youth are not interested in agriculture as it is not economically satisfying and a motivating experience to them.

the farmers from entering into direct contract with any bulk processor or manufactures, as the produce is required to be routed through these regulated markets. Though almost 70 percent of the agricultural produce goes through the APMC market (mandi), it is extremely localised and highly fragmented with a large number of intermediaries involved in the farm-to-fork value chain.

• Land Preparation	• Quality Check	• Storing	• Back-end inventory management	• Selling
• Irrigation	• Drying	• Transport	• Training	• Interfacing with customer
• Fertilizing	• Cleaning & sorting			
	• Packaging			

Fig. 1: Agricultural Value Chain
Source: Author

Subsequently the Ministry of Agriculture had formulated a model law on agricultural marketing (Model APMC Act, 2003) that provided for the freedom of farmers to sell their produce directly to contract sponsors, processors, retailers or private bodies.

Currently, MT retailers prefer to procure directly from the farmers and create their own sourcing and distribution networking the value chain (Figure 1).

Crop production- This involves land preparation, irrigation and fertilizing by the farmers. **Land preparation** entails ploughing the field to make it arable. Proper tilling helps recycle plant nutrients and allows decomposition. Also it provides a soft soil mass for direct seeding and helps to enrich the soil. **Irrigation** is to artificially and systematically add water to get better crop production. It affects temperature conditions by regulating the temperature of the external layer of the soil and the ground layer of the air. **Fertilizing** is to add substances comprising chemical essentials such as manure or mixture of nitrates that increase the growth of plants. They give nutrition to the crops.

Harvesting - Harvesting is the cutting and gathering of the mature crop by the farmers. Crops are harvested manually, mechanically or as a combination of the two. Harvesting is the most labor-intensive activity of the growing season. Quality of the produce cannot be enhanced after harvesting; therefore it is

Collection centre - In the collection centre of the retailer, **quality checks** are done on the produce that the farmers bring in, to provide customers with products that are attractive and clean with minimal risk of microbial contamination. **Drying** is the process of the removal of water (moisture) from hygroscopic materials by means of evaporation. It is one of the most important post-harvest treatments being adopted worldwide to reduce the spoilage and increase the shelf life or storage durability of agricultural products. Examples of the products that are dehydrated include fruits, vegetables and meats (Pabis et al., 1998; Sokhansanj and Jayas, 2006). **Cleaning & sorting** involve freeing the produce of any visible soil/other materials and removing portions of product that may carry a risk for reducing shelf life and/or contamination by a microbial organism. Crops are to be washed and dried properly before **Packaging**. Its dimension and design must be suited to the available transport in order to load the packages neatly and firmly. Packaging should prevent physical damage to the crop and be easy to handle.

Distribution center – At the distribution centre of the retailer which acts as the hub for the agricultural produce, **storing** extends the shelf life of the product. Temperatures below 41°Fahrenheitwill reduce the risk of microbial growth for the fruits and vegetables. Storage area should be separated from the processing area for preparing shipments as per store orders and are to be kept clean using good housekeeping practices. Storage racks should be away from walls to allow cleaning and air circulation. **Transport** includes following a "First-In", "First-Out" system for inventory control, as an established good practice. Precautions are to be taken for minimising risk of microbial contamination during transit. Separate refrigerated and non-refrigerated vehicles are to be use for highway transport.

Retail stores – Activities at the retailer's physical store entail back-end inventory management and training to store employees. **Back-end inventory management** deals with stocking products that customers want, using pricing, promotions to sell profitably and maintaining inventory at levels that meet demand. **Training** provides knowledge to workers in proper food handling techniques, food security basics, personal hygiene and sanitary practices to decrease the post-harvest losses and wastages.

Customer – Retail **selling** to customers is based on accurate demand forecasting and proper feedback methods. Strong supply chain leads to cost savings and higher profitability. Existing practices are monitored regularly to

Case Study – Observation and Field Analysis

A field visit was conducted to observe and analyse the post-harvest value chain process that MT retailers undertake. A farmland and a Collection Center in Barasat area were visited for monitoring the aggregation process of vegetables. The farm areas covered under the Barasat Collection Centre are Amdanga, Madhavpur and Nilgunge. Farmers bring their vegetables to the Collection Center where the vegetables are sorted based on their quality and sent to the Distribution Center every evening, for onwards supply to the retail outlets.

The MT retailers provide some selected farmers (who are receptive to learning innovative methods in farming) with the services of agronomists who advise them on scientific methods of growing crops and also provide them access to good quality seeds. The retailers also connect the farmers to the representatives of fertilizer and pesticide companies, who advise these farmers on proper usage and also give them an opportunity to buy the product.

In spite of the above, a large amount of wastage happens in the fields. Due to inclement weather such as heavy rainfall, the crops (e.g. tomatoes) get damaged and are left to rot in the open fields. The farmers lack prior information and are unable to take preventive measures to retrieve the produce, prior to the weather condition. Also, they do not have access to spare laborers who can salvage the crop from the fields immediately after the bad weather passes. Hence, lack of timely harvesting creates huge loss of produce to the farmers. A farmer's ability to successfully harvest and handle his crops even under abnormal weather conditions could be the difference between his financial success and failure.

At the Collection Center the farmers bring their produce. Each item is individually hand-sorted and checked for quality by the local employees of the MT retailer, as per specifications laid out to them for monitoring the firmness, shape, color, size and texture of the produce. Approximately 150-160 farmers are associated with a Collection Center. This association is not based on any formal contract but on mutual understanding and benefits that are derived by both the parties. For the MT retailer, there is an ***assured quality of produce*** as the farmers are producing the vegetables with good quality seeds, drip irrigation, right amount of fertilizers, pesticides etc. The MT retailers also get access to a ***consistent amount of supply*** of vegetables from the farmers for meeting their retail store requirements, as apart from the facilities, they offer remunerative prices to the farmers. The vegetables that meet the specifications are then weighed and payments are transferred to the bank account of the farmers within a day.

the produce is used as cattle fodder, while the remaining produce that show some signs of decay are thrown away in open pits, as there is no means of preventing/salvaging the wastes. This wastage creation can be depicted in the following Figure 2.

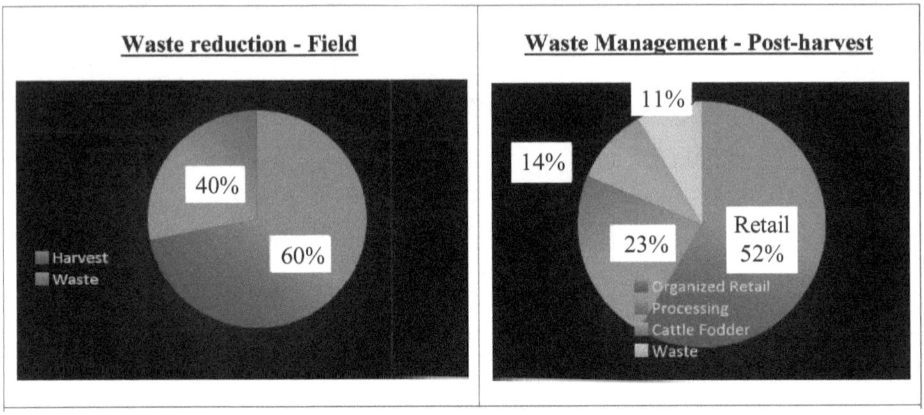

Fig. 2: Wastage in agri - produce

On a national level as per industry estimates, the total amount of such harvest and post-harvest wastes can be ascribed to 40 percent of the agricultural produce. It is to be noted that most of the farmers are marginal farmers with small land holdings which is 1-2 hectares as per the agricultural census 2010-11(a marginal farmer often has a bare survival level of income from his own land and sometimes he works as an agricultural labourer on other farmers' lands to provide himself an additional income). They grow the same range of crops for years and are excessively dependent on climatic conditions for harvesting. They lack access to cold storage infrastructure, weather updates and other related inputs, that leave them devoid of any major intervention towards undertaking sustainable farming practices.

Recommendations: Way Forward

This section of the study makes an attempt to suggest solutions that may mitigate the wastages created on the field and during post-harvest situations.

Waste management during the harvesting period can be done by **Mechanisation.** It can help to expedite the farming processes in the field, such as sowing seeds, irrigation and harvesting. However, the major constraint

Mechanisation can raise the efficiency of labour and enhance the farm production per worker. Co-operative form of equipment usage may be considered useful.

During the post-harvesting period, waste management can be done by effective **Sorting and Grading** at the farm. The agricultural produce usually comprises of ripe, unripe, rotten, and fungus-attacked, disease infected or bird damaged crops. These are often harvested together in bulk. Most of these crops can be graded into categories before leaving the farm / farm storage. This ensures that the good crops are not mixed with the bad ones. Effective sorting in quality terms and grading will also give right/higher price to the farmer.

Post-sorting and grading, as per their quality, the produce can be classified (as an example, grade A+, A, B+, B, etc. have been used, A + being the best quality produce) and managed following the different recommendations below:

- **Quality A+ –Food for Export** – The excess produce can be exported to countries globally for which bodies like Agricultural and Processed Food Products Export Development Authority (APEDA) can play an important role in expanding the export potential of Indian agricultural and food products.
- **Quality A –Cold Storage for round-the-year supply** – Each agricultural produce may be best stored in different temperature ranges. Cold does not kill the spoilage agents, but greatly reduces their activity. The current facilities are accessible only to the big farmers and middlemen, who usually engage in unfair practices such as hoarding the crops when supplies peak, leading to huge price fluctuations. The small farmers lose out as they have to sell their produce at very low prices right after harvest. Increasing cold storage capacity will ensure that agricultural production can be continued perennially. This will ensure there is less wastage of agri food produce.
- **Quality B+ – Food Processing Industry** – Food processing companies play a vital role in reducing the wastage of perishable agricultural produce by enhancing the shelf-life of agri produce through indigenous drying and conversions into value-added products, such as pickles, reserves, etc. Food and beverage companies procure their raw materials from the farmers. In the process they can help farmers with supportable farming and capacity-building initiatives, building associations with global companies for knowledge transfer of farm-level technologies, prioritising farm-

self. In order to preserve them as long as possible, conservation techniques such as salting, pickling or drying processes were practiced from earlier times, that in due course has given way to other progressively sophisticated categories such as preserves, frozen food, etc.

- **Quality B – Up-cycle waste in Beauty and Pharmaceutical industry–** Some bio molecules that can be derived from crop waste also have anti-oxidant, anti-inflammatory, anti-microbial, anti-cancer or gut-health properties that can also be used for treating people. Such waste can be utilised by up-cycling through biotechnology to produce medicines for treatment of animal diseases. Compounds and extracts originating from agronomical disposable wastes can be used for making cosmetics. They are inexpensive and bio-sustainable, and thus can be a valid substitute to the regular plant-derived extracts, that are more commonly used in manufacturing cosmetics.
- **Quality C – Re-purpose waste into Tableware and Packaging, use in Cattle fodder–**Agricultural wastes such as banana and cabbage leaves can be purchased from farmers to make biodegradable packaging and tableware such as banana and cabbage plates. The patented technology converts agro-waste into self-binding fibers by churning them with water in huge machines. The end-products through this process of re-purposing are sustainable packaging and tableware that takes only three months to biodegrade. Also, by-products of plant origin consisting of milling industry by-products, bran, waste flour, wheat, corn and rye germs, hulls of some seeds (e.g. pea, barley, etc.),wastes resulting from grain cleaning processes, crop residues, animal and poultry manure can also be used as cattle fodder and a feed component of livestock. This will result in effective utilisation of wastages.
- **Quality D – Recycle waste into Bio-compost, Alternative Source of Energy–** Farm waste can often contain some of the most recyclable materials. Organic materials, animal manure and decaying straw and hay can all be recycled to make materials such as compost, which can then be put back into the earth for growing crops, plants, vegetables and more. Agricultural wastes can also be an alternative source of energy. Small units can be founded to manufacture fuel brigades from these wastes. The raw materials can be purchased directly from the cultivators from the adjoining areas. This helps in keeping the cost of production low since

It may be noted that the drivers such as mechanisation, information dissemination, and infrastructure development are most vital for tackling the agricultural wastage issues that exist in the farm-to-fork value chain. In the long run, ***adoption of technologies*** by farmers to lessen inefficiencies such as wastages, and to subsequently improve their income, is the ultimate objective of most agricultural research. However, it also poses the biggest challenge – that is ensuring availability of the technology in a form that can be understood by farmers and ensuing adoption of the technology by the farmers in their fields. ***Capacity building initiatives*** are to be taken for providing the farmers with training on efficient and effective usage of resources, and good farming practices for overall reduction of agricultural wastages. ***Information Management*** such as timely availability of information on weather forecasts, technologies in farming, crop rotation, demand forecasting on types and quantity of vegetables to be produced, Minimum Support Price (MSP) will help the farmer to minimise wastages. Initiatives that will make relevant information seamless, accessible by and available to the farmer at the appropriate time help the farmer's community to take decisions for sustained growth of agricultural activity. Additionally, ***infrastructure development*** like cold storages and refrigerated container for transport of agricultural produce will help to improve post-harvest productivity. New incentives and policies for ensuring the sustainability of agriculture and ecosystem services are crucial if India is to meet the demands of improving yields and enhancing the benefits that may flow to all the stakeholders in the agricultural ecosystem. The government progressively is incentivising private sector companies to introduce technological and business model innovations to minimise wastages and increase value chain productivity through ***Public Private Partnership models***. Further scope for research lies in exploring joint interventions by private players, government agencies, non-profit organisations and entrepreneurs in public-private partnership models or through development clusters may pave the way ahead for achieving the above objectives.

References

Alexandratos, N., and J. Bruinsma. 2012. "World agriculture towards 2030/2050: the saving water. From Field to Fork-Curbing Losses and Wastage in the Food Chain 2012 revision." Working paper: FAO: ESA No. 12-03, p.4.

Associated Chambers of Commerce of India report on post-harvest losses: https://www.intellecap.com/wp-content/themes/intellecap/pdf/Public-Facing-Report.pdf

Aujla, K.M., Shah, N.A., Ishaq, M. and Fraooq, A. (2011), "Postharvest losses and marketing

Choudhury, M.L. (2006), "Recent developments in reducing postharvest losses in the Asia-Pacific region", Postharvest Management of Fruit and Vegetables in the Asia-Pacific Region, Vol. 1 No. 1, pp. 15-22.

Eisenhardt, K. M. (2002). Building theories from case study research // In: Huberman A. M., Miles M. B. (Eds.). The Qualitative Researchers' Companion. Thousand Oaks, CA: Sage Publications. 5–36 p

Elkington, J. (2004), "Enter the triple bottom line", in Russo, M.V. (Ed.), The Triple Bottom Line: Does It All Add Up, SAGE, Eugene, pp. 49-66, available at: http://kmhassociates.ca/resources/1/TripleBottom Line a history 1961-2001.pdf

Estimated losses in fruits and vegetables in India: file:///C:/Users/admin/Downloads/PostharvestSituationandLossesinIndia.pdf

FAO report 2016 http://www.fao.org/3/a-i5555e.pdf

Fehr, M. and Romão, D.C. (2001), "Measurement of fruit and vegetable losses in Brazil: a case study", Environment, Development and Sustainability, Vol. 3 No. 3, pp. 253-263.

Food for export https://www.ibef.org/exports/agriculture-and-food-industry-india.aspx

Gustavsson, J., Cederberg, C. and Sonesson, U. (2011), "Global food losses and food waste, Food and Agriculture, available at: www.madr.ro/docs/ind-alimentara/risipa_alimentara/presentation_food_waste.pdf

Henriques, A. and Richardson, J. (2013), The Triple Bottom Line: Does It All Add Up, Routledge, available at: https://books.google.co.in/books?hl=en&lr=&id=bZbb2Y7Y GvMC&oi=fnd&pg=PR1& dq=elkington+Enter+ the+triple+bottom+line.+In:+ Henriques,+A.,+Richardson&ots =G0UFwx7R4v&sig=pytdI5dR3eX6VzkxQm49ea8nrRs

Hill, T., Westbrook R. (1997). SWOT Analysis: It's Time for a Product Recall - Long Range Planning. Vol. 30. Issue 1: 46–52.

https://books.google.co.in/books?hl=en&lr=&id=0OWqJxuB7GkC&oi=fnd&g=PP1&dq=agri+food+ commodity+waste&ots=hKeDZcxg JR&sig=D_gwrpp VwcZeWKQNQzoSvXG0Tvo

Kader, A.A. (2004), "Increasing food availability by reducing postharvest losses of fresh produce", Procedia 5th International Postharvest Symposium, Vol. 682 No. 1, pp. 2169-2176.

Kasso, M. and Bekele, A. (2016), "Post-harvest loss and quality deterioration of horticultural crops in Dire Dawa Region, Ethiopia", Journal of the Saudi Society of Agricultural Sciences, Vol. 1 No. 1, pp. 1-9.

Kereth, G.A., Lyimo, M., Mbwana, H.A., Mongi, R.J. and Ruhembe, C.C. (2013), "Assessment of postharvest handling practices: knowledge and losses of fruits in Bagamoyo District of Tanzania", Food Science and Quality Management, Vol. 11 No. 1, pp. 8-15.

Kiaya V. (2014), "Post-harvest losses and strategies to reduce them", Technical Paper on Post-Harvest Losses, Vol. 1 No. 1, pp. 1-25.

Kosseva, M. and Webb, C. (2013), Food Industry Wastes: Assessment and Recuperation of Commodities, Academic Press, available at:

Lipinski, B., Hanson, C., Lomax, J. and Kitinoja, L. (2013), "Reducing food loss and waste", working paper, May/June, pp. 1-40, available at: http://staging.unep.org/wed/2013/docs/WRI-UNEPReducing-Food-Loss-and-Waste.pdf

M. De Lucia, and D. Assennato, Agricultural engineering in development: Post-harvest operations and management of food grains, FAO Agricultural Services Bulletin No. 93. Rome: FAO, 1994.

Maheshwar, C. and Chanakwa, T.S. 2006. Post-Harvest Losses due to Gaps in Cold Chain in India – A Solution. Acta Hort. (ISHS). 712:777-784

Masood, A., Gupta, S. and Basu, P. S. 2009. Higher levels of warming in North India will affect crop productivity. The Hindu Survey of Indian Agriculture. The Hindu group of Publications, pp: 44-48.

McCutcheon and Meredith (1993), "Conducting case study research in operations management", Journal of Operations Management, Vol. 11, pp. 239-56.

Musasa, S.T., Mvumi, B.M., Manditsera, F.A., Chinhanga, J., Musiyandaka, S. and Chigwedere, C. (2013), "Postharvest orange losses and small-scale farmers' perceptions on the loss causes in the fruit value chain: a case study of Rusitu Valley, Zimbabwe", Journal of Food Science and Quality Management, Vol. 18 No. 1, pp. 1-9.

National Sample Survey Organization (2005) https://www.intellecap.com/wp-content/themes/intellecap/pdf/Public-Facing-Report.pdf

Oelofse, S.H. and Nahman, A. (2013), "Estimating the magnitude of food waste generated in South Africa", Waste Management & Research, Vol. 31 No. 1, pp. 80-86.

Pabis, S., Jayas, D.S., Cenkowski, S., 1998. Grain Drying: Theory and Practice. John Wiley & Sons, Inc., New York, NY

Parfitt, J., Barthel, M. and Macnaughton, S. (2010), "Food waste within food supply chains:

Pharmaceutical: http://theleadsouthaustralia.com.au/industries/primary-industries/from-farmer-to-pharma-waste-provides-food-for-thought-in-south-australia/

Quantification and potential for change to 2050", Philosophical Transactions of the Royal Society of London, Series B, Biological Sciences, Vol. 365 No. 1554, pp. 3065-3081, available at: http://doi.org/10.1098/rstb.2010.0126

Rajasri et al., 2010; Maheshwar and Chanakwa, 2006; Rolle, 2006; Ali, 2004 file:///C:/Users/admin/Downloads/Post-harvest Situation and Losses in India.pdf

Reducing Post-harvest Losses in India: Key Initiatives and Opportunities, Intellecap, supported by The Rockefeller Foundation https://www.intellecap.com/wp-content/themes/intellecap/pdf/Public-Facing-Report.pdf, 2016

Report on Assessment of Quantitative Harvest and Post-Harvest Losses of Major crops/Commodities in India, 2015, ICAR

Rolle, R.S. (2006), "Improving postharvest management and marketing in the Asia-Pacific region: issues and challenges", Postharvest Management of Fruit and Vegetables in the Asia-Pacific Region, Vol. 1 No. 1, pp. 23-31.

Singh, M. 2011. Prime Minister's address at the IFPRI Conference on 'Leveraging Agriculture for improving Nutrition and Health. Available at http://pib.nic.in/newsite/erelease.aspx

Small Holder Farmers in India: Food Security and Agriculture Policy, FAO http://www.apaari.org/wp-content/uploads/2009/08/small-farmers-in-india1.pdf

Sokhansanj, S & Jayas, D.S. 2007. Drying of foodstuffs. In A.S. Mujumdar (Ed.), Handbook of industrial drying (pp. 521-546). (3rd ed.). Boca Raton: Taylor & Francis Group.

Steps Taken to Reduce Post Harvest Food Losses, PIB, Feb 2016 http://pib.nic.in/newsite/PrintRelease.aspx?relid=136922

Traditional Agricultural Supply Chain Model: https://www.flickr.com/photos/analectic/

6

Packaging Metamorphosis in the Food Processing Industry in India

Tanusree Das and Kavitha Sundararajan

Abstract

Packaging industry is considered to be one of the world's largest industrial sectors. In the past few years, food processing has undergone several paradigm changes with respect to production, distribution, storage, processing and retailing. This increasing dynamism in the food industry, while on one hand placing a lot of challenges on the packaging industries, is on the other hand opening up opportunities for entrepreneurs to foray into food processing and also packaging industries and develop appropriate solutions in response to the needs of the market and environment. This study aims at exploring the state of packaging industry and packaging technologies in developing countries, with special emphasis on India, against the backdrop of increasing concern for prevention of food losses and therefore highlighting the need for new innovative ideas for food packaging. The authors posit that customer awareness about safety of processed food has given rise to tremendous possibilities of entrepreneurship opportunities in the area of safe and hygiene packaging. However market preferences, state reputations and cost benefit analysis play major roles in packaging of processed food products.

Keywords: Packaging industry, Food processing, Entrepreneurs.

Introduction

The food-processing industry is widely touted as a 'sunrise sector' in India with massive potential for double-digit growth. A vital segment of the food-processing

Packaging is one of the most important business processes to maintain the quality of food products for storage, transportation and consumption both at input and output stage of food processing. It prevents quality deterioration of inputs and facilitates distribution and marketing of outputs. The sole purpose of a good packaging is to retain the quality and quantity of the product till it reaches the end consumer. Besides, packaging also fosters convenience in product handling along with the scope of marketing communication, which therefore contributes to the profit of the business concern. Food industry uses a lot of variations in packaging and even a small reduction in the amount of material used for each package would result in a significant cost reduction, and may improve the problems of solid waste.

In the past few years, food processing has undergone several changes with respect to production, distribution, storage, processing and retailing. This increasing dynamism in this industry is not only creating a lot of challenges on the packaging industries, but is also opening up opportunities for entrepreneurs to foray into this industry and develop appropriate solutions in response to the needs of the environment.

This study aims at exploring the state of packaging and packaging technologies in developing countries, with special emphasis on India, against the backdrop of increasing concern for prevention of food losses and therefore highlighting the need for new innovative ideas for food packaging.

Objective

This study is an exploratory study which looks into different types of packaging, both conventional and contemporary, available innovations in the field of packaging of processed food in India and exploring the tools and techniques which have made packaging effective in food preservation. The paper aims to highlight the available opportunities in the field of processed food packaging that may lead to entrepreneurial opportunities.

Packaging Metamorphosis: Innovations in Food Packaging

The food-processing industry in India is one of the fastest in terms of growth in India. As per the recent Annual Report of Ministry of Food Processing Industries (MoFPI), Government of India, the food processing sector between the years 2011-12 to 2015-16 has shown an average growth rate of 2.88 percent which is greater than the growth rate of the agriculture sector during the same period

- Increase in disposable income has substantially changed the consumption pattern of the masses; leading to more convenient consumption.
- Rise in disposable income causing increased spending on food
- Rise in nuclear families with more working women and increase in double-income families.
- Growing urbanisation which in turn is affecting people's lifestyle
- Demand for nutrient-rich, easy-to-prepare, on-the-go, functional foods
- Expansion of organised retail and penetration of private labels in food products

In fact, the contribution of food-processing industry to the Gross Value Added in Manufacturing Sector ranged from 8 percent to 10.50 percent between 2011-12 and 2015-16 (Ministry of Food Processing Industries, Government of India, 2018).

The increasing requirement for processed foods, along with advances in food processing technique requires optimum packaging solutions to address the increased needs for food preservation. The general approach of preservation relies on how well the processed food is protected against adverse environmental conditions, which is only accomplished by effective packaging. Packaging is, therefore, *sine qua non* of the prevailing food system, whose role from a mere parcel has evolved, to become a mechanism that assures safe handling and delivery of fresh and processed food products from the production-point to the end user, at the same time handling various information needs related to the food product. Also contributing to the development of packaging techniques, is the demand for safe and high quality foods. This demand supplemented by the changing consumer preferences, has boosted technological developments in food processing and enhancements in food packaging tools.

As per a recent study (2018) conducted by Associated Chambers of Commerce of India and Ernst & Young, the size of India's packaging industry is slated to reach USD 72.6 billion by financial year 2020 due to rising population and income levels. A significant portion of the market is occupied by processed food-packaging. An earlier report of the New Delhi based Centre for Market Research & Social Development, estimated in 2015 that the packaging for processed food represented 48 percent of the packaging market.

materials which are recyclable, environment-friendly packaging and at the same time, attractive.

In order to address these needs of a consumer, two packaging innovations came into existence that revolutionised food packaging in India – Active Packaging and Intelligent Packaging. Active Packaging refers to all those processes which ensure that food products remain in good condition from the stage of food processing till it reaches the end consumer in the supply chain. On the other hand, Intelligent Packaging acts as an indicator of a product's freshness or perishability and informs the same to the consumer or retailer. In fact the current packaging systems use a combination of different types of packaging, which is referred to as Smart Packaging. It covers the entire gamut of various packaging activities like Aseptic Packaging, Sustainable Packaging, and Interactive Packaging. Technological developments in Smart Packaging at present, offer new prospects to reduce losses, maintain quality, add value and extend shelf-life of agricultural produce and consequently secure the food system.

Notwithstanding the rise in modern packaging techniques, the Annual Report of MoFPI (2018), states major infrastructural gaps in supply chain that must be addressed; one of which is the need for a Sustainable Packaging industry. There exists a pressing need for enhancing packaging industry at all levels - from logistical and consumer packaging, building suitable machinery to making available adequate packaging materials for building sustainable food & beverage supply system in India. According to N. C. Saha, the Director of Indian Institute of Packaging Kolkata, (2017), "Food processing and packaging are complementary to each other". He also mentioned that "packaging sector is growing rapidly in India at the rate of 15 percent per annum and by 2020, $30 billion worth of investment is expected in the food packaging sector".

The food packaging industry, therefore, offers extensive opportunities for new entrepreneurial ventures and domestic technology-driven startups to foray into the areas such as, intelligent, flexible, sustainable and interactive Packaging.

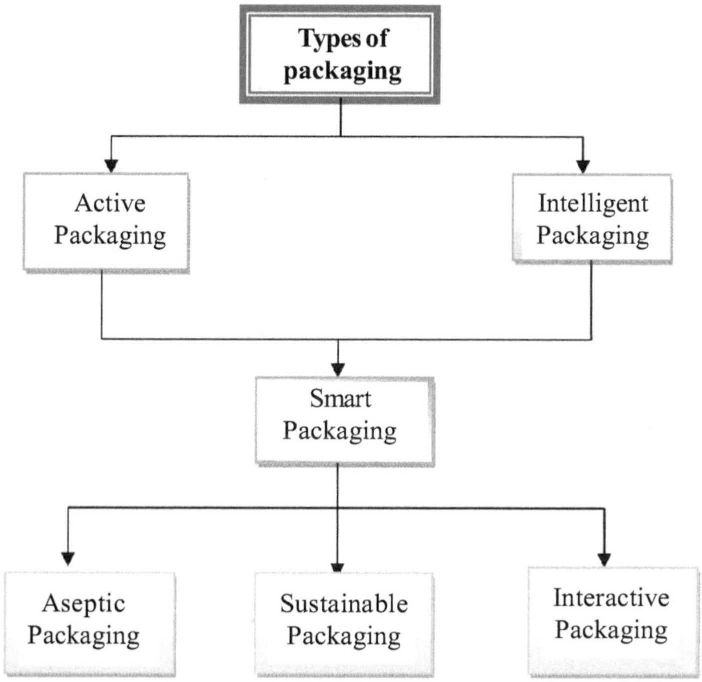

Fig. 1: Types of Food Packaging
Source: Compiled by the authors

Active Packaging

Packaging may be termed active when it performs some role other than providing an inert barrier to the external environment (Rooney, 1995). Active Packaging is a system in which the product, package and the environment interact in a positive way to extend the shelf life or attain some distinctiveness in the product (Miltz et al., 1995).

The sole purpose is to enhance the preservation of food in the package. Extended shelf life involves application of various strategies like temperature control, oxygen removal, moisture control, addition of chemicals such as salt, sugar, carbon dioxide or natural acids or a combination of these with effective packaging.

Types of Active Packaging

- **Oxygen scavengers**

colour changes and nutritional degradation and overall shelf life stability of muscle foods (Hogan and Kerry, 2008). Thus oxygen level in food needs to be controlled in order to minimise the spoilage. Oxygen-sensitive foods can be packed in modified atmosphere packaging (MAP) or vacuum packaging, but that does not make them completely oxygen-free since oxygen permeates through the thin packaging films which can only be removed by the use of oxygen scavengers.

- **Carbon dioxide absorbers and emitters**

Carbon dioxide can be added to the packaging environment to suppress the microbial growth in certain products such as fresh meat, poultry, fish, cheese, and backed goods (Lopez Rubio et al., 2004) and to reduce the respiration rate of fresh produce (Labuza, 1996). Therefore high carbon dioxide levels (10–80 percent) are desirable for such food items to extend the shelf life (Labuza, 1996).

- **Antimicrobial packing**

Antimicrobial packing is a form of Active Packaging in which the packaging acts to reduce, inhibit or retard the growth of microorganisms that may be present in the packaged food or packaging material itself (Appendini and Hotchkiss, 2002). To control unwanted effect of microorganisms on foods, antimicrobial substances can be built-in or coated onto food packaging materials (Labuza and Breene, 1989). These agents can be either natural or artificially created. Natural antimicrobial agents include extracts from spices like cinnamon, clove, thyme, rosemary, oregano and other plant extracts like onion, garlic, radish mustard and horseradish. Cinnamaldehyde is also used as a fungicide which is effective on over 40 different crops. It is typically applied to the root systems of plants and due to its low toxicity and well-known properties, it ideal for agricultural activities. Polylactic acid (PLA) films, generated from lactic acid, have shown the highest commercial potential and are now produced on a comparatively large scale.

- **Moisture control**

One reason for food spoilage is the presence of moisture. The moisture-regulator reduces the water activity of the product to suppress the microbial growth (Vermeiren et al., 1999). In case of fresh fruits and vegetables, due to condensation, when one part of the package is cooler than the other areas, soluble nutrients leak into the moisture that is retained inside the package, thereby

Vermeiren et al., 1999). Moisture absorbent pads, sheets and blankets are used to control the wetness due to moisture secretion from foods like fish, meat, poultry, fruits and vegetables.

• Antioxidant release

Antioxidants are widely used in food to improve the oxidation stability of the food which in turn prolongs the shelf life. Antioxidants are incorporated in packaging films as a source in some foods, due to its increased demand. Antioxidant incorporation can also stabilise the polymer in order to safeguard the films from degradation (Smith et al., 1990; Rooney, 1995).

• Flavour or odour absorbers and releasers

The volatile compounds that gather inside the package due to gradual decomposition of food, such as aldehydes, amines and sulphides, can be selectively removed (Day, 2008). Flavour scavengers avert the cross-contamination of pungent odours. Odour proof packages were developed for the transportation of Durian fruit by Morris (1999). The package consists of an odour impermeable plastic like polyethylene tetraphthalate (PET) or polyethylene of suitable thickness, together with a port to allow for the emission of respiratory gases and a sachet made from a blend of charcoal and nickel to absorb odour.

• Ethylene scavengers

Ethylene is a hormone for plant growth, which speeds up respiration of fruits and vegetables, induces fruit ripening and fruit softening (Abeles et al., 1992). It causes yellowing of vegetables, russet spotting on lettuce and has detrimental impact on shelf life of many fruits and vegetables (Zagory, 1995). Potassium permanganate immobilised on inert minerals is available in sachets for packages and blankets that can be placed in product-holding rooms without integrating into the food contact packaging material and activated carbon base with various metal catalysts, facilitates in removing ethylene effectively.

Active Packaging is an essential in Indian agriculture sector. Jain et al. (2017) highlight how Active Packaging is evolving in the area of post-harvest handling of fresh horticultural to help in preservation, protection and safe transportation of products during storage and handling. One of the challenges of Active Packaging is to keep meat products fresh. The preservation requirements are many while packaging meat and meat-products to prevents its exposure to oxygen, which may spoil it. Packaging with oxygen barrier improves the shelf

High Pressure Processing (HPP) is a technique of cold pasteurisation wherein packaged foods are placed in a high-pressure chamber. In this chamber the product is subjected to high isostatic pressures crested by water. This pressure from the water helps to destroy microbes and protein in the form of enzymes, which are the major causes of food deterioration but at the same time, prevents loss of nutrition, color, texture, aroma, and flavor. The Indian company Rakyan Beverages Private Limited with its brand Raw Pressery uses this technique to processes fresh fruits and vegetables to manufacture high quality juices in hygienic packages.

Intelligent Packaging

Intelligent packaging is a type of packaging which monitors or provides information on a product and its quality, safety, or location during transport, storage, sales and use.

It involves use of intelligent materials and articles which monitor the state of packaged food or the environment surrounding the food, thereby facilitating decision-making related to packing. Intelligent packaging systems provide the user with information on the conditions of the food or its environment (temperature, pH levels, etc.). It is an extension of the communication function of traditional packaging and communicates to the consumer based on its ability to detect sense and record the changes in the products environment (Restuccia et al., 2010; Realini and Marcos, 2014). Contrary to Active Packaging solutions, intelligent components do not emit any element into the food. It rather, helps to identify processes that strongly affect the quality attributes and efficiently improve the final food quality (Vanderroost et al., 2014). Generally there exist three popular intelligent systems - sensors, indicators and radiofrequency identification (RFID) systems.

- Sensors are one of the easiest to use innovative technologies, which are implemented in Intelligent Packaging systems. These generally include devices or systems with control and processing electronics, network system and software. These devices then detect, locate, or quantify, by giving a signal by measuring or detecting a physical or chemical property, to which the device responds.
- Radio frequency identification (RFID) is a system that uses radio waves to keep track of items wirelessly. RFID has today has numerous applications in the food industry, ranging from food monitoring and

retail level. RFID technology also provides security for food companies through tracing the origin of supplies.

- Indicators provide information related to the presence or absence of a substance, the degree of a reaction between two or more substances, or the level of concentration of a specific substance or class of substances. Indicators generally include three types - time-temperature indicators, freshness indicators and gas indicators. These solutions include packages that help in enhancing product quality and are one of the most widely used devices for food packaging applications.

Intelligent packaging thus, relates to adding additional information or functions to packaging, often in the form of sensors or communication features. A wide variety of potential applications like, tracking a package along the supply chain, discovering the expiration date of a product and using sensors informing consumers when the product is close to this date, monitoring food safety, tracking delivery of items via embedded security tags, are some of the many uses for Intelligent Packaging. A number of studies have been done on the use of Intelligent Packaging in Indian agriculture with many of the current works on use of nanotechnology in packaging. Many studies by Sastry et al. (2010), Rai et al. (2015), Bhagat et al. (2015) have highlighted how nanotechnology has been integrated in a number of food and food packaging products. Pacquit et al. (2007) identified that such packaging may also be used to identify inadequacies in supply chain, reduce costs and errors, improve product performance and ultimately increase profit margins. For instance, Finland-based Magic Add uses Internet of Things in packaging. It embeds coding in its packages, which can capture data along the supply chain and supplies information to customers.

Aseptic Packaging

The Aseptic Packaging technology is referred to as one of the most important food packaging innovations of the 20th Century by the Institute of Food Technologists (Verma, 2017). An aseptic package is one which is sterilised prior to filling with sterilised or UHT (Ultra High Temperature) treated food, resulting in a product which can be shelved for over six months. Heat treatment of products is one of the main techniques in the food industry for food conservation, as it stops bacterial and enzyme activity and prevents loss of quality and keeps food non-perishable. Aseptic Packaging is therefore, filling of a commercially sterile product into a sterile container. This form of packaging

Packaging Metamorphosis: Rise of Interactive Packaging

The paper observes that Packaging metamorphosis is the evolution in the role of packaging from a component of logistics to an important tool of marketing. This is especially true for the final-level package that actually reaches the end-user. Such packages are a vital element in the decision-making process of a consumer, as it is the first component of a product that communicates with consumers at the point-of-sale and helps them make the final buy. Today, packaging apart from being used for storage, protection, preservation and extension of shelf-life of foodstuff has developed into an important section of integrated marketing communication in the food-processing industry. Nowadays, packaging has acquired an interactive role by incorporating new technologies to improve engagement of consumer with the product, creating more awareness and refining brand communication. These packaging solutions allow the consumer to connect with the brand digitally. With the increased usage of mobile phones and other hand-held electronic devices, today companies can interact with the consumer beyond the shelf using the internet. Food packaging has become a powerful tool of consumer engagement with the use some of these common tools -

- QR (Quick Response) code - These are black and white two-dimensional matrix barcode that can be easily seen on a package. Scanning these using a mobile app takes the consumers to a product or company's website or social media page or to a video link that provides detailed information about the product – from showing the packaging details, usage of the product, entire product range, suggesting recipes, to creating awareness about any social campaigns. The MNC Tetra Pak is going to introduce Dynamic QR codes for liquid food packaging which will enable each package to be tracked, monitored and traced throughout the supply chain, helping in efficient stock management, distribution and creating opportunities for consumer interaction too. Nestle has added QR code which allows its consumers to use mobile phones to find out more about its products, their nutritional value, etc.

- Image Recognition - This involves scanning the existing package with an image recognition app, thereby removing the need for any separate space in the package for QR codes. After scanning the pack using this technology, the consumer can access links to websites, videos, visuals, blogs, product reviews etc., about the product.

This is possible when consumers direct their mobile phone or tablets on a package, which activates the screen by displaying attractive visuals and three-dimensional interaction.

The new interactive food packaging component therefore, translates any encoded information related to the product to an audible, visual and/or tactile message and makes it available either before, during or after consuming the food product. It is emerging as an important tool of promotion by allowing consumers to differentiate among competing brands, through regular customer engagement such as providing useful information or entertainment.

Marketers are of the opinion that a vital consideration that influences consumers buying behavior is not just the visual element, but rather the tactile element. The interaction that a consumer has with touching a product acts as a major purchase stimuli. It is this that Interactive Packaging solutions nowadays seek to capture. Interactive Packaging adds value to the buying-process by converting it into an experience, through interactions using QR Codes, augmented reality (AR) and image-recognition technology, etc. It provides tangible access to the product without having the need to open the packaging.

Interactive Packaging offers a number of benefits. Companies are today leveraging these mobile-based technologies, to better understand customer interests and behaviours. In case of customers, it enables them to check the quality and origin of the food products displayed by simply scanning an item with an application which is loaded on their hand-held mobile devices. Many a times, a customer can get details of the entire supply chain of the product. When a mobile device, like a smartphone or tablet is directed at a package, the image of the cover of the package, on the mobile application changes and provides pre-loaded interactive custom-made online content which customers can access by just looking at the package through the device.

London-based Blippar uses AR that engages customers to interact directly with their brands by providing relevant content and developing personalised digital interface which users can unlock by through a mobile application built by the company.

Interactive Packaging may add to the cost of packaging, but second-generation QR codes and easily available universal QR code application on the mobile devices may be used to reduce costs.

communication has become vital. However, one of the major drawbacks of the rise in food packaging is the damage it is causing to the environment. Packaging has moreover become a liability, due to its reliance on limited-energy resources and the lack of appropriate systems to deal with wastes caused by disposal of packages. It is one of the major causes for the increasing waste levels, as most of the packaging material ends-up as landfill after use. This is especially true for packages that are disposed after a single-use. In the recent past, the packaging industry has received severe flak for the rising levels of packaging waste and is faced by a pressing need to improve recyclability and reuse of packaging material. Sustainability is one of the 'buzz' words that are highly discussed in the area of packaging nowadays (Nordin and Selke, 2010). Today packaging is required to incorporate not only the consumer or the people-aspect but also address the environment or the planet-aspect. The need to integrate environmental facets in a product-packaging has given rise to a whole new range of packaging elements viz., Sustainable Packaging. Defining Sustainable Packaging is not easy as it can be assimilated at different levels of supply chain.

One of the earliest bodies to work extensively in giving a theoretical framework to Sustainable Packaging is the Sustainable Packaging Alliance (SPA) based in Australia (Lewis et al., 2007). The SPA initially identified four principles of Sustainable Packaging as:

- 'effective' meaning a packaging system that incorporates value-addition to society along with securing contents of the package and making consumers aware as a product travels through the supply chain, thereby, improving the functional aspect of the product but ensuring commensurate use of packaging material and reducing wastage.
- 'efficient' which requires resources, whether raw-materials, energy or natural resources, to be used optimally throughout the life cycle of a product.
- 'cyclic' dimension of a packaging wherein the package can be returned, reused or recycled, and lastly
- 'clean' which entails that ingredients used to prepare a package do not harm the ecosystems of the planet. In doing so it cuts down on emissions, toxic wastes and lowers level of landfills.

These principles were further developed by organisations like Sustainable principles. The concept today has been embraced by many corporations. In fact, the American multinational retail corporation Wal-Mart in 2006 introduced the Sustainable Packaging Scorecard or commonly known as the "7 R's of Packaging" – Remove, Reduce, Reuse, Renew, Recycle, Revenue and Read, which is used as a tool by many companies to measure how environmentally-safe product packaging can be made without denting company's viability in terms of costs.

Sustainable Packaging is difficult to define but it is equally challenging to practice. Even using recyclable materials in packaging does not make an organisation sustainable. Collecting the used packaging materials back from consumers and undertaking the reuse or recycling process for the package is a major hurdle for many companies. Moreover, only 14 percent of the plastic packaging used globally is recycled (Ellen MacArthur Foundation, 2017).

The many challenges of Sustainable Packaging require reasonable solutions. It requires mission-oriented entrepreneurs, who will not only serve their business objectives but at the same time address environmental causes. Sustainable Packaging provides opportunities, which may help these businesses to discover new revenue-streams and provide them with competitive advantage. As consumers become more environmentally conscious and hold businesses and their packaging standards to account, the hope is that businesses will be incentivised to produce and package more responsibly (Lacy and Splinder, 2019).

Conclusion

The development of active and intelligent packaging will fundamentally depend on the perception of the manufacturer or the distributor about the benefits of its implementation. As compared with traditional as well as active systems, this particular type of food packaging offers the ability to acquire process, communicate and also preserve food as well as display information related to it. Such smart solutions also enable monitoring and providing knowledge about the quality and safety of food products or their location during transportation, storage, retail sale, as well as during their use.

There undoubtedly exists, a wide array of Smart Packaging concepts, which can be converted to functional and dependable systems. It is an onerous task but offers myriad prospects as discussed above, for organised businesses to come forward and build practical solutions to address growing demands of the packaging industry. Wastage of food is a serious burden for the food industry.

viewed in isolation, rather, a complete packaging solution today needs to combine both active and intelligent competencies and at the same time assure sustainability.

The most significant advantage of Smart Packaging is extending the shelf life of food, enhanced control of its storage conditions, as well as suitable perception of the brand by consumers. It is also worth noting that the introduction of new and innovative technologies in this area, like Interactive Packaging, will raise the present status of packaging, from a mere instrument of marketing communication, to a more informative and interactive mechanism, which therefore will act as an efficient tool for decision making. However, additional effort should be given on overcoming the technical constraints and high costs associated with these technologies, which have been the main factors obstructing wider implementation and the development of additional commercial applications for new types of packaging materials in this industry. On the other hand, advances in nanotechnology offer great potential for overcoming the existing challenges associated with packaging materials and cost reduction.

Finally, to increase the safety and effectiveness of new food packaging technologies and ensure the sustainable growth of modern societies, continuous research and development should be performed based on collaboration between government regulatory agencies, industries, consumers and multidisciplinary experts.

References

Balasubramanian, S & Sharma, Rajiv. (2009). Aseptic Packaging of food and food products. Processed Food Industry. 36-41.

Bhagat, Y., Gangadhara, K., Rabinal, C., Chaudhari, G., & Ugale, P. (2015). Nanotechnology in agriculture: a review. J Pure App Microbiol, 9, 737-47.

Biji, K. B., Ravishankar, C. N., Mohan, C. O., & Gopal, T. S. (2015). Smart Packaging systems for food applications: a review. Journal of food science and technology, 52(10), 6125-6135.

Brody, A. L., Bugusu, B., Han, J. H., Sand, C. K., & McHugh, T. H. (2008). Scientific status summary: innovative food packaging solutions. Journal of food science, 73(8), R107-R116.

Brody, A. L., Strupinsky, E. P., & Kline, L. R. (2001). Active Packaging for food applications. CRC press.

Coles, R., & Kirwan, M. J. (Eds.). (2011). Food and beverage packaging technology. Hoboken, NJ: Wiley-Blackwell.

Costa, C., Antonucci, F., Pallottino, F., Aguzzi, J., Sarriá, D., & Menesatti, P. (2013). A review on agri-food supply chain traceability by means of RFID technology. Food and bioprocess

Ghaani, M., Cozzolino, C.A., Castelli, G. and Farris, S., 2016. An overview of the intelligent packaging technologies in the food sector. Trends in Food Science & Technology, 51, pp.1-11.

Investigating active and intelligent packaging. (n.d.). Retrieved from https://sml-rfid.com/in-the-news/investigating-active-intelligent-packaging/

Jain, Vikas & K Singh, Anil & Tiwari, Anupam & Maurya, Ashish & Pal, Sumit & Kanth, Neeharika & S Hada, T. (2017). Active Packaging of Horticultural Produce.

Kaur and Puri, S, (2017). Active and intelligent packaging: A boon to food packaging. International Journal of Food Science and Nutrition, Volume 2, 15-18.

Kit: Food Packaging in India-Technopak Advisors - https://www.business-standard.com/article/management/kit-food-packaging-in-india-112070900039_1.html

Kotler P, Keller K. 2006. Marketing management. 12th ed. Upper Saddle River, N.J.: Pearson. 729 p.

Ministry of Food Processing Industries | Goi-http://mofpi.nic.in/documents/reports/annual-report

Packaging Innovation To Boost Food Sector- New Indian Xpress - http://www.newindianexpress.com/states/odisha/2017/mar/11/packaging-innovation-to-boost-food-sector-1580157.html

Packaging Innovation. (2019). The future of Interactive Packaging. [online] Available at: https://www.packaginginnovation.com/packaging-design/innovative-packaging-2/future-interative-packaging-will-electronics-change-industry/.

Pareeratanasomporn, N. (2018). Consumer Preferences in Food Interactive Packaging.

Patil R, Birhade V and Jadhav, V, (2015). Innovative Food Packaging. International Journal of Science and Research, Volume 6, 1287-1291.Han, J.H. ed., 2005. Innovations in food packaging. Elsevier.

Popa, A., Hnatiuc, M., Paun, M., Geman, O., Hemanth, D. J., Dorcea, D. & Ghita, S. (2019). An Intelligent IoT-Based Food Quality Monitoring Approach Using Low-Cost Sensors. Symmetry, 11(3), 374.

Rai, M., Ribeiro, C., Mattoso, L., & Duran, N. (Eds.). (2015). Nanotechnologies in food and agriculture (p. 347). Cham/Heidelberg/New York/Dordrecht/London: Springer.

Rundh, B. (2009). Packaging design: creating competitive advantage with product packaging. British Food Journal, 111(9), 988-1002.

Rundh, B. (2016). The role of packaging within marketing and value creation. British Food Journal, 118(10), 2491-2511.

Sastry, R. K., & Rao, N. H. (2013). Emerging Technologies for Enhancing Indian Agriculture-Case of Nanobiotechnology. Asian Biotechnology & Development Review, 15(1).

Subramanian, K. S., & Tarafdar, J. C. (2011). Prospects of nanotechnology in Indian farming. Indian Journal of Agricultural Sciences, 81(10), 887-93.

Surintrspanont, S. (2003). U.S. Patent No. 6,525,660. Washington, DC: U.S. Patent and Trademark Office.

Yes Bank, & FICCI. (2018). Startup-Report [PDF]. FICCI.

Part-II: Government Policies and Interventions in Entrepreneurship

7

Agricultural Insurance Schemes in West Bengal: Assessment & Entrepreneurship Opportunities

Debisree Banerjee

Abstract

Entrepreneurship essentially involves economic and dynamic activities, risk- assuming and idea generation that help in developing, organising and managing a business opportunity for profits. Entrepreneurship in agriculture is not merely confined to farm activities but also involves activities interlinked and interdependent with core and peripheral agricultural activities. Impediments in the pathway of agricultural entrepreneurship in West Bengal are characterised by fragmented land-holding, low financial resources and thereby debt stickiness & dependence on short-term agricultural loan. Though disbursements of short-term credit have increased substantially, the rate of increase is low. For most farmers, insurance for financial or crop crisis is unheard or have hardly any implication. The paper tries to explain the performance of various agricultural insurance schemes in terms of coverage and the benefits being delivered in India and in West Bengal. The paper analyses whether the recipients consider the schemes as an effective risk mitigation tool or merely a habit of credit-dependence in West Bengal through a diffusion model. The paper concludes with the focus on possible entrepreneurial opportunities that may offer more customised agri-insurance policies, where regional disparities could be considered and individual interests be given little more importance.

Keywords: Agriculture, Agricultural Insurance, Diffusion, Entrepreneurship, Risk.

Introduction

Entrepreneurship essentially involves motive for profit, economic and dynamic activities, risk-assuming and idea generation that help in developing, organising, and managing a business environment. Entrepreneurship in agriculture is not merely confined to farm activities such as growing crops or raising cattle to make profit. Agriculture and allied activities involve a wide range of activities which is tightly interlinked and interdependent with core agricultural activities. Examples of such agri-enterprises can be industries such as dairy, food processing, handlooms; and mechanisms supporting them such as agricultural-credit, marketing, insurance.

Though, today India's service sector is the largest sector contributing about 54 percent of the country's GVA (Gross Value Added) at current prices in 2016-17, still the importance of agriculture cannot be ignored. Agriculture contributes about 16 percent of country's total GDP and more than 49 percent of total working population is dependent on it (Economic Survey, 2017-18). The volatility in Indian agriculture is also quite high. The position of West Bengal in agriculture is also vulnerable. The agricultural economy is greatly dependent on monsoon and flood, land erosion, drought and other natural calamities which often affect production in agriculture. Due to high density of population and concentration of industrial and agricultural activities there is increase in risk due to natural and man-made disasters. There are also traces of other natural disasters like landslides in hilly region, subsidence in mining areas and little risk from earthquakes.

Though risks involved in agriculture are multi-faceted, vagaries of weather have been the most common risk associated with agriculture. According to Crisis Management Plan on Drought 2012, 16 percent of the country's total area is drought prone exposing about 50 million people to the crisis of drought. Rainfall is erratic in four out of ten years enhancing the trouble for farmers. Further, depletion of ground water and limitation of surface water indicates that not all the net sown area is amenable to irrigation, which in turn makes the farmers dependent upon weather conditions again. Apart from that, agriculture has also been subject to yield risks, market risks, technological risks and many more.

The obvious question that arises is about the strategies and policies that should be adopted for mitigating those risks. Risk management strategies may be classified in several ways majorly, ex-ante and ex-post and/or formal and informal.

Table 1: Table showing risk management strategies

Strategies	Formal Mechanism	Informal Mechanism
Ex-ante strategies	• Co-operative farming • Pest control management • Soil testing • Supply of quality input, etc.	• Crop diversification • Mixed farming • Precautionary savings • Low investment, etc.
Ex-post strategies	• Government relief programme • Formal credit • Minimum guaranteed procurement price • Agricultural insurance etc.	• -Sale of assets • Reducing consumption • Overtime in other jobs • Migration, etc.

Source: Adapted from Rosenzweig R. and Binswanger P. (1993) "Wealth, Weather Risk and the Composition and Profitability of Agricultural Investments".

Among various policies adapted at individual and at gross levels, Agricultural Insurance (A.I.) is one of the most important and widely discussed risk management tools for entrepreneurship.

Agricultural Insurance (A. I.) In India And In West Bengal

A.I. as a concept has been employed long time back in India. The Central Legislature for the first time discussed the subject of crop insurance in 1947. However, the first ever crop insurance scheme was introduced in India in 1972 during the Fourth Five Year Plan. The scheme was simple based on individual approach which covered yield losses of a few farmers. The scheme was implemented in six states including West Bengal and suffered losses paying about ten times more claims than premium collected. Soon it was realised that a scheme based on individual approach is not viable in the Indian scenario. The scheme was withdrawn in 1978 after it suffered huge losses by covering only a handful of farmers.

In 1979 a Pilot Crop Insurance Scheme was introduced based on the recommendations of Professor V. M. Dandekar (also known as Father of Crop Insurance). The scheme was based on Homogeneous Area Approach and participation was voluntary for the states. The scheme ran till 1984-85 in 13 states. The scheme covered 627 thousand farmers for a premium of Rs 19.6 Million against a claim of Rs 15.6 Million. Though the scheme did not suffer losses like the previous scheme, it was unable to gain confidence of the farmers. Finally, the scheme was replaced by Comprehensive Crop Insurance Scheme (CCIS) in 1985. The Government of India initiated the CCIS in 1985-86 jointly

Million farmers. The scheme was discontinued as it served limited purposes. Finally, the CCIS was replaced by National Agricultural Insurance Scheme (NAIS) in 1999-2000, which was the longest running and most widely operated crop insurance scheme of the country. Traditional yield-based crop insurance scheme was inadequate to cover the diverse risks involved in farming activities. Considering this limiting factor, government introduced Weather Based Crop Insurance Scheme (WBCIS) in 2007. The scheme was innovative as it protected the insured farmers against the likelihood of financial loss on account of anticipated crop loss resulting from incidence of adverse conditions of weather parameters like rainfall, temperature, frost, humidity, etc. It operated on the basis of area approach. The reference area was linked with a reference weather station, on the basis of which current weather data and claims would be processed. However, all the schemes have been criticised on several grounds, based on which these were modified and re- modified several times. One such initiative was National Crop Insurance Programme (NCIP) 2013. The central government introduced the National Agricultural Insurance Scheme (NAIS) with Pilot Modified National Agricultural Insurance Scheme (MNAIS), Pilot Weather Based Crop Insurance Scheme (WBCIS), and Pilot Coconut Palm Insurance Scheme (CPIS). Again, with the introduction of Pradhan Mantri Fasal Bima Yojana (PMFBY) and Restructured Weather Based Crop Insurance Scheme (RWBCIS), NAIS also came to an end.

The above discussion briefly gives an overview about the major agricultural insurance schemes in India. It is observed that through various experimentations and policy changes based on trial and error method, the presently running schemes have evolved. West Bengal has also followed a similar road-map. The paper attempts firstly to look into the issue of relevance of agricultural insurance, its limitations in applicability and suggests a few unusual opportunities in the area that may be explored for entrepreneurship opportunities. In the succeeding section, a brief analysis of relevant literatures has been covered.

Review of Literature

Agricultural risk is uncontrollable and therefore the role of insurance becomes significant. According to Bhende (2002), a properly designed crop insurance programme would protect the small and marginal farmers from hardships, bring in stability in the farm income and help in increasing farm production. Agricultural insurance in India has certain distinct features. In India the major form of agricultural insurance is the crop insurance (which is highly subsidised by the that experience in developed countries is not a good model for the developing countries due to lack of fiscal resources as compared to developed nations. Further the risk management strategies of the developed nations are also much about income transfer, but such models are not affordable for the developing countries due to the dependence of large segment of population on the farming sector with small land-holding pattern and no access to global re- insurance market. Mehrotra (2010) studied the pattern of small and marginal farmers in Indian agriculture. The author observed that though their share in agricultural output has increased, their share in agricultural credit has declined over time. Even the effort in terms of doubling of agricultural credit was not able to even out the regional inequalities in agriculture credit flow despite the fact that agricultural credit grew substantially.

Crop credit insurance is favoured as it would automatically make the borrowers a subscriber of crop insurance (Dandekar,1985; Prabhu and Ramachandran 1986). However, dependence on agricultural credit may keep a large portion of farmers uncovered. Moreover, the problem of corruption and bias favoured large farmers. Insurance policies should not be made a mandatory condition to access credit because it may make it difficult to measure both the bank's and insurance company's capacity to evaluate creditworthiness, measure risk, and assess farmer management capacity (Prabhu and Ramachandran, 1986; Wenner 2005). Further, the problem of adverse selection and moral hazard is common with ineffective actuarial rates. The scheme is also often not preferred by the farmers as there are complications involved with it including delays in claim settlement (Bhalla, 2006; Raju and Chand, 2007, 2008a, 2008b, 2009; Banerjee and Bhattacharya, 2011).

Ifft (2001), stated that Government sponsored Comprehensive Crop Insurance scheme replaced by NAIS is just a replacement of a flawed scheme by a slightly less-flawed scheme. The author argued that both in developed and developing countries, government sponsored crop insurance schemes suffered losses and private insurance does not exist even where it is feasible. The author criticised the schemes and considered that income guarantee scheme would be beneficial instead of schemes based on yield, price or area covered. Most of the government sponsored crop insurance schemes have suffered losses due to several factors including insufficient coverage and lack of awareness (Bhalla, 2006; Raju and Chand, 2007; 2008a, 2008b, 2009; Narayanan and Sarvanan, 2011; Goudappa S.B. et al., 2012. Sundar and Ramakrishnan (2013), firstly measured the awareness level of farmers and their source of awareness,

The review of the above literary works of India and across the globe brings out a common view on A.I. i.e. low penetration, too much experimentation and lack of awareness, which justifies the need for the present study. Thus, in this backdrop the paper attempts to cover the objectives as stated in the subsequent section.

Objectives

1. To study the performance of different A.I. schemes (past and present) of India.
2. To understand the nature of spread of the NAIS through diffusion model in West Bengal and to ascertain the positioning of the districts on the basis of estimated parameters of the diffusion model.
3. To suggest entrepreneurial opportunities in the field of A.I.

Data Source And Methodology

Data Source

Secondary data has been utilised for the study. Publications of Agriculture Insurance Company of India Ltd. (AICL) and Dept. of Agriculture and Co-operation, Ministry of Agriculture, Govt. of India and reports of the Department of Agriculture and Co-operation, West Bengal are the major sources of relevant information used in this paper.

Methodology

The performance of various A.I. schemes has been explained through analysis of ratios, percentage analysis and graphical representation. Further, in order to explain the spread of NAIS in West Bengal a diffusion model has been prepared. It is done in SPSS 16 through multiple regression analysis.

The model is specified as:

$st = \alpha . St\text{-}1 + (M - St\text{-}1).\beta$

Where, st= Number of farmers/area covered at time t for a district. St= Cumulative no. of farmers/ area covered at time t for a district. α = coefficient of repetitions.

β = coefficient of awareness. M= Market size.

The second part is a fraction (β) of that part which is not covered under the scheme till (t-1). Therefore β can be taken as a measure to reflect the level of awareness.

The above model could be reduced to:

$st= M.\beta + (\alpha- \beta).St$

Estimation of the diffusion model using NAIS data-set for West Bengal has been done, considering two variables, one being number of farmers covered and the other one being area covered under the scheme in different districts of West Bengal from 2000-01to 2010-11.

The model is estimated as $s_t = a + b.St$

Therefore, it is simply regression of st on St. Where, $\beta = aM$ and $\alpha = b + \beta$ The next section depicts the major findings and discussion of the study.

Findings And Discussion

National Agricultural Insurance Scheme (NAIS)

NAIS, also known as '*Rashtriya Krishi Bima Yojna*', since its inception in 1999 till Rabi 2015-16 covered 27,25,40,000 farmers and 39,17,18,000 hectares of area. In aggregate all over India three hundred fifty percent more claim is paid than what premium has been collected, indicating loss of operation. West Bengal is considered to be a mediocre performer in terms of performance of the NAIS. It benefitted about 24 percentage of the farmers covered with claim premium ratio being 113.34 as compared to 31 percentage benefit being delivered in India with higher loss of operation indicated through 349 percentage claim premium ratio.

Table 2: NAIS in India and in West Bengal (1999-2000 to Rabi 2015-16)

State / UT	Beneficiary Ratio* (%)	Claim to premium# (%)	Premium to sum insured$ (%)	Claim to Sum Insured* (%)
WestBengal	23.72	113.34	7.22	8.18
India	31.26	349.00	3.44	11.99

Source: Calculations based on data from the AICL

**Beneficiary Ratio = No. of farmers benefited/ No. of farmers covered * 100.*

*#Claim to Premium Ratio= Claims paid/Premium collected*100.*

$Premium/Claim to Sum Insured Ratio= Premium collected or Claim Paid / Total Sum

percentage of farmers covered as compared to 8.84 percentages of farmers in India, in 2013-14 West Bengal. had 19.17 percentage of its farmers covered as against 11.55 percentage of farmers covered overall India (Figure 1).

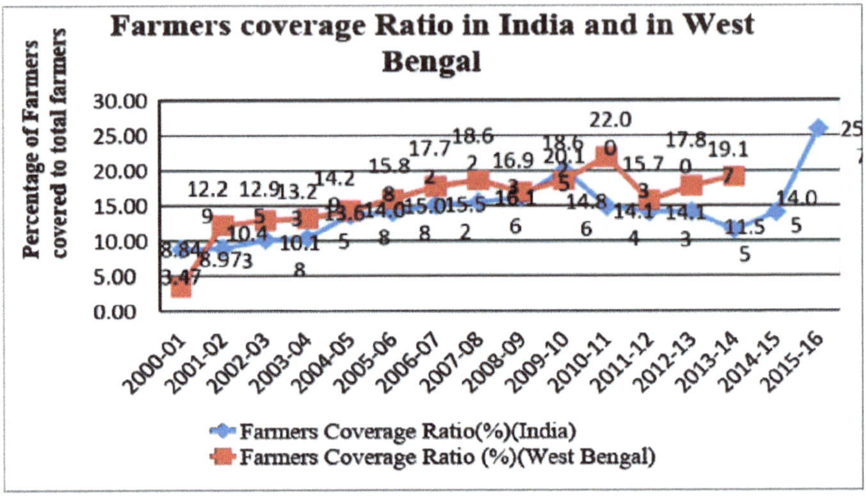

Fig. 1: Comparison of Farmers Covered (%) under NAIS in India and in West Bengal
Source: Calculations based on data from the AICl
*Detailed data on NAIS in West Bengal available till 2013-14

On comparing the area coverage ratios, West Bengal started with merely 1.90 percentage of Net Area Sown as compared to 11.55 percentage of Net Area Sown in the whole of India. In 2013-14 in India where it increased to 14.64 percentage, in West Bengal the coverage increased to 10.40 percentage (Figure 2). Thus, indicating comparatively take- up was more in West Bengal in comparison to India in overall.

Thus, it can be stated that in West Bengal though the benefits delivered were little less than the aggregate level, the increase in coverage was more here. Further, loss of operation was also lower than that of rest of India. Still there were certain limitations of the scheme. In order to improvise the scheme, Modified National Insurance Scheme (MNAIS) was initiated.

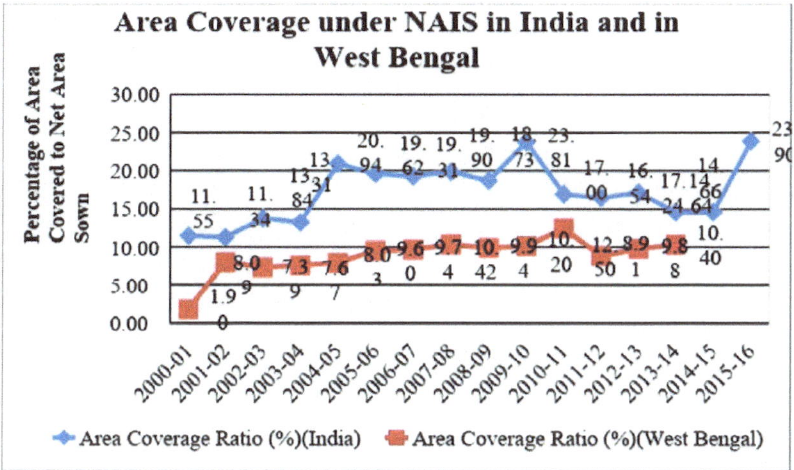

Fig. 2: Comparison of Area Covered (%) under NAIS in India and in West Bengal
Source: Calculations based on data from the AICl
*Detailed data on NAIS in West Bengal available till 2013-14

Modified National Agricultural Insurance Scheme (MNAIS) (*Rabi* 2010-11 to *Kharif* 2014)

In its four years of operation since Rabi 2010-11 to Kharif 2014 it covered 1,21,28,000 farmers and 1,35,25,000 hectares of land in India. The scheme was initiated in 2010 in 50 selected districts and then merged under National Crop Insurance Program of the then Central Government in 2013. In these years it delivered more than 28 percent of benefit in aggregate (see **Table 3**). However, too much similarity of the scheme with NAIS did not allow it to gain much popularity. Finally, the scheme became dysfunctional with the introduction of Pradhan Mantri Fasal Bima Yojana (PMFBY).

Table 3: Performance of the MNAIS (*Rabi* 2010-11 to *Kharif* 2014)

State / UT	Beneficiary Ratio (%)	Claim Ratio (%)	Claim to Sum insured (%)	Premium to Sum Insured (%)
WestBengal	27.13	35.11	7.38	21.01
India	28.10	55.89	7.74	13.85

Source: Calculations Based on Data from AICL

In recent years another similar natured scheme has been initiated by the Government of India, which attempts to give an answer to the criticisms faced by the age-old NAIS. The scheme is PMFBY, which is being implemented from *Kharif* 2016 in all the states of India.

On comparing the schemes, though some major differences can be identified, the similarities are also not rare. The major improvements are reduction of unit area, private participation, use of technology and on account payment of claim (Table 4).

Table 4: A Comparison between National Agricultural Insurance Scheme (NAIS) and Pradhan Mantri Fasal Bima Yojana (PMFBY)

NAIS (1999)	PMFBY(2016)
Scale of finance or value of Threshold yield or 150% of value of Average Yield.	For loanee farmers scale of finance fixed by the District Level Technical Committee. For voluntary participants value of threshold yield
(1.5 to 3.5)% for major kharif and Rabi crops. Actuarial rate of Annual Horticultural and commercial crops.	(1.5 to 2)% for major Kharif and Rabi crops. 5% of Sum Insured or Actuarial rate whichever is low for Annual Horticultural and commercial crops.
CCE- Taluka/ Tehsil/ Block- 16, Mandal/ Phirka/any other unit comprising (8-10 villages)- 10, Gram Panchayat (4-5villages)- 08.	CCE- District- 24, Taluka/ Tehsil/ Block- 16, Mandal/ Hobli/ Phirka etc- 10, Village/ Gram Panchayat etc.- 4 for major crops and 10 for other crops.
Implementing Agency-Government	Implementing Agency-Government and Private.
No on account payment.	On account payment.

Source: Comparison based on information from AICL

In the next section an attempt has been made to analyse the impact of PMFBY in the country and in West Bengal.

Pradhan Mantri Fasal Bima Yojana (PMFBY) an analysis (*Kharif 2016 to Rabi 2017-18*) in India and in West Bengal

PMFBY has been implemented by replacing NAIS and MNAIS in India. In its four seasons of operation the scheme covered 3,96,41,000 farmers and covered 3,95,16,000 hectares of land and benefitted nearly about 20 percent of the farmers covered. The claim premium ratio is just about 29 percent indicating that just 29 percent of claims are being paid out of the premium collected. West Bengal implemented PMFBY since 2016 in its different districts through two formance of PMFBY in India (*Kharif* 2016 to *Rabi* 2017-18)

	No. of Farmers Insured (000')	No. of Farmers benefitted (000')	Percentage of Farmers Benefitted	Total Premium (Rs. in Milli on)	Sum Insured (Rs in Milli on)	Claims (Rs in Mil lion)	Claim to Premium (%)	Premium to Sum Insured (%)	Claim to Sum Insured (%)
	3131	152	4.85	7600	89980	450	5.92	8.45	0.50
	39641	7792	19.66	281280	1390410	81300	28.90	20.23	5.85

ulations based on Data from AICL

All the above mentioned schemes are similar in some ways; they are yield-based schemes and none of the schemes' coverage increased substantially, nor did they benefit more than fifty percentage of the farmers covered. Considering other varieties of A.I. schemes, the most significant is weather insurance. Weather insurance is often considered to be a parallel risk management entrepreneurship tool.

Weather Based Crop Insurance Scheme (WBCIS) - a study (*Kharif* 2007 to 2015-16)

WBCIS is unique in its own way as it aims at mitigating the hardships of the insured farmers against financial losses for crop loss on account of weather parameters. Government of India initiated WBCIS on pilot basis from *Kharif* 2007 in different selected districts of the country. In its almost a decade of operation, the scheme covered 36,567,000 farmers of which 23,258,000 farmers were benefitted i.e. more than 60 percent of total farmers covered; in West Bengal which is even higher (82 percent). The claim to premium ratio is just about 50 percent indicating that 50 percent of premium collected is paid as claim. This is again established through the difference in premium to sum insured and claim to sum insured ratios, which shows a profit in operation of more than two times (Table 6).

On analysing the performance of the scheme in India the most positive aspect is the claim settlement ratio and the percentage of beneficiaries. Figure 3 shows that WBCIS has been highly beneficial since its inception. There has been constant increase in beneficiaries from about 33 percent of farmers covered in 2007-08 to more than 83 percent of farmers covered in 2015-16. Still there has been no significant increase in farmers' covered or area insured. Similarly in West Bengal also, though WBCIS has been implemented since Rabi 2008-09, there has been no significant increase in percentage of farmers covered or area covered (Table 7).

India Business Snapshot of WBCIS (*Kharif* 2007 to *Rabi* 2015-16)

	No. of Farmers Insured (000')	No. of Farmers benefitted (000')	Beneficiary Ratio (%)	Sum Insured (Rs in Millions)	Gross Premium (Rs in Millions)	Claim (Rs in Millions)	Claim to Premium (%)	Premium to Sum Insured (%)	Claim to Sum Insure d (%)
	39	32	82.05	543.2	89.2	50.1	56.17	9.79	9.22
	36567	23258	63.60	709781.1	111933.1	5558 6.6	49.66	15.77	7.83

ulation based on Data from AICL

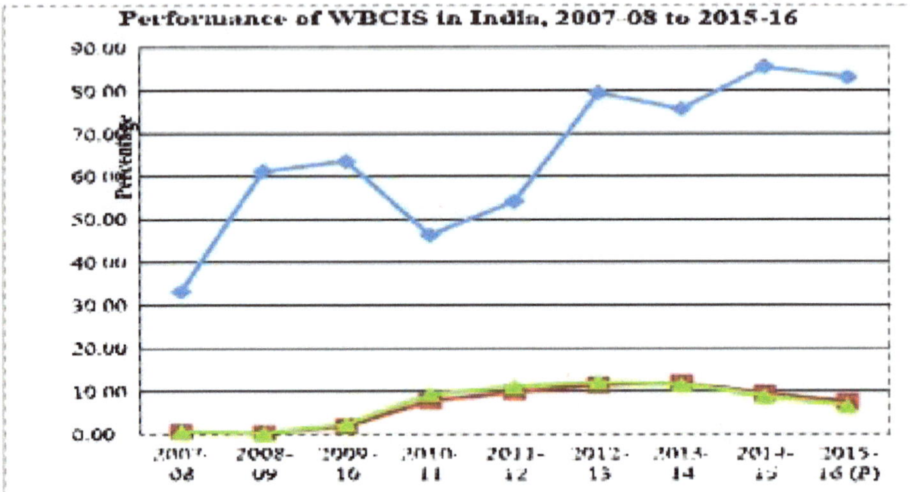

Fig. 3: Performance of WBCIS in India over the years (2007-08 to 2015- 16)
Source: Calculations based on data from Agricultural Statistics at a Glance, 2016

Table 7: Over the Years' Performance of WBCIS in West Bengal

Year	Farmers covered to total cultivators (%)	Area insured to total netarea sown (%)	Beneficiary ratio (%)
2008-09	0.019	0.018	97.044
2009-10	0.038	0.058	73.302
2010-11	0.062	0.131	72.543
2011-12	0.055	0.136	96.485
2012-13	0.021	0.010	28.301
2013-14	0.032	0.017	98.967

Source: Calculations based on data from AICL and Agricultural Statistics at a Glance, 2016

Though WBCIS seems to be beneficial from the farmer's point of view there are certain features of the scheme making it difficult to implement on a large scale. Government of India launched Restructured Weather Based Crop Insurance Scheme (RWBCIS) on 18th February, 2016. 12 states implemented the scheme in Kharif 2016 whereas nine states have implemented the scheme in Rabi 2016-17. Approximately 1.5 Million farmers have been insured in the Kharif 2016 for 1.695 Million hectares of land at premium of Rs 9839.6 Million for a sum insured of Rs 85365.3 Million as per figures available on 31.03.2017.

The above analyses give an idea about the performance of various agricultural developing an understanding about the challenges in nature of spread i.e. underlying reasons for participation in agricultural insurance. This has been attempted through formulation of a simple diffusion model on the NAIS in West Bengal.

The Diffusion Process of the NAIS in West Bengal

The model segregates the coverage under the NAIS both in terms of farmers covered and area covered into two parts, namely - through repetitions and through awareness. It is evident from the analysis that in West Bengal and in all its districts, coverage is mostly due to repetition (See Table 1 in Appendix). On ranking the districts based on the above parameters it was observed that Hooghly and Burdwan are the two districts which tops the list both in terms of farmers covered and area covered and also in terms of á and â, followed by Midnapore East and West respectively. Thus, the age-old agricultural insurance scheme of India lags in its implementation, owing to which coverage and farmer's effective participation was found to be discouraging.

Table 8: Results showing positioning of different districts of West Bengal in terms of (á) and (â), 2000-01 to 2010-11

Districts	Rank			
	Coefficient of Repetition (á)		Coefficient of Awareness (â)	
	No. of Farmers	Area	No. of Farmers	Area
Bankura	7	5	5	5
Burdwan	2	1	2	3
Birbhum	6	6	7	4
Howrah	4	8	4	6
Hooghly	1	2	1	2
Jalpaiguri	11	10	6	17
Maldah	10	11	9	9
Midnapore W	3	7	3	7
Murshidabad	8	13	11	15
Nadia	14	12	12	13
24-Parganas (N)	15	17	10	12
Purulia	17	15	15	10
Uttar Dinajpur	16	16	13	11
Cooch Behar	5	3	17	16
Midnapore E	12	4	16	1
24-Parganas (S)	13	14	14	14
Dakshin Dinajpur	9	9	8	8

Summary and Concluding Observations

A.I. is not the first opportunity that knocks on the door of agricultural entrepreneurship. This is because quick growth and profit making and innovation are the two basic features that we understand from the definition of entrepreneurship. However, the widened view of entrepreneurship focuses on creation of new ideas, which could support other businesses in earning profit/ reducing losses. Thus, in the broadened view A.I. is an important risk management entrepreneurship mechanism which will not only bring profits to the entrepreneur but also certainty of profits to the customer.

Indian agriculture contributes immensely to the economy's well-being. Considering its significance to the economy, agriculture has always received importance from the very beginning of the planning era. A.I. also caught the eyes of the policy framers way back in 1947. However, in a country like India with so much regional disparity and an overpopulated, financially unstable farming community, it was really a tough job to implement. The government succeeded to a certain extent with the implementation of the NAIS in 1999-2000. However, a lot of work was still to be done as the scheme was not flawless and was often being heavily criticised. Two of the major criticisms were firstly, low coverage keeping out large number of farmers uncovered/ insecure and secondly, huge loss of operation suffered by scheme, not generating expected benefits (both from insurer and insured's point of view). The government kept on experimenting and improvising the schemes in order to cope up with gaps associated with its implementation. WBCIS was found to have little more impact on the farmers as benefits delivered was way higher than that of the age-old yield based schemes. Further, the loss in operation of the scheme was also found to be quite lower than that of the previously implemented schemes. However, difficulty in application of the scheme due to huge implementation, administrative and maintenance expenditure involved with it, did not allow its mass implementation. It is still being implemented in notified areas on notified crops in selected districts as Restructured WBCIS (RWBCIS). Recently, through the implementation of PMFBY, which took into account most of the previously held criticisms of agricultural insurance in India, a lot of positive expectations come from the farming community.

The author posits, agricultural insurance as a risk management entrepreneurship mechanism has immense potential in the Indian agrarian sector. The government is making room for the private entrepreneurs in this area after providing performance or progress of such initiatives, this could be considered as a leap forward.

The paper attempted to study the performance of agricultural insurance in India and in West Bengal, and pointed out the positives and negatives associated with each of the schemes and gave an explanation for the low participation of farmers in agricultural insurance through the diffusion model, as a case study in West Bengal. The age-old agricultural insurance scheme of India lags somewhere in its implementation, owing to which coverage and farmer's effective participation was found not to be encouraging. It can be stated that entrepreneurial opportunities are dormant in more customised policies, where regional disparities could be considered and individual interests be given little more importance. This could be achieved through encouragement to entrepreneurs in the private insurance domain and advanced use of technology for A.I. The entrepreneur may exploit the information asymmetry due to lack of awareness being a big hindrance in this area. So it may be recommended that both government and the private enterprises may partner to design entrepreneurial models to enhance farmers' participation in A.I. This could be achieved through effective utilisation of electronic media and more trained ground level workers. The paper leaves much scope for future research in the area of effective implementation of agricultural insurance risk management entrepreneurship mechanism.

Acknowledgement

My sincere thanks to my teachers Dr. Uttam Kumar Bhattacharya, Associate Professor (Retired) of Institute of Development Studies, Kolkata (IDSK) and Shri. Arabinda Bhattacharya, Associate Professor (Retired) of Department of Business Management, University of Calcutta without whose support and guidance it would have been difficult to complete this work.

References

Banerjee, D. and Bhattacharya, U. (2011). Innovations in Agricultural Insurance in India- Retrospect and Prospect , Indian Journal of Agricultural Economics, ISSN No.- 0019-5014, July- September 2011, vol- 66 No. 3, pp- 457-471.

Bhalla, G.S. (2006). Condition of Indian Peasantry, New Delhi: National Book Trust.

Bhende, M.J. (2002). 'An analysis of crop insurance scheme in Karnataka', available online, Institute of Social and Economic Change (ISEC).

Dandekar, V.M. (1985). Crop Insurance in India: A Review, 1976-77 to 1984- 85', Economic and Political weekly, June, pp. A46-A59.

Goudappa, S.B., Reddy B. S. and Chandrashekhar S.M. (2012), Farmers Perception and Awareness about Crop Insurance in Karnataka, Indian Research Journal of Extension

Mehrotra, Nirupam (2010). 'Emerging Patterns in Share of Small Farms in Production and Credit: Implications for Policy Formulation', Indira Gandhi Institute of Development Research Mumbai, March 2010, pp 1-17.

Ministry of Finance, Government of India, Economic Survey (2017-18) New Delhi, Ministry of Finance, OXFORD.

Ministry of Finance, Government of West Bengal (2012-13), Economic Review (2011- 12) Ministry of Finance, Kolkata.

Narayanan, A.G.V. and Saravanan, T.P. (2011). A study on customers' perception towards General Insurance products (livestock and crop insurance) with special reference to Erode Rural, Tamil Nadu, India, European Journal of Social Sciences, vol. 25, November 2011, pp 219- 232.

Prabhu, K.Seeta and Ramachandram, Saroja (1986). Crop-Credit Insurance: Some Disturbing Features, Economic and Political Weekly, October 18, pp1866-1869.

Raju, S.S. and Chand, Ramesh (2007), Progress and problems in Agricultural Insurance, Economic and political Weekly, May 26, pp. 1905-1908.

Raju, S.S. and Chand, Ramesh (2008 a). A study on the performance of National Agricultural Insurance Scheme and Suggestions to make it more effective, Agricultural Economics Research Review, January-June 2008, pp11-19.

Raju, S.S. and Chand, Ramesh (2008 b). Agricultural Insurance in India Problems and Prospects, National Centre for Agricultural Economics and Policy Research (Indian Council of Agricultural Research), New Delhi, March 2008.

Raju, S.S. and Chand, Ramesh (2009), Problems and Prospects in Agricultural Insurance in India, NCAP Policy Brief, July 2009.

Rosenweig, R. Mark and Binswanger, P. Hans (1993). Wealth, Weather Risk and the Composition and Profitability of Agricultural Investments, The Economic Journal, Jan 1993, pp 56-78.

Sundar, J. and Ramakrishnan, L. (2013). A study on Farmers' Awareness, Perception and willing to Join and Pay for Crop Insurance, Indian Journal of Business and Management Inventions, Volume 2 Issue 1, January 2013, pp 48-54

Wenner, Mark. (2005). Agricultural Insurance Revisited: New Developments and Perspectives in Latin America and the Caribbean, Rural Development Unit Sustainable Development Department, Inter-American Development Bank, New York

World Bank (2005). Managing Agricultural Production Risks: Innovations in Developing Countries, The World Bank Agriculture and Rural Development Department, pp 1-54.

Appendix

Table 1: Results showing spread of the NAIS through repetitions (α) and through awareness (β) in terms of Farmers Covered and Area covered in different districts of West Bengal, 2000-01 to 2010-11

Districts	Farmers (F) / Area (A)	a	B	M	α	β
Bankura	F	54010.121	5.926e-02	439957	0.182022	0.122762
	A	37191.124	2.461e-02	264089	0.165438	0.140828
Burdwan	F	109856.0	5.447e-02	361687	0.358202	0.303732
	A	88683.857	4.943e-02	452462	0.245433	0.196003
Birbhum	F	29710.118	7.123e-02	260955	0.185081	0.113851
	A	17781.823	6.383e-02	319956	0.119406	0.185081
Howrah	F	17399.802	1.577e-02	74935	0.247969	0.232199
	A	8164.201	-4.31e-03	79413	0.098497	0.102807
Hooghly	F	103287.9	4.535e-02	277901	0.417022	0.371672
	A	45088.88	2.877e-02	212407	0.241046	0.212276
Jalpaiguri	F	31985.466	-5.47e-02	269944	0.063789	0.118489
	A	6927.742	6.619e-02	334127	0.086924	0.020734
Maldah	F	25521.134	-2.00e-02	279276	0.071383	0.091383
	A	15255.734	-1.80e-02	217984	0.051986	0.069986
Midnapore (W)	F	127019.4	1.329e-02	527462	0.254102	0.240812
	A	45050.198	2.479e-02	486199	0.117448	0.092658
Murshidabad	F	26141.921	1.407e-02	375172	0.08375	0.06968
	A	9002.146	2.451e-02	395958	0.047245	0.022735
Nadia	F	20333.528	-1.78e-02	320464	0.04565	0.06345
	A	8593.062	2.064e-02	290447	0.050226	0.029586
24-Parganas (N)	F	22863.164	-3.63e-02	300930	0.039675	0.075975
	A	10847.771	-4.22e-03	358401	0.026047	0.030267
Purulia	F	13629.174	-3.58e-02	352712	0.002841	0.038641
	A	13769.580	-2.47e-02	226134	0.036191	0.060891
Uttar Dinajpur	F	17298.439	-4.21e-02	276731	0.02041	0.06251
	A	9629.855	-2.17e-03	274768	0.032877	0.035047
Coochbehar	F	9846.017	0.207	361840	0.234211	0.027211
	A	5247.931	0.212	250611	0.232941	0.020941
Midnapore (E)	F	166073.2	2.788e-02	5274622	0.059365	0.031485
	A	61942.654	3.616e-03	288052	0.218656	0.21504
24-Parganas (S)	F	15330.697	1.053e-02	362110	0.052867	0.042337
	A	9672.826	1.648e-02	358401	0.043469	0.026989
Dakshin Dinajpur	F	18986.451	-2.10e-02	189814	0.079027	0.100027
	A	12891.639	2.318e-02	183615	0.09339	0.07021

Source: Secondary Data collected from AICL, West Bengal

8

Staple Food Pricing in *Mandis* of Selected States

Manisha Dey

Abstract

Among the 29 Indian states, 14 are linked with 585 regulated mandis with electronic national agricultural market. Across the states, 7.35 million farmers with 53,163 commission agents are registered in these regulated mandis. Every year Government of India announces modified agricultural policies to safeguard the interest of the farming community. Amongst the policies, one of the mechanisms to protect the producers from price fluctuations is Minimum Support Price (MSP). While determining MSP, government takes into account cost of production, cost of living, as well as economic and socio-political factors. For the past two decades, it has been observed that one MSP graph is moving upward but still the farming community seems dissatisfied. The reasons behind MSP variation among states include offering bonus prices additionally with MSP by some states, due to variation in government procurement procedures and policies. As a result, MSP is playing an important role in manoeuvring of prices amongst the various state markets. MSP deviation provides chances for the private sector to take undue advantage and the farmers are adversely affected. The study analyses existence of deviation in mandi prices of staple food between two states from year 2007 to 2018. It will disclose whether centralized price system reduce the cost of government and aid the farmer to get fair valuation.

Keywords- Agricultural price deviation, MSP, Rice and Wheat Mandi Prices

Introduction

by providing various policies and regulations in agriculture sector. E-Bhoomi project in Karnataka, Bargadar system in West Bengal, Pradhan Mantri Fasal Bima Yojana at an all-India level, are some major projects run by government to embolden farmers. Another mechanism to improve the performance of regulated market is the Agricultural Produce Marketing Committee (APMC) enacted by respective state government to safeguard the farmers. Only 18 states and union territories are utilising this model. APMC provides a common platform to farmers and integrates wholesale *mandi*s. According to APMC Act (2017) state governments have divided the geographical area of the state into markets which are headed by Market Committee. The motive of the APMC is to provide fair price to the farmers for their cultivation through open market operations. This open market operation ensures better price discovery and immediate settlement of payments.

Other than APMC model, government announces minimum support price and procurement quantity from various regions. Indian government announces the MPS for 22 crops prior to each sowing season mainly in the month of July to October to encourage farmers to cultivate more of each variety of crops. But the physical procurement by Food Corporation of India (FCI) and by State Agencies takes place only for the staple food i.e. wheat and rice and other crops do not fall under that cohort. It has also been observed that after procurement it is troublesome for FCI to manage the surplus stock because of insufficient storage capacity. Online reports from PRS Legislative Research of a survey conducted by NITI Ayog found that only 10% of the farmers were aware about MSP before sowing of the seeds and 62% came to know about it after sowing. The reason behind the announcement of MSP prior to sowing is to help farmers to decide which crops to cultivate. But this MSP generates price variation in agriculture product prices among the various different states because of additional bonus attached with MSP. Most of the State government declares additional bonus advantage along with minimum support price to farmers which again creates differentiation in prices between the states. Another major problem with MSP is that it does not differentiate between quality grades. Due to this, farmers are tempted to produce lower varieties crops. According to online reports from PRS Legislative Research, in the year 1950-51 India was only producing 21 million tonnes of rice and 6 million tonnes of wheat whereas in 2015-16 it increased to 104 million tonnes of rice and 94 million tonnes of wheat. Therefore over the span of 66 years post-independence in India, productivity increased by 395 times in rice and 1466 times in wheat whereas ribution of area, production and yield of rice and wheat

	Area (Million hectare)			Production (Million Tonnes)			Yield (kg/hectare)		
	2014-15	2015-16	2016-17	2014-15	2015-16	2016-17	2014-15	2015-16	2016-17
	44.11	43.499	43.194	105.48	104.41	110.15	2391	2400	2550
	31.465	30.418	30.597	86.53	92.29	98.38	2750	3034	3216

artment of Agriculture, cooperation and farmers welfare

According to Table 1, average production of rice based on last three years' figures is 2390 Kg and 2872 Kg of wheat, per hectare of land respectively. The percentage increase in yield is 10% in 2015-16 and 5% in 2016-17 as compared to previous year. On the other hand percentage increase in yield of rice is 6% in 2016-17 and 6.6% in 2016-17 as compared to previous year. So it may be presumed, this enormous improvement in productivity happened after adaptation of modern technology and methods to cultivate.

This study is conducted to find whether producers are really benefitted from open market operation headed by APMC and also to find whether they are satisfied by the procurement quantity announced by government. The study will also reveal whether the price movement is unidirectional or bidirectional between the states. This paper is undertaken to understand various complexities between MSP and *mandi* prices as found in various states APMC.

Literature Review

A pioneering study by Schultz, The Economics of Research and Agricultural Productivity (1979),stated the level of agriculture productivity depends more on the government measures than on technical consideration. The study undertaken by Ashok Kumar Tripathi on Agriculture price policy, output and farm profitability examined linkages during post-reform period in India (2013) has undertaken in-depth analysis of cost and returns on paddy and wheat. The analysis showed a significant improvement in net

profitability of wheat over rice. A paper on Irrigation Facility Differential and Productivity Variation in Paddy Cultivation by Field Evidences from Udalguri District of Assam by Phanindra Goyari (2014) examined the season variation in irrigation and high technology adoption leading to increase in productivity in summer season. A paper on Price distortion in agriculture and its effects: An international comparison (Bale and Lutz,1981) explained the pricing policies pursued by developing and developed countries. The analysis was undertaken on nine countries based on various parameters like output, rural employment, consumption and trade. It stated the effects of price distortion on distribution of income between producers and consumers and also on government revenue and foreign exchange by calculating net social losses arising from agricultural policies. Another review paper based on World Bank database on Agricultural price distortion trends and volatility, past and prospective, by Kym Anderson (2012) gauge agricultural incentives and government responses due to fluctuation

Agricultural price distortion and their effects on the Nigerian economy: An empirical study by Benedict(2015) examined the effect of agricultural price distortion on agriculture output. The major implication of the study is to bring reforms in agricultural pricing policies so that Nigerian economic growth gets accelerated. The study "Price distortion in Indian agriculture" by Shweta Saini and Ashok Gulati (2017) on 11 states who are major producers of 15 agriculture commodities for the period of 10 years from 2004-05 to 2013-14, has provided implications which should be considered while setting policies like allowing future markets to operate freely and also to allow private players to have unified markets.

Another research had been undertaken by ShikhaJha, P.V. Srinivasan and Maurice Landes on Indian Wheat and Rice Sector Policies and the Implications of Reform (2007).It stated how the recent agricultural policy changes in rice and wheat created impact on producers and consumers interest. It found that decentralization, distribution and procurement process from central to state government reduced the rebalance between producer, consumers and traders. Minimum support price, input policies, price stabilisation, income support, subsidies in fertilizer, power and irrigation water policies, food and distribution policies revamped the agricultural market in favour of small producers.

Primary Objective

- To find whether there exists any variation in *mandi* prices of rice between two states.
- To find whether there exists any variation in *mandi* prices of rice in states with MSP.
- To find whether there exists any variation in *mandi* prices of wheat between two states.
- To find whether there exists any variation in *mandi* prices of wheat in states with MSP.

Data Collection and Methodology

The secondary source of data has been collected from agriculture marketing websites and also various government websites like Department of Food and Distribution, Food Corporation of India, Ministry of Agriculture, Central Statistical Office, Department of Agriculture Cooperation and Farmers' Welfare, Indian prices of rice and wheat, data has been taken from agriculture market from the year 2008 to 2018.

Hypothesis

H1-There is no difference in *mandi price* of rice between the states of West Bengal and Karnataka from 2008 to 2018.

H2-There is no difference in *mandi price* of wheat between the states of Uttar Pradesh and West Bengal from 2008 to 2018.

H3-There is no deviation in *mandi* prices of rice and wheat of the selected states with minimum support price (MSP).

Data Analysis

About Rice

Rice is one of the major producing crops in India occupying 23% of cropping area. To produce 1kg of rice it is estimated that 1000 litres of water is required. As per the data of National Sample Survey Office (NSSO) survey 2013, 59% of households are involved in cultivation of paddy. The government intervention in pricing decision of the paddy pushes the farmers towards paddy production. There are three seasons for growing rice: winter, autumn and summer. Autumn is known as pre-Kharif, winter crops are known as Kharif and summer crops are known as Rabi. The sowing time for Kharif crops is June-July and harvesting time is November-December. Whereas Rabi crop sowing time is November to February and harvesting time is March to June.

This study is based on two states of India, one is major producer and other is the lowest producer of rice, to find the price variation that exists between them. West Bengal is one of the highest rice producing states in India consists of 18 districts with 62 market centres out of which 4 districts fall under high productive groups, whereas Karnataka as an average producer of rice has 20 districts with 32 market centres.

To analyse whether there is any existence of difference in *mandi*s price of states, West Bengal and Karnataka are selected.

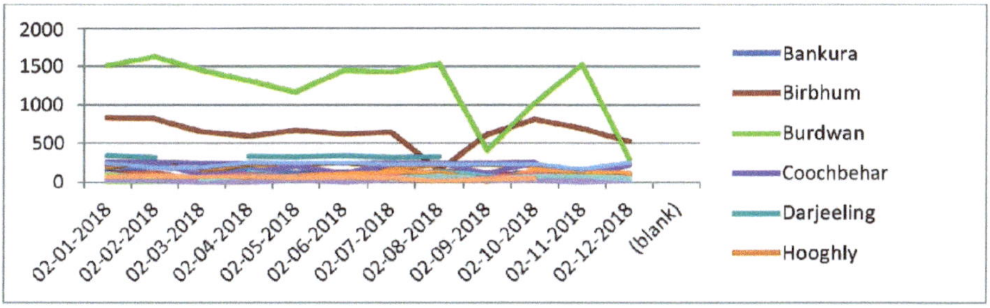

Fig. 1: Arrival quantity of rice in district *mandis* of West Bengal for the year 2018(tonnes)
Source: www.agmarknet.gov.in

In West Bengal pre-Kharif is known as *Aus.* The sowing time is from the month of April to July in Northern region and from May to September in southern region. The winter or monsoon crops are known as *Amam*. The sowing time is June and harvest time is in the month of December.

The graph is formed from the daily *mandi* prices data of West Bengal for the year 2018. The graph shows that Burdwan, Kolkata, Birbhum, Bankura, North and south 24 Parganas district of West Bengal are the highest producers of rice. As per the graph, on average arrival quantity in *mandi* is below 400 tonnes in most of the *mandi*s except the *mandis* of Kolkata and Birbhum. Overall the arrival status is very poor in the *mandi*s of West Bengal.

The highest rice crop producing districts in Karnataka are Bangalore, Kolar and Mysore. The harvesting time in Karnataka for Kharif paddy crop is from September to October, Rabi crop is from the month of January to February and summer paddy is from the month of May to June. The *mandi*s arrival quantity is more than the *mandi*s of West Bengal. On an average 1000 tonnes of rice arrive in all the *mandi*s of Karnataka. The arrival of crop is high in the month of April and also in the month of July.

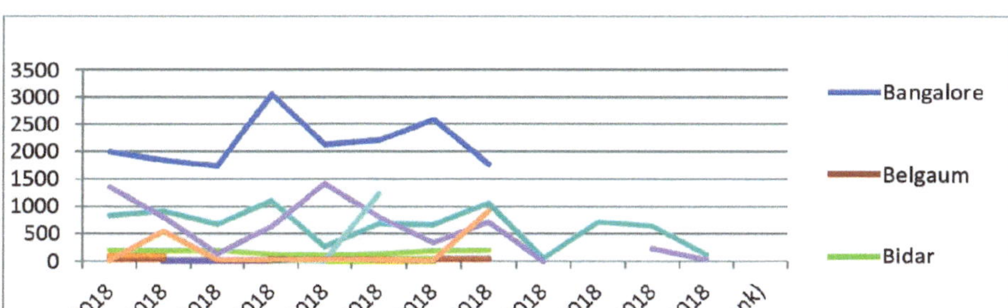

About Wheat

Wheat is another major crop in India occupying 16% of the cropping area. As per NSSO survey data 39% of households involves in cultivation of wheat. India is second largest country after China in wheat production. At the time of Independence, productivity of wheat in India was quite low but scenario has completely changed after implementing green revolution which makes our country self-dependent. Mainly three varieties of wheat grow in India. They are T. aestivium, T. durum and T.dicoccum.

This paper throws light on two states of India i.e. Uttar Pradesh and West Bengal to find their individual contribution in wheat production and also focus on input by their respective districts. The study focuses on wheat price variation existing between the states.

Uttar Pradesh is one of the top producers of wheat consisting of 69 districts with 223 market centres. Prices in Uttar Pradesh will be compared with West Bengal's18 districts and 62 market centres where trading of wheat takes place.

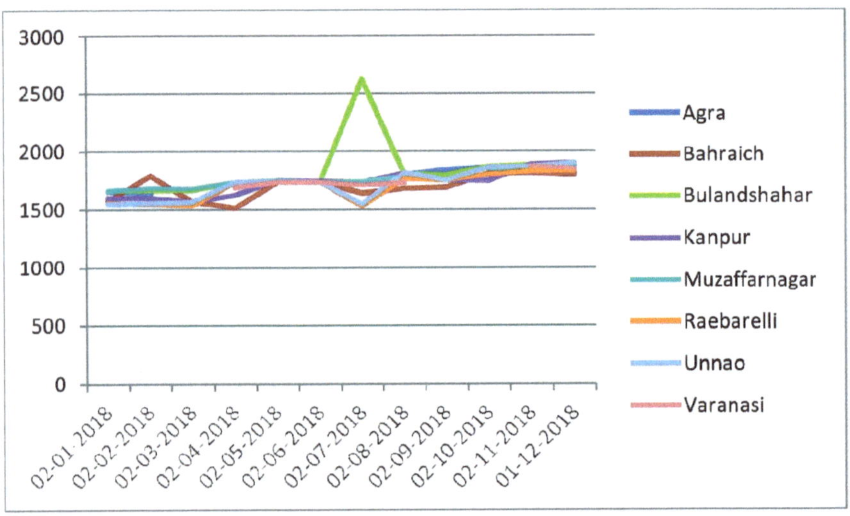

Fig. 3: Arrival quantity of wheat in district *mandis* of Uttar Pradesh for the year 2018
Source: www.agmarknet.gov.in

In Uttar Pradesh there are 232 districts, but the highest productive districts are Agra, Bahraich, Kanpur, Raebralli, etc. According to the agriculture calendar, sowing time of wheat in Uttar Pradesh begins from February to March and harvesting time is from October to January. The graph is showing almost a

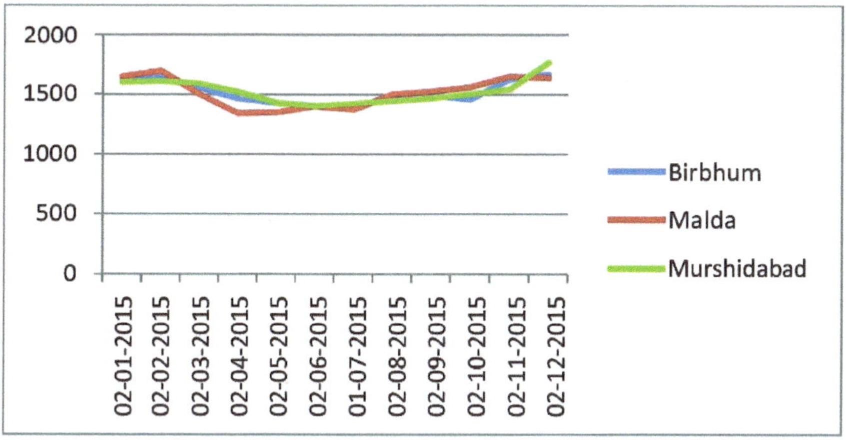

Fig. 4: Arrival quantity of wheat in district *mandis* of West Bengal for the year 2018
Source: www.agmarknet.gov.in

The arrival of wheat in West Bengal *mandis* is high in Birbhum, Malda and Murshidabad district. The sowing time in West Bengal begins from November to December and harvesting time is from March to April. The impact of arrival during the harvesting month is insignificant and gives an uneven picture through the year. The graph is not oscillating throughout the year, stating on an average 1600 tonnes of arrivals in the *mandi*s of West Bengal. The production of crops is different in various *mandi*s of the two states due to type of soil, rainfall and demand, etc.

Analysis

The daily *mandi* prices have been collected from agricultural marketing website for 11 months. From the daily *mandi* prices, average monthly prices have been calculated to analyse the presence of price deviation between the district *mandi*s. The main motive of this study is to examine the role of APMC in price discovery of staple food grain through open market operation. The *mandi* operation becomes successful not only with the participation of farmers and consumers but also with the licensed commission agents who are allotted shops in the *mandi*s. To throw light on *mandi* prices, comparative study of average monthly prices between states are shown below:

The above is the average monthly price trend of rice of West Bengal and Karnataka showing insignificant variation of prices between them. From the

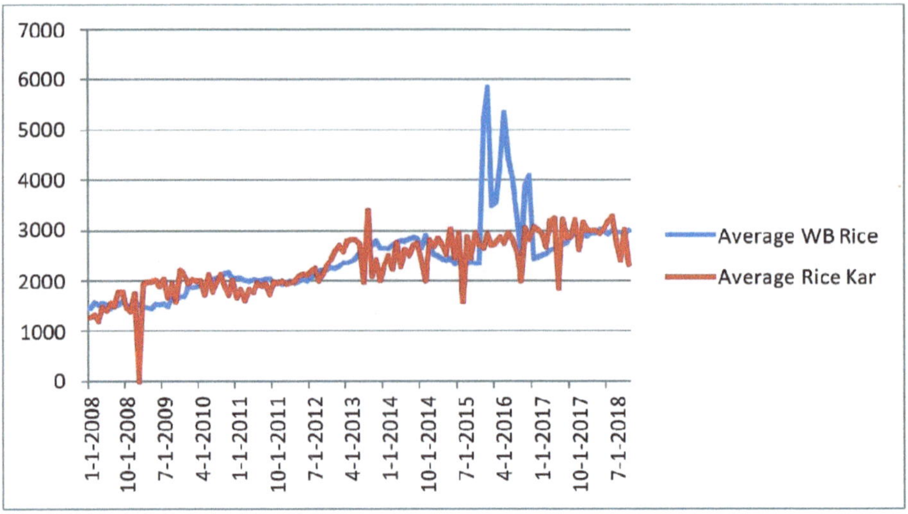

Fig. 5: Average monthly prices of rice in West Bengal and Karnataka
Source: www.agmarknet.gov.in

To find the *mandi* price difference, t-test is applied on the average monthly *mandi* prices of West Bengal and Karnataka. The results are as follows:

Table 2: T-Test is applied on average monthly *mandi* prices of rice of West Bengal and Karnataka from the year 2008 to 2018

	West Bengal	Karnataka
Mean	Rs. 2414.043054	Rs. 2306.9955
Variance	594219.6909	321319.3909
Observations	132	132
Pooled Variance	457769.5409	
Hypothesized Mean Difference	0	
df	262	
t Stat	1.285361448	
P(T<=t) one-tail	0.099900513	
t Critical one-tail	1.650690284	
P(T<=t) two-tail	0.199801025	
t Critical two-tail	1.969059715	

Source: www.agmarknet.gov.in

Table 2 states that there is insignificant difference of *mandi* prices of rice between West Bengal and Karnataka, after application of t-test on average monthly *mandi* prices for both the states. The p-value is approximately 9%

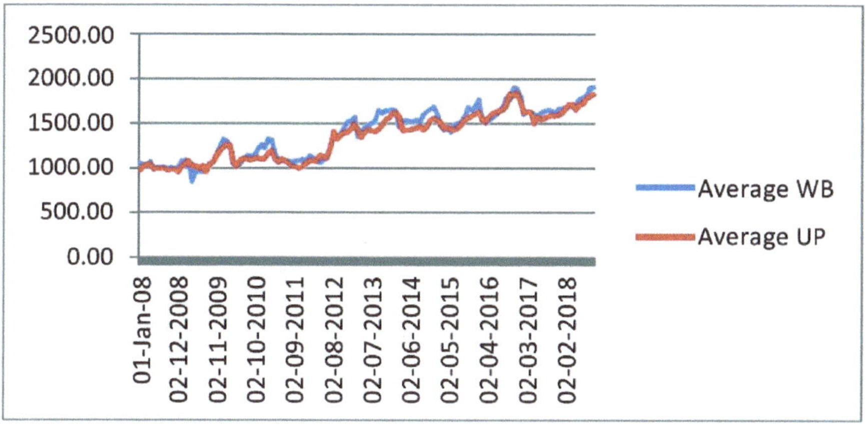

Fig. 6: Average monthly wheat prices of West Bengal and Uttar Pradesh
Source: www.agmarknet.gov.in

The above graph shows the average monthly *mandi price* trends of wheat of Uttar Pradesh and West Bengal which is moving in a unidirectional way. It reveals that there is an existence of uniformity in the market prices of Uttar Pradesh and West Bengal. To prove the above trends, t-test is applied on the average monthly *mandi* prices of wheat of both the states to find the level of significance between them. The result is given below:

Table 3: T-Test is applied on average monthly *mandi* prices of wheat for West Bengal and Uttar Pradesh from 2008 to 2018

	West Bengal	Uttar Pradesh
Mean	Rs. 1384.701922	Rs. 1347.029271
Variance	78722.96546	69432.39699
Observations	132	132
Pooled Variance	74077.68123	
Hypothesized Mean Difference	0	
df	262	
t Stat	1.124487058	
P(T<=t) one-tail	0.130917809	
t Critical one-tail	1.650690284	
P(T<=t) two-tail	0.261835617	
t Critical two-tail	1.969059715	

Source:www.agmarknet.gov.in

Table 3 depicts that no significant price difference exists between the two *mandi* prices of wheat in Uttar Pradesh and West Bengal, as

To scrutinise the price deviation between the average monthly *mandi* prices of rice with MSP of the two states and to find the dissimilitude in average *mandi* price of the states with the MSP, the t- test is applied.

Table 4: Deviation of monthly average *mandi price* of rice in West Bengal and Karnataka in terms of MSP

	West Bengal	MSP	Karnataka
Mean	Rs. 2414.043054	Rs. 1289.09091	Rs. 2306.9955
Variance	594219.6909	58102.984	321319.391
Observations	132	132	132
Pooled Variance	326161.3375		189711.187
Hypothesized Mean Difference	0		0
df	262		262
t Stat	16.00257149		18.9859603
P(T<=t) one-tail	5.6744E-41		1.8925E-51
t Critical one-tail	1.650690284		1.65069028
P(T<=t) two-tail	1.13488E-40		3.785E-51
t Critical two-tail	1.969059715		1.96905972

Source:www.agmarknet.gov.in

Table 4 exhibits no dissimilitude between average *mandi* prices of rice of West Bengal and Karnataka with MSP. The test states insignificant variation between the average *mandi* prices with MSP. Therefore the result draws the inference that, null hypothesis of no deviation in *mandi prices* of rice of West Bengal and Karnataka in terms of MSP, is accepted.

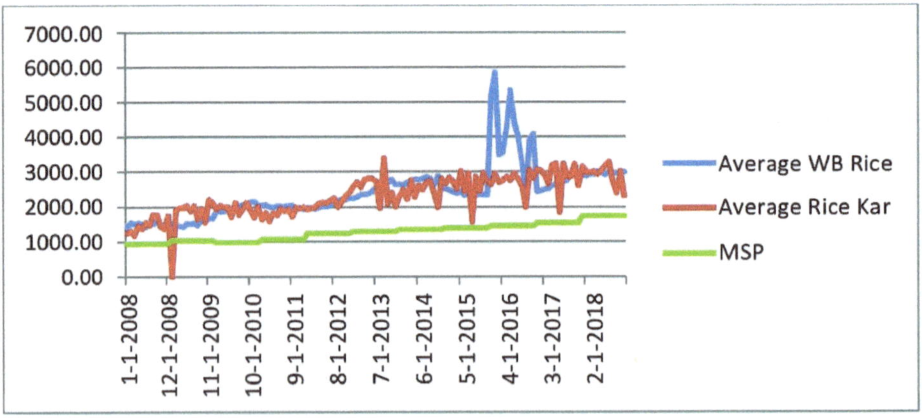

Fig. 7: Graphical presentation of average *mandi* prices of West Bengal and Karnataka

The graph reveals position of the *mandi* prices of the states with MSP. The prices of the *mandis* with MSP show positive correlation between each other.

Table 5: Deviation of monthly average *mandi price* of wheat in West Bengal and Uttar Pradesh in terms of MSP

	West Bengal	MSP	Uttar Pradesh
Mean	Rs. 1384.702	Rs. 1338.182	Rs. 1347.029
Variance	78722.97	51294.38	69432.4
Observations	132	132	132
Pooled Variance	65008.67		60363.39
Hypothesized Mean Difference	0		0
df	262		262
t Stat	1.482269		0.292552
P(T<=t) one-tail	0.069735		0.385048
t Critical one-tail	1.65069		1.65069
P(T<=t) two-tail	0.139471		0.770096
t Critical two-tail	1.96906		1.96906

Source:www.agmarknet.gov.in

Here, t-test with two sample assuming equal variables is applied to find the presence of distortion in wheat prices in the states of West Bengal and Uttar Pradesh with MSP. The test shows probability level is insignificant at 5% and at 10%. Therefore the result draws the inference that null hypothesis of no deviation is accepted which means that there is no deviation in average *mandi price* of wheat of West Bengal and Uttar Pradesh in terms of MSP.

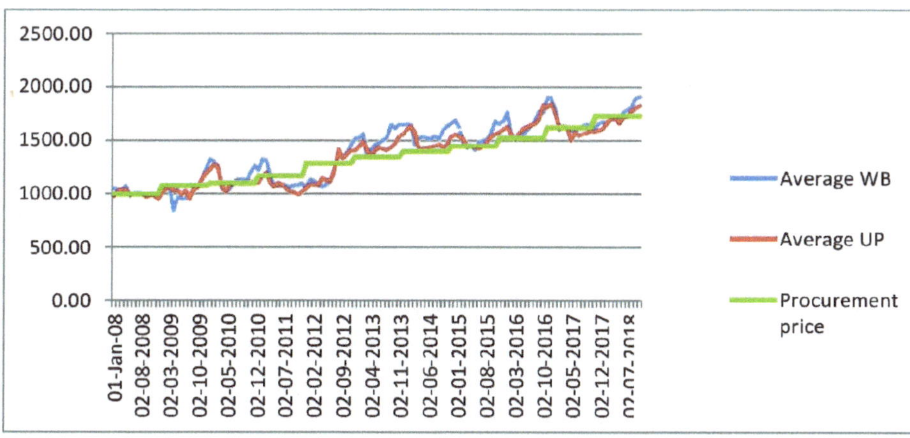

Fig. 8: Average *mandi* prices and MSP of wheat in West Bengal and Uttar Pradesh

The trend of average prices of wheat with respect to two states, that is West Bengal and Karnataka, are going in the same direction stating positive correlation between them. Hence the procurement price provided by the Centre is fair price for the farmers compared to market price.

A reason behind the presence of uniformity between the *mandi* prices of the states is because of consistent procurement of rice and wheat every marketing season by the Central Government.

Caveat of the Above Analysis

Are Indian farmer entrepreneurs or just producers? The answer to this question differs according to the scenario of various States in India. If we compare Punjab with West Bengal, it is observed that Punjab is one of the major producers of paddy where farmers use advanced and modern technology to ameliorate agricultural cultivation and where paddy procurement is done by FCI at a large scale. On the other hand, West Bengal is far behind in the race of cultivation.

The other factor where West Bengal is behind Punjab is mainly in the land holding percentage. The majority of farmers in West Bengal belong to the category of marginal farmers (0.5 hectares<1 hectares) whereas in Punjab they belong to the category of semi- medium (range 2 to 4 hectares) and medium holding (range 4 to 10 hectares).

Government provides funds to establish Agricultural Price Marketing Committee (APMC) in every state to help farmers get fair prices. This statutory body under agricultural marketing department operates through Krishak Bazaar (*mandi*) in every district providing better marketing infrastructure and modernized marketing facilities. The aim of these Krishak bazaars is not only for the trading of crop but also to impart training for spreading awareness of modern practices in agriculture.

In process of procurement undertaken by Krishak Bazaar, farmers of West Bengal are facing several problems such as-

- Farmers have to show the Record of Right (ROR) i.e. land holding, on the basis of which eligibility of procurement is ensured by Krishak Bazaar. But nowadays Krishak Bazaars do not follow the eligibility criteria because of which brokers and middlemen take superfluous advantage of those benefits for which they are not entitled. Thus, actual gain goes in the hand of brokers who purchase the paddy from the market and sell the less than minimum support prices. Government is primarily concerned about the target of procurement of paddy and not about the market-mechanism of acquisition of paddy.

- Secondly, procurement on the basis of fair average quantity specification criteria is not maintained by Krishak Bazaar. The criteria which the farmer should follow before selling the paddy to Krishak Bazaar is that it should be free from moulds, weevils, obnoxious smell and also the paddy should be uniform in colour and size. This entails the farmers to ensure that the paddy is clear from all types of deleterious substances. But even if the paddy is clean, the farmers are deprived and are compelled to sell their produce with a cut off percentage, of the quantity of paddy.

Growth in the system is only possible when the system follows the rules and maintains the policies. The problem in West Bengal lies with the system which binds the farmers to supply the paddy with the known fact that they will not get the fair price of their effort.

The data reveals that 31.33% of the state's total paddy production arrives in the *mandi*s of West Bengal and the rest goes to the hands of private players. The private players show that they are dissatisfied with the paddy quality because of deleterious substance and non-uniformity in colour and size because of which they offer lower prices than MSP to farmers. Hence, farmers suffer both in the hands of the private players and the Krishak Bazaar. Every year after harvesting, farmers are rushing towards the search of perfect seller who will offer them a fair price so that they may continue maintaining their livelihood. The farmers of West Bengal are only worried about how to maintain their livelihood because majorities are marginal farmers whose only motive is how to sustain themselves and overcome the impoverished condition.

The author posits that the environment poses a challenge to Agricultural entrepreneurship for West Bengal, specifically in terms of crops like rice and paddy. State policies make survival an issue rather than supporting the farmers. It is difficult for them to get a fair deal for the produce and build on their business ventures. On a different note, as land holding is significantly high in the hands of farmers in Punjab, it enables them to take entrepreneurial risk and develop their business.

In West Bengal, therefore the Government should take measures and policies to convert farmers from producers to entrepreneurs.

Conclusion

From the above study it can be suggested that APMC is providing substantive support to farmers by providing them a platform to trade for their produce and also in getting a fair price of their deals. The analysis apprises that prices are moving in unidirectional manner stating no discrepancy between MSP and *mandi* prices, in the states under study.

To gauge the importance of the equality between the *mandi* prices and MSP it is important to understand the implications of the deviations from the equilibrium point. If in the market MSP would be higher than the *mandi* prices, the government would be facing the excess financial burden of procuring the entire crop from the farmer and simultaneously resulting in the problem of a huge food grain stock for the government to manage, given its infrastructural constraint. At the same time, even though the farmer could sell to the government at a premium, their lack of awareness about the MSP prices, the debt obligations to the local traders and the poor infrastructure of warehousing of the farmers result in the immediate sale to middlemen and local market at *mandi* prices. Thus this deviation of MSP being higher than mandi prices, leads to challenges both to the farmer and the government.

On the other hand, if the MSP is lesser than the *mandi* prices, it would imply the government's failure to duly compensate the farmers for their toil and efforts. The importance of MSP is undermined as it is not just a number but is a tool for the farmers' growth and productivity enhancement. In this case the farmers would prefer to sell at the *mandi* prices but if they have a supply which exceeds demand at *mandi* level, in case of a bumper production, the farmers will be unable to sell their entire produce which would lead to agricultural wastage. Thus it would be an inefficient outcome.

It is clear that farmers lose at both ends. Hence for optimum allocation and production it is imperative that the MSP is in line with the *mandi* prices. This equality holds true especially in case of small and marginal farmers in the agriculturally backward parts of India as they are the ones with least awareness, having poorest infrastructure for storage and in most cases, they are financially heavily burdened. If such equality exists, then the farmers would be saved of possible exploitation at the hands of private local traders and middlemen, while being assured that their entire produce would be sold at the *mandi*s and if any excess remains, it would be procured by the government.

- Amongst the district *mandi*s of West Bengal, Burdwan, Birbhum and North 24 Parganas are the highest rice producers of the states. On the contrary, amongst the district *mandi*s of Karnataka, Bangalore, Kolar and Mysore are the highest producers of rice. State agencies' procurement of rice from West Bengal on an average is 1.6% of the total production whereas from the state of Karnataka it is only .05%.
- Amongst the district *mandi*s of Uttar Pradesh, Agra, Bahraich, Kanpur, Raebralli are the highest producers of the wheat. At the same time the district *mandi*s of West Bengal, Birbhum, Malda and Murshidabad are the highest producers of wheat. The state agencies' procurement of wheat is almost zero from the state of West Bengal but from the state of Uttar Pradesh, state agencies' procurement is on an average 2% of the total production.

Similar equilibrium can be achieved in multiple states if the MSP would include more crops. MSP should also be calculated as an efficient and accurate estimator of the farmers' costs of production and provide sufficient incentive to the farmers to continue and enhance production. The awareness about MSP in cases of small and marginal farmers is poor and needs to be addressed. Also, the presence of *mandis* in crop deficit states is beyond the reach of small farmers due to lack of infrastructure, accessibility and unawareness of *mandis*. It is not possible for the farmers to visit the *mandis* often to sell their products due to time and cost constraints. Due to the monopoly of the richer and well-endowed farmers, the market prices are controlled by them and the small farmers are forced to sell at a price lesser than their costs of production.

One of the major contributing factors that lead to such problems is the location of these *mandis*. In states like West Bengal, marginal farmers having low quantity produce are unable to avail the benefits of these platforms, as they have to bear the additional cost of carrying and transportation, along with the cost of production. Another factor is the involvement of middlemen or agents, who tend to favour certain producers/farmers in trading their produce in the *mandis*. Due to these factors, the marginal farmers tend to search for other alternative avenues in order to sell their produce. Farmers tend to lose due to the cut off percentage in quantity at the time of procurement by the government and the cut off percentage moves even higher if the same commodity is purchased by any private player. In spite of the farmer supplying the quantity specified by the buyer, they are often exploited by not getting the promised MSP. To add to it,

The government needs to refine the underlying mechanism of the open market operation, should open more *mandi*s near to the farmlands and also needs to bring a coherent policy of the various states, so as to provide fair value to the farmers. Central government should take proper measures not only to sanction more funds for the development of *mandis* but also to ensure frequent monitoring and administration of the allotted funds. Hence this paper draws out the equilibrium condition of a few states but prescribes suggestions for those states where equilibrium does not exist. The equality of MSP and *mandi* prices in most cases, provides a cushion for the small famers, but in the absence of this, the role of the State and sometimes the private operators, deserve special mention.

References

Agricultural price distortion and their effects on the Nigerian economy: An empirical study by Benedict (2015),European Journal of Research in Social Sciences Vol. 3 No. 1, 2015 ISSN 2056-5429.

Anderson Kym (2012), Agricultural price distortion trends and volatility, past and prospective, Working Paper No. 2013/01

Bale, M. D., & Lutz, E. (1981). Price distortions in agriculture and their effects: An international comparison. American Journal of Agricultural Economics, 63(1), 8-22.

Bale, M. D., & Lutz, E. (1981). Price distortions in agriculture and their effects: An international comparison. American Journal of Agricultural Economics, Vol. 63 No. 1, 8-22.

Dasgupta, D., Dubey, R. N., & Satish, R. (2011). Domestic wheat price formation and food inflation in India: International prices, domestic drivers (stocks, weather, public policy), and the efficacy of public policy interventions in wheat markets (No. id: 4291).

Goyari, P. (2014). Irrigation Difference and Productivity Variations in Paddy Cultivation: Field Evidences from Udalguri District of Assam, Indian Journal of Agricultural Economics, 69(902-2016-67968), 90.

Jha, S., Srinivasan, P. V., & Landes, M. R. (2007). Indian wheat and rice sector policies and the implications of reform. USDA-ERS Economic Research Report, (41).

NSSO survey 2013 accessed on 24th March 2019 (http://mospi.nic.in/sites/default/files/publication_reports/KI_70_33_19dec14.pdf)

Saini S & Gulati A (2017): Price distortion in Indian agriculture, International Bank for Reconstruction and Development / The World Bank 1818 H Street NW

Schultz, T. W. (1979). The economics of research and agricultural productivity. In Instituto de Investigaciones Agropecuarias, Santiago (Chile). Universidad de Chile, Santiago. Facultad de Agronomia. Universidad Catolica de Chile, Santiago. Facultad de Agronomia. Seminario sobre los Aspectos Socioeconomicos de la Investigacion Agricola en los Paises en Desarrollo. Santiago (Chile). 7 May 1979.

Tripathi, Ashok Kumar (2013),Agriculture price policy, output and farm profitability examined a linkages during post reform period in India, Asian Journal of Agriculture and Development, Vol. 10, No. 1.

USDA Foreign Agriculture Services grain report (https://www.fas.usda.gov/data/grain-world-markets-and-trade)

9

Intellectual Property Rights and Indian Agriculture: Some Policy Issues

Arundhati Ray

Abstract

Trade Related Agreements on Intellectual Property Rights (TRIPS) widely affects the agricultural sector which is largely unorganised in India. At the same time this sector remains the bread winner for majority of the population of the country. The Intellectual Property Rights (IPRs) affect the extensive and intensive margins in agricultural trade. This paper draws attention of enterprises in the field of agricultural biotechnology which has genetic modification (GM) as one of its core activity. GM is of benefit in terms of value additive features but also of great concern for the community in conservation of biodiversity. Food & Agricultural Organisation (FAO), being aware of the pitfalls of implementing IPRs in agriculture, constituted an expert panel to study the issues pertaining to the sector. They came up with very clear directives to the FAO on the course of action. This paper aims to focus on this area to identify the micro-level dynamics of IPRs in agriculture and its effects on the rural enterprises in India. The impact of IPRs and its ramifications, the issues of agricultural productivity and its future trajectory, are to be understood from the perspective of an entrepreneur's policy decisions. This will lead to identification of policies that would help in harnessing IPRs for the growth of Indian agriculture.

Keywords: IPRs, TRIPS, Agricultural Biotechnology

Introduction

1930, which ushered the application of Intellectual Property Rights (IPRs) in agriculture. This was further accentuated by the needs of research and development in agriculture to feed the growing population of the world. Different countries adopted different approaches in accordance with the socio-political system prevailing in the country.

Research in the field of agriculture is very expensive and time consuming. It takes at least 12 to 15 years from conceptualisation to a commercially viable application. The long gestation from the discovery of a particular development possibility to convincingly prove the concept, to the early stages of development, the advanced stages of preparation leading to pre-launch (pilot production) for commercial exploitation, needs funding. In India, the need for research for development of agriculture was recognised by the colonial rulers. The Imperial Council was founded in 1929 to conduct research in agriculture. After Independence, the council was renamed Indian Council for Agricultural Research (ICAR) and was empowered as the apex body to conduct research in the areas of agriculture, horticulture and animal husbandry. It guided the establishment of the first agricultural university in Pantnagar, Uttarakhand. Gradually a large number of agricultural universities and research institutions came into being. Indian Council of Agricultural Research (ICAR) acts as the apex body and the research is conducted by the different agencies under it.

The activities led by ICAR continued unhindered by the imposition of IPRs, till the advent of World Trade Organization (WTO) and Trade Related Agreements on Intellectual Property Rights (TRIPS) in mid-nineties. India, being a member of WTO and signatory of the TRIPS agreement was under obligation to frame stringent intellectual property rights laws and impose binding rules in all the fields of trade including agriculture. This has created serious concern for conventional entrepreneurs operating with indigenous products and processes, preservation of traditional knowledge generated and practiced through thousands of years, possibilities of bio-piracy and destruction of bio-diversity

The paper aims to cover issues important for development of agricultural enterprises.It begins with a discussion on TRIPS Agreement and its ramifications. The next discussion covers IPR Laws pertaining to agriculture. The practical problems in implementation of IPRs are discussed next. The paper then looks at policy issues and discusses some additional ideas. The next section studies how agricultural enterprises can use this knowledge and how their decisions are impacted by IPRs. The ideas are then concisely spelt in a conclusion.

TRIPS Agreement and its Ramifications on Indian Agriculture

The International Trade Policy is being discussed, debated and negotiated from the days of mercantile practices. After the devastation of the Second World War, three institutions were created, ostensibly, for the purpose of peace and prosperity through mutual assistance, trade with diminishing barriers and strengthening of private sector in the developing countries. The first two were International Monetary Fund (IMF) and World Bank (WB), formed in the conference of Breton Woods in 1944 and the third was General Agreement on Tariff and Trade (GATT) in 1946. The agreement on reduction of trade barriers and bringing in more openness, expected from rounds of discussion in GATT produced result in the form of World Trade Organization (WTO) in 1994 in the Uruguay Round. Some discussion on the backdrop of the success of this Round may indicate what can be expected from this organisation.

Post World War II, the devastation in the developed world (Mainly Western Europe and Japan) called for huge investment for reconstruction. Non-aligned countries like India could follow a middle path with support from the Soviet Block and pursue independent paths for the country's development. But the whole scenario gradually changed with the resurgence of the developed world and weakening of the Soviet Block economy. In the late eighties and early nineties India faced a very serious balance of payments crisis. In an earlier period in 1966, in a similar situation, India had to devalue its currency as per the dictates of IMF but could afford to avoid implementation of the other terms of IMF on opening up of the economy. During petroleum price hike of 1970s, Soviet oil supply on rupee payment helped India to ford over the crisis. The scenario changed in the '80s. The fissures in the Soviet economy were visible. Ultimately, it crumbled under its own internal contradictions on 26th December, 1991. Now the world suddenly became unipolar. Not only India, all the developing countries faced similar problem of having very limited choice. In this scenario, The Uruguay Round of GATT (1986-94) culminated into formation of WTO with 132 members. One significant development was the inclusion of Intellectual Property Rights (IPRs) as an important issue in multilateral trade agreements. This was effected through Annexure 1c of the agreement signed in Marrakesh, Morocco, to form the World Trade Organization.

Intellectual Property Rights were part of the legal system of the industrially developed countries from 15th and 16th Century. Application in agriculture is a late development and the earliest manifestation was a lawsuit in the United independent states to frame laws and rules applicable within the country was compromised to accommodate the provisions of TRIPS in the country's legal framework. WTO was bestowed with the power of implementation of the TRIPS Provisions in each member country.

Indian IPR Laws Relating To Agriculture

In this section the main thrust of the IPRs in agriculture will be discussed to delineate the IPR provisions and how they affect the entrepreneurs. (Desai, 2018)

In agricultural sector, there are several provisions to protect and provide impetus for innovation in agriculture. Patenting new innovations is most prominent of them. Other provisions are safeguards for plant breeders' rights; geographical indicators of any particular produce (like Darjeeling Tea); trade secrets and trademarks. Patents are the most important IPRs and patents are allowed for patentable plants, animals and biotechnological processes for their production. Patent rights are provided on the basis of three criteria:-

1. Novelty – which is a new development, not available earlier
2. Non-obviousness - which calls for some inventive activity and is significantly different from available products or processes
3. Usefulness – which calls for its actual application in production and/ or process

The way in which mercantilism and industrial revolution could affect developed countries, did not happen here. In India, the developments in the agricultural sector were more of a community activity, whose benefits were shared by the community. Later, in the post- independence period, research was structured around ICAR, agricultural universities and research institutes in the state sector. Any development was for the common good. Culturally, Indian agricultural sector was not ready for legal intervention.

The WTO and its offshoot – Agreement on Trade Related Intellectual Property Rights (TRIPS) operates as a quasi-judicial body. The 132 signatories of the TRIPS Agreement are obliged to frame and implement laws related to IPRs which must conform to the TRIPS articles and provisions. TRIPS were heavily favourable to the developed countries. The developing and the less developed countries fought for recognition of their apprehensions and introduction of some corrective measure. This came in the form of phased implementation of

The Government of India being a signatory of the TRIPS Agreement was under obligation to introduce IPRs in agriculture. But India's unpreparedness was also quite obvious. The government passed laws relating to IPRs, which also affected agricultural sector. A brief study of the laws affecting the agricultural sector would enable interested readers to understand their ramifications on the agri-sector.

Patent Rights and Trade Mark are the major concerns for all interested groups (companies using patent rights to secure the market for the patented product, trademark to make their products identifiable to the users of the products and the government). This has been addressed by passing the Trade Mark Act of 1999, which fully complies with TRIPS requirements. The Copyrights Act has been modified to accommodate computer programmes as original literary work. The Patents Act of 1957 has been modified in 1999, 2002 and 2005 to align it with TRIPS requirements. The Designs Act of 1911 has been scrapped and a new law – The Designs Act of 2000, has been put in place. The new areas of innovation have been covered through the passing of the following laws:

a) The Geographical Indication of Goods (Registration and Protection) Act, 1999

b) The Semiconductor Integrated Circuits Layout Design Act, 2000(not being discussed here, as it is not affecting the agriculture directly)

c) The Protection of Plant & Varieties and Farmers' Rights Act, 2001

d) The Biological Diversity Act, 2002

This section covers three of these new acts that need a careful understanding as they affect the agriculture sector in myriad ways:

The Geographical Indication of Goods (Registration and Protection) Act, 1999

Section 3 of the TRIPS Agreement covers provisions for Geographical Indication of Goods (GI). The Indian Act provides for certification of goods connected to a particular place to indicate a specific quality, characteristic or reputation which can be associated with its geographic origin where it is harvested or manufactured. GI (Geographical Indication) registration remains valid for 10 years. During this period, there is provision for the following:

a) Right to seek and receive relief in case of infringement of GI mark.

The producers of the countries which have established region-specific product would surely benefit from this Act.

The Protection of Plant & Varieties and Farmers' Rights Act, 2001

This act has been framed to provide safeguards in accordance with the Article 27.3(b) of TRIPS Agreement. The article provides for two options for the member countries – (a) Protection under patent right or protection under "SUI GENERIS" system. This covers areas related to plant variety and protection of farmers' rights. India has opted for Sui Generis System. The following features indicate the nature of safeguards for the farmers of the developing countries:

- The safeguard is provided for the products developed through public and private research through patenting.
- The rights of the farmers and the traditional communities have been protected through ensuring their legal right to save the seed for sowing and re-sowing, exchanging and even selling. But farmers cannot sell any branded seed of any variety protected under this Act.
- This Act has thrust on encouraging the plant breeders and researchers to develop improved varieties that may be patented and remain out of sales purview of the farmers and the traditional community.
- The Act provides for establishment of "Protection of Plant Varieties and Farmers' Rights Authority" (PPV&FRA), which is responsible for granting registration of new varieties and adjudication of claims of benefit from such development.
- The infringement of the registered varieties can be dealt with in civil and criminal legal procedure under this Act.
- The Act strives to strike a balance between the farmers and the traditional communities on the one hand and plant breeders and researchers on the other. The farmers and traditional groups are rewarded for their effort in conservation and development of the traditional seeds through National Gene Fund. It also encourages the researchers and plant breeders through registration of the outcome of their effort.

The registration can be claimed in two situations –

(1) If the registration claim is for a new variety that must be novel and distinct; must provide a standard uniform process and the whole process must be

Here, the "Extant Variety" could be any of the following:

a) A variety that has been notified in The Seeds Act, 1966, Section 5.

b) A Farmers' Variety - developed by farmers or traditional cultivators in their field and which is in the common knowledge of the farmers.

c) Any variety which is commonly known by the cultivators.

d) Any other variety which is in the public knowledge.

The protection provided by the Act remains valid for the following period:

a) For trees and vines – 18 years

b) For "Extant Variety" – 15 years

c) In all other cases – 15 years

The Biological Diversity Act, 2002

The Biological Diversity refers to the variability among living organisms which are part of a complex ecosystem and comprises organisms from all sources within the complex of which they are a part. Any differentiation within the species and differentiation between the species within the ecosystem are also contained in the concept of biological diversity. The Biological Diversity concepts are offshoots of the Convention on Biological Diversity (CBD). India is a member of CBD and this Act was put in place to honour the resolutions of the convention.

The objective of the Act is:

a) To conserve the biodiversity prevailing in India.

b) Sustainable use of the components of biodiversity.

c) Fair and equitable distribution of the benefits when the "Biological Resources" are put to use.

Here, the term "Biological Resources" denotes plants, animals and micro-organisms, their parts, their genetic material, and by-products which have potential use or value. This list does not include human genetic material and any value-added part.

The most important creation of this act is constitution of National Biodiversity Authority (NBA). The Authority has very wide ranging power. The following are some of the controls exercised by the Authority:

2. Foreign nationals have to seek prior permission from the Authority for research and export of the knowledge. Foreign nationals are defined as those who are not Indian citizens.

3. Even Indians, intending to export any knowledge or information in this field will have to take approval from the Authority.

4. Any benefits accruing from IPRs in this field needs to be shared and NBA has power to establish ground rules for such sharing.

Benefits for agri-entrepreneurs

1. The GI registration must be availed of for all the possibilities prevailing in the country– this will open gates of wider market to many local products and in the process will help in retaining the traditional knowledge that goes into the product.

2. Seeds of all traditional products must be patented and preserved to (a) deter bio- piracy; (b) safeguard traditional knowledge; (c) develop improved strain from them which retain the positives of the mother material.

3. Every effort must be made to retain/bring back the biodiversity prevalent before the advent of rampant use of pesticides, herbicides and fertilizers.

4. Record keeping is essential and hence all attempts to improvements in the product and/or process field are to be recorded.

Challenges before agri-entrepreneurs

1. Lack of general awareness, which has to be eliminated on war footingamong the user sectors.

2. Absence of the notion of treating agriculture as any other industrial sector. Present day agriculture operates like any industrial sector. It is driven by innovation to meet the market demand. The price is market-driven. Hence, control of input cost like control of raw material cost in industry and continuous process improvement are necessities that are to be structurally addressed.

Application of IPRS and its Consquences for Indian Agri-Sector

The first and foremost cause of concern for Indian agri-sector with regard to

Knowledge (TK) was established from European documents where the strain Nap Hal was mentioned as collected from UP. The case of Basmati Rice is a mixture of success and defeat as Rice Tek, the American Company had to lose only 3 clauses of the total 18 clauses of the patented right. There are many interested groups seeking to take advantage of unawareness of the indigenous users of Indian TK to identify the medicinal properties of fruits, plants, barks and roots to patent them as original inventions. Jamun, brinjal and bitter gourd are good examples of that endeavour. A New Jersey based company of non-resident Indians patented the anti diabetic medicinal property of these vegetables. This was, in spite of their reference in ancient texts as having properties curative for diabetes was not their invention.

Apart from bio piracy, the loss of traditional varieties of fruits, vegetables and grains has been substantial. The lure of high yield has led to loss of many traditional rice varieties and varieties of other cereals. The intercropping practice to sustain the fertility of the land also got lost. As an illustration it may be cited that Genetically Modified (GM) brinjal is being touted for high yield, though its hypoglycaemic properties have not been examined.

Many such plants with healing properties in specific applications are getting lostdue to an absence of endeavour to conserve them.

The case of mango is also noteworthy. The Andhra Pradesh Government has been declared as owner of the Geographical Indication (GI) Tag for *Banganapalli* mangoes grown in that region. 5 districts ofMaharastra have received the GI tag for *Alphonso* mangoes. The farmers of Krishnagiri district of TamilNadu are planning to apply for GI tag for *Thothapuri* mangoes produced in the district. This acts as an impetus to farmers of the particular crop and encourages more focussed growth in these specific sections.

Briefly, it can be stated that Indian agriculture has been mostly supported, guided andgoverned by public sector agencies, which operated through the government channels and mainly provided service to the sector for improvement of productivity. There was no pecuniaryinvolvement of the farmer entrepreneur. Everything was informally operated and based on trust. All this changed with TRIPS. The layman farmer, unaware of the effects of the products of multinational corporations (MNC) in the local environment, were influenced by the promises doled out in the advertisements and under dire need for inputs to safeguard the produce, latched to them. This has crucially affected biodiversity in the rural areas as birds and reptiles have been eliminated in large numbers

The unfortunate specific case of the Vidarbha region of Maharastra which became the hotbed for farmers' suicide is a burning example of the problem. Vidarbha is a cotton cultivating area and they had shifted to genetically modified cotton (BT Cotton). This type of cotton farming calls for more inputs and cost of each input has been going up. With the draught situation in the region, the productivity was low and price was non remunerative. The rural economy became dependent on unorganised moneylenders whochargedvery high interest rate. The cumulative effect was deplorable economic condition of the farmerresulting in large number of suicides.

Conclusion

India is an economy with average 7% Gross Domestic Product (GDP) growth rate maintained for quite some time. For substantiating this growth engine, innovation is imperative. And there is a specific need for understanding the dynamics between growth and innovation. India's indigenous Research & Development (R&D) is not adequate and there is a need to avail of the fruits of global R&D. This makes a robust IPR Regime as a prerequisite. Even growth in agriculture will be dependent on assimilation of new technologies and IPR support would be essential.

The author posits that rural enterprises must be aware of all necessary technological information to take a conscious decision about the technology to be adopted by the enterprise with a clear idea of the paths for improvement to be followed. Whenever the enterprise is using any patented technology in any area of operation, from seed to agricultural implements to methodology, use of herbicides and pesticides, application of fertilizer technology use insowing, de-weeding and harvesting, it must collect data on compatibility of the technology with local regulations. If the enterprise is using any innovation, that must be properly documented and authenticated to establish the claim of the enterprise on the innovation. The enterprise should be aware of the biodiversity and must aim to preserve that and in the process make gains from the Biodiversity Act. The enterprise must take adequate initiative to avail of the protection from IPRs which can be used to protect biotechnology innovations initiated by the enterprise.

IPRs have close impact on agri-entrepreneurship. Any traditional knowledge or innovation needs the support of IPRs to reap the full benefit. Hence Indians entrepreneurs – the owners of TK, and the innovators engaged in every sector that strong IPR regime under the TRIPS Agreement is a given situation and the nation must be prepared to make best use of the same.

The Patent is a necessary precondition for thrust on innovation. New ideas take shape from the necessities felt by people in the work environment. Problems call for solutions and any solution is an innovation. A novel solution which is not obvious and is found to be useful is an opportunity for patenting. The benefits of patenting motivate entrepreneurs to be innovative. Hence the entrepreneur needs to be aware and his task is to remain vigilant, so that indigenous practices are not controlled by private sector patenting.

GI Tag is a great opportunity for the farm sector. The tag would help to create awareness about the agricultural product throughout the world and would help in better marketing communication. Protection of Plant Variety and Farmers' Rights can help to improve the lot of the farmers. Entrepreneurs as a community should take initiative in preserving and recycling indigenous varieties of agricultural produce and thereby become eligible for benefits from National Gene Fund.

There has to be a general awareness about the Biological Diversity Act. This will help the farm sector to stop any plundering of resources. The endeavour should be to make the NBA not only active but proactive to the ground situation.

To remain a proactive player in the global agricultural market, the entrepreneurs in India have to evolve an ecosystem with profound knowledge about the IPRs'laws governing the sector. Any loopholes or slips will be devastating not only for one entrepreneur but for the entire community. The entrepreneur needs to have balanced exchanges with the private and public sector agencies because there is an unavoidable inter-linkage between the stakeholders. All stakeholders have an equally responsible role in maintaining a healthy ecosystem of the agri-business sector. Knowledge has the power to build or break that balance. Hence the information on IPR with reference to agribusiness has an important role in the ecosystem.

References

C. Ramasamy, (2013), Indian Agricultural R&D: An Introspection & Way Forward, Agricultural Economics Research Review – Vol. 26 (No. 1)January to June, 2013, PP 1 – 20

Campi Mercedes (2016) The effect of Intellectual Property Rightson Agricultural Productivity, The Journalof the International Association of Agricultural Economists

Can intellectual Property Rights (IPRs) Help Promote Agriculture and Food Security in Devel-

Desai Nishith Associates, Legal and Tax Consultants Worldwide, Intellectual Property Law in India – Legal, Regulatory & Tax (January 2018) Intellectual_ Property_ Law_ in_ India_ 4.pdf

Dewan Mohan-IPR Protection in agriculture – An Overview, R. K. Dewan & Co., Trademark & Patent Attorneys, Poddar Chambers, S. A. Badri road, Fort, Mumbai – 400001.

http://pdfs.semanticscholar.org/b4ee/de95ibb/59f8a63bc802e40b50d928d525ea.pdf Intellectual property Rights in the USA

https://ageconsearch.unm.edu/bitstream/152078/2/1-Presidential -address.pdf

https://assets.publishing.service.gov.uk/government/uploads/attachment_data/file/456368/IP_rights_in_usa.pdf

https://doi.org/10.1111/agel.12337

https://krishi.icar.gov.in/jspui/bitstream/123456789/697/1/pb4.pdf docs.manupatra.in/newsline/articles/upload/81628268-050d-4557-84A4- 48EE74BD6086.pdf

https://odi.org/events/2400-con-intellectual-property-rights-iprs-help-promote- agriculture-food-security-developing - countries

https://www. Ncbi.nlm.nih.gov/pmc/articles/PMC3217699/

https://www.academicjournal.org/AJB

https://www.researchgate.net/publication/262120917_Intellectual_Property_Rights_and_Agricultural_Technology_Interplay_and_Implications_for_India

Intellectual Property Law in India – Legal, Regulatory and Tax by Nishith Desai Associates, Legal and tax Consultants Worldwide, January 2018.

Intellectual Property rights and Indian Agriculture, Policy Brief (4), ICAR

Jewell Catherine, (2015), Who Benefits from IP Rights in Agricultural Innovation, WIPO Magazine, August 2015.

K. Venkataraman and S. SwrnaLatha, (2008), Intellectual property rights, Traditional Knowledge and Biodiversity of India, Journal of Intellectual Property Rights, Volume 13, pp 326-335

Kumar Sinha 2014 status and prospect of research and development in agriculture In India

Kumar Surinder and MisraAditya -Impact of TRIPS Agreement on Indian Agriculture, Bharati Law review, July – Sept. 2016 pp234

Prasad Ram, Bagde U. S. and VermaAjit(2012),An overview of intellectual Property rights in Relation to Agricultural Biotechnology, Volume 11. No.73

R. Silva Repetto & M. Cavalcanti, Legal office, Provisions of the TRIPS Agreement Relevant to Agriculture (Part I)

Saha Chandranath and Bhattacharya Sanjib(2011), Intellectual Property Rights: An Overview and implications in Pharmaceutical Industries, Volume 2.2

Vikas Kumar and KunalSinha, Ph.D., Status & Prospect of research and Development in Agriculture in India, Journal of Science Policy & Governance

WatulJayashree (1998), Intellectual Property Rights in Indian Agriculture,Indian Council for Research on International Economic Relations,July 1998.

www.fao.org/docrep/003/x7355e/x7355e03.htm

www.fao.org/docrep/014/i2043e/i2043eo2d.pdf

10

Corporate Governance in Agricultural and Allied Companies in India

Amitava Roy and Ananda Mohan Pal

Abstract

The agriculture and allied sector provide livelihood for 58% of India's population. A large population and rising disposable incomes are key growth drivers. Growing external demand has increased its contribution to exports. The demand for processed food has also led to increasing requirements for agricultural inputs, hybrid seeds, machinery and fertilizers. Investment opportunities in storage infrastructure and agrochemicals also present immense opportunities. Organised retail has made India attractive for multinationals. The industry has a combination of multiple organisational forms, like associations, co-operatives, government (departmental) undertakings, foreign entities, trusts and companies, private and public. Unlisted companies encompass a vast range (private limited companies, family business, group-owned firms, and joint ventures are major actors.) The form and complexity of business ownership highlights Corporate Governance (CG) debate. Given this background, our objective is to understand the CG characteristics of unlisted agricultural and allied companies operating in India, the driving forces for improving CG practices, and the need for a policy framework in supporting good CG. We propose to examine the extent of control in the various types of entities and explore the mechanisms that contribute to the development of an efficient CG framework. Using data from the Prowess database, on 2,879 firms, from 2012-2013 to 2016-17, we analysed how CG problems are caused and how it can be alleviated. The results provide stakeholders and agri entrepreneurs with an overview of the policy and managerial issues that arise in the debate on CG of

Introduction

India has a large agriculture sector and it supports the livelihood for 58% of country's population. The food and grocery segments are the sixth largest in the world. India has abundant livestock. Farmers are shifting towards the production of horticulture crops to cash in on the growing demand. The food processing sector poised for growth as demand for processed food has grown manifold. India is emerging as a sourcing hub due to cost competitiveness. The food processing industry contributes 32% of this sector, contributing to 13% of total exports and 6% of industrial investment[1]. Investment in storage facilities and food infrastructure is rising. It is estimated that the required infrastructure to enable the growth of food processing industry is 7,845 cold storage chains with a capacity of 35.88 million tonnes and 42 mega food parks sanctioned as of 2017. Out of these, 25 mega food parks were to be operationalised by 2018-end[2]. This phenomenal argi growth has led to increasing requirements for agricultural inputs like, hybrid seeds, machinery and fertilizers. The agrochemicals industries also present immense opportunities.

The key growth drivers, on the domestic demand side, include a large population and rising disposable incomes. External demand is also on the rise and the industry is poised for growth thereby increasing its contribution to exports. On the supply side, hybrid and genetically modified seeds, favourable climate, wide variety of crops and improvement in irrigational facilities have been instrumental in driving demand. Policy support focussing on institutional credit facilities and increase in the minimum support price has fuelled growth. Further, liberalisation and growth of the organised retail sector has made India more attractive for multinationals operating in the agricultural and allied industry.

The agricultural and allied industry in India has a combination of multiple organisational forms. Firms have devised different legal business forms to structure their organisation and includes non-corporate (with unlimited liability) to companies (with limited liability. Among the companies operating, both public and private, majority are unlisted companies. Unlisted companies encompass a vast range (private limited companies, family business, group-owned firms, and joint ventures) and have been instrumental in amassing resources estimated at Rs. 17.67 trillion in gross value-added (hereafter, GVA) terms during the year 2018. Agriculture and allied sector's GVA at constant of 2011-12 prices grew at CAGR of 2.75%between the years 2012 to 2018[3]. Also, lured by the size and returns of the Indian market, foreign entities have entered the market. The

The firms operating in this sector do not fit into a single mould and use varied legal business forms to structure their organisation. The form and complexity of business ownership brings us to the Corporate Governance (CG) debate and challenges in this sector. The choice of the organisation form defines and determines the extent of the CG mechanism. For instance, the chosen legal business form may allow for a CG structure in which the owners only may constitute the board. Other business forms may permit the promoter group, through a nexus of cross holding, to control the firm. Relevant for this study, the major CG concern emerges from the domination of the unlisted companies in this sector and the different CG mechanisms adopted by them. The challenges of CG practices in these companies arise out of the ownership and control structures prevalent in the operating entities and the lack of a proper regulatory and follow up mechanism. Literature has focused extensively on listed companies, and firms with dispersed shareholding, but unlisted companies are relatively unexplored and deserve attention, especially in a sector that is so vital. Further, the relevance of CG in today's progressive and aggressive business environment is an accepted phenomenon. Reforms - trade and regulatory, are manifestations of the policymaker's desire to place the efficient allocation and use of resources at the core of economic activity. Besides other things, this depends upon whether the owners (and management) can be induced to use the resources effectively and efficiently. Thus, we focus on the CG features and mechanisms that are characteristic of the vast majority of the unlisted companies operating in this sector, like: ownership and control; role of professional management; and transparency. Central to the theme of this research is the need for understanding and creating sets of effective internal and external mechanisms for unlisted companies and the requirement for improved institutions to stimulate social welfare and economic growth in the agricultural and allied sector.

Employing a sample of unlisted companies, this study has been developed to foster an understanding of their ownership and control structure. With limited data, we observe that unlisted firms typically operate as a closely held company with concentrated ownership. While there are similarities in the problems (and solutions) devised for both unlisted and listed companies, the typical organisational structure of unlisted companies seems to demand an alternative and robust CG approach.

The rest of the paper is organised in this manner. We begin with a brief presentation on the theoretical background followed by the details of the sample

Literature Review

Extant literature offers two theories with contradictory views regarding the role of CG in unlisted firm. Jensen and Meckling, 1976 observed, CG mechanisms are expensive to implement, and therefore, value reducing. Schulze, Lubatkin, Dino, and Buchholtz, 2001 argued, the benefits of CG system outweigh its costs and unlisted firms will surely benefit from a good CG structure. Literature suggests, CG mechanisms may be classified as, internal and external. Internal mechanisms include, the ownership and control structures, board of directors, executive compensation, financial transparency and adequate information disclosure. External or market-based techniques are designed to reinforce the internal CG structure of the firm and include the competitive and regulatory environment and the market for corporate control (which is weak in India). An effective CG system depends on the presence of both internal and external mechanisms that are sufficiently responsive to the CG problems that surface.

Ownership structure is an internal CG feature. At its root, CG is a concern when ownership and control are separated, and it gives rise to agency cost. The seminal work of Berle and Means, 1932 lays the foundation for examining the relationship between CG and ownership structures. The premise of their work was the recognition of problems associated with the separation of ownership and management. Jensen and Meckling, 1976 elaborated these ideas and formulated the agency theory. They suggested, a firm represents a nexus of contracts between the owners (principals) and managers (agents) and that they have contradictory risk preferences leading to managerial decisions that depart from shareholders' preferences. Extant literature has questioned the extent to which manager and shareholder preferences diverge (Ghoshal, 2005) and research relying on agency theory demonstrates that this assumption resonates (Dalton et al., 2007).

Separation of ownership and management raises conflicts between the goals of owners and managers, which may be due to different managerial effort and attitudes toward risk. Agency costs within firms are complex, depend upon a wide range of motives, incentives and structures and occur between shareholders and managers as a result of incomplete contracting. This Type I (or Vertical) agency costs result when the goals of the shareholders and managers are non-aligned, resulting in managers resorting to higher perquisite consumption and expropriation of shareholders' wealth. This type of agency costs and risk can be reduced by sharing the ownership of the firm (Bozec and Bozec, 2007).

ownership of 20 largest companies in 27countries and found that most companies are closely held by a small number of controlling shareholders. They noted "the principal agency problem in large corporations around the world is that of restricting expropriation of minority shareholders by the controlling shareholders, rather than that of restricting empire building by professional managers unaccountable to shareholders". This brings forth another type of agency cost, known as Type II (or Horizontal) agency costs. Concentrated ownership may frustrate the reduction in type II agency costs since the degree of control that can be exerted by the owners of concentrated holdings may lead to decisions intended to maximise their personal wealth. Another source of agency costs for unlisted, private (closely held) firms is the threat of self-control, often expressed through providing secure employment and other privileges to family members or within the promoter group. Further, the inability to offer competitive compensation and promotional opportunities may result in human resource policies that may be inferior to those of professionally managed firm. These distinct set of agency problems for unlisted private firms may impact their financial performance and survival.

A review of literature suggests that ownership structure may be used as an effective CG mechanism. The role of ownership in mitigating Type I agency problems provides us two solutions. First, to offer ownership stakes to the management which will align the interests of the managers with the dispersed shareholders (Jensen and Meckling, 1976; Morck et al., 1988). Second, the constructive role played the outside block holders or institutional owners, with relatively large equity positions, in alleviating this type of agency problem. Type II agency problem may be minimised in three ways. First, by focusing on the financing structure of unlisted companies and encouraging the role of institutional investors, particularly the banks. Another way of addressing this problem is to ensure proper succession planning and conflict resolution mechanisms are in place. Third, the role of a strong policy framework in strengthening CG structure of unlisted companies.

Objective

The objective of this study is to understand the nature of CG problems in unlisted firms which is dependent on their ownership structures, and the regulatory framework in which they operate. Specifically, the paper reviews the firm's ownership structure, as it acts as a control mechanism. Further, given the nature of the business forms, the need here is to design and implement an institutional effective CG mechanism in place that ensures transparency and provides sufficient information monitoring.

Sample Construct

We sourced our data from the Prowess data base supported by the Centre for Monitoring Indian Economy. It includes information on corporates and non-corporates. It is widely used for firm-level research on India (for example, Khanna and Palepu, 2000, Gopalan et. al., 2007, Sarkar and Sarkar, 2009). The Prowess[4] database includes information on non-corporate entities, as well as, private (listed and unlisted) companies. This database provides us with 2,879 non-corporate and unlisted firms (as on 31 March, 2017) operating in the agriculture and allied sector in India, with operations ranging from manufacturing to trading and marketing. We constructed our data set considering the period of five-years, from 2012–2013 to 2016–2017.

Analysis and Discussions

The sample includes firms engaged in a plethora of activities ranging from agriculture in food and cash crops; fruits; floriculture; oils and fats; animal husbandry and dairy; poultry and marine products; meat and derived products like sauces, dressings; and consumer food products (like, alcoholic beverages, soft drinks, and packaged drinking water). Firms engaged in rubber, spices, tea and other cash crops make up 13.4% of the sample followed by oil and fat with 10.3%. The allied and other business firms, accounting for 33.1%, are engaged in trade of various kinds of agricultural products. The sales of processed food have been increasing at a fast pace and it includes, pasta and noodles; sweet and savoury snacks; bakery, confectionery and condiments; and ice cream and frozen desserts. The sample also includes firms engaged in the manufacture of agricultural machinery, fertilizers and pesticides. Table 1 lists the classification of firms, based on product/service group, operating in the agricultural and allied sector.

Table 1: Classification of firms, based on product/service group, operating in the agricultural and allied sector

Main product/service group	Number of firms	Percentage of firms
Tea	190	0.066
Agricultural machinery	3	0.001
Bakery products	26	0.009

Fertilisers	22	0.008
Floriculture	53	0.018
Marine products, fish and shrimps	70	0.024
Wheat and cereal	50	0.017
Rubber, spices, and other cash crops	385	0.134
Paper and pulp	59	0.020
Pesticides	19	0.007
Poultry	34	0.012
Processed food	169	0.059
Rubber based	13	0.005
Sugar	198	0.069
Oil and fat	296	0.103
Agri-based products	106	0.037
Plywood	14	0.005
Other allied business	954	0.331
Total	2,879	1.000

Source: Authors' calculations based on data from Prowess

As already explained, the business scenario in India comprises of a mix of non-corporate and corporate entities. Corporates include, family/promoter group owned, corporate groups, multinationals, professionally managed standalone and government enterprises. These firms may further be reclassified as listed or unlisted. The agricultural and allied sector has firms having different business forms, both non-corporate and corporate. Our data set shows that there are twenty-eight non-corporate entities (i.e., one percent of the sample, as given in Panel A of Table 1) and the balance 2,851 is corporates (see Panel B of Table 1). Thus, ninety-nine% of the sample comprises of, both private and public limited, unlisted companies. We, therefore, focus on the unlisted corporates (comprising of 99% of the sample) and exclude from the scope of this study the non-corporates since they make up a miniscule portion (i.e., 1% of the sample).

Table 2 describes the distribution of firms across ownership groups.

Table 2: Distribution of firms across ownership groups operating in the agricultural and allied sector

Business forms	Number	Percentage
A. Non-corporate entities		
Associations/Federations	5	0.002
Co-operatives	10	0.003
Departmental undertakings/Boards	2	0.001
Foreign Entities	3	0.001

B. Corporate entities		
Private Ltd. companies	923	0.321
Public Ltd. companies – unlisted	1928	0.669
Total number of corporate entities	2,851	0.990
Total number of sampled firms	2,879	1.000

Source: Authors' calculations based on data from Prowess

Theoretical perspectives on CG span across different disciplines and among them the influential theoretical paradigm in finance literature is the agency theory or the corporate finance perspective. According to this perspective, as Shleifer and Vishny, 1997 observed, CG deals with the ways in which the suppliers of finance to the corporation exercise control and ensure accountability of the company's management in order to ensure they get the best possible return on their investment. CG in such cases seeks to limit managerial discretion or provide incentives to help align the interests of managers and shareholders. Without CG mechanisms in place the firm's debt investors may be unwilling to provide low cost external financing thereby limiting new investment and growth.

In India, concentrated ownership and control is the rule rather than the exception and this is further aggravated by the fact that a vast majority of the firms operating in this sector are unlisted. We, therefore, restricted the scope of this study to the ownership structure of unlisted companies only. Hansmann, 1996 defined unlisted companies to include, closely held companies whose shares, unlike those of publicly held companies; do not trade freely in impersonal markets, either because the shares are held by a small number of persons or because they are subject to restrictions that limit their transferability. It includes family and promoter-controlled firms. Another feature of such firms is that the owners may control the management through persons acting in concert[5], which are usually other private companies controlled and operated by the controlling owners. Thus, divergence between ownership and control is present in the family or promoter-controlled firms leading to the possibility of expropriation of minority shareholders' wealth.

According to the classification of ownership structure adopted by the Prowess database, promoters are controlling shareholders who are either individuals or corporates. Individual promoters as per Prowess includes, the directors and their relatives who control the firm. Non-promoters are non-controlling shareholders and include institutional investors, corporates and the public. Institutional investors are reclassified as domestic (like, banks and financial institutions, mutual funds, insurance companies) and foreign institutional investors.

undivided family (mean holding of 37.12%) and corporate bodies (mean holding of 21.87%). They constitute the main group of shareholders. Three companies were promoted by the Central and/or State Government and only one firm was promoted by domestic institutions and banks. Bulk of the foreign promoters' contribution are by corporate bodies and only eight companies have been promoted by them. In Tables 3 and 4 the extent of shareholding by the different classes of domestic and foreign promoters, respectively, are exhibited.

Table 3: Ownership structure - extent of domestic promoters' shareholding

	Maximum (%)	Minimum (%)	Mean (%)
Individuals and Hindu undivided family	100	0	37.12
Corporate Bodies	83.70	0	21.87
Central and/or State Government	31.53	0	0.24
Indian Institutions & Banks	24.88	0	0.23
Other Promoters	55.28	0	2.60
Persons acting in concert as promoters	34.02	0	7.82

Source: Authors' calculations based on data from Prowess

Table 4: Ownership structure - extent of foreign promoters' shareholding

	Maximum (%)	Minimum (%)	Mean (%)
Individuals (NRIs)	21.81	0	0.75
Corporate Bodies	74.33	7.73	38.27
Foreign Institutions	0	0	0

Source: Authors' calculations based on data from Prowess

The bulk of the non-promoters' shares are held by small investors with average holding of 47.66%. Banks, financial institutions, and insurance companies have invested in only thirty-nine companies. Table 5 shows the extent of shareholding by the different classes of non-promoter groups.

Table 5: Ownership structure - extent of non-promoters' shareholding

	Maximum (%)	Minimum (%)	Mean (%)
Institutions	59.98	0	3.77
Banks, Financial Institutions, and Insurance Companies	48.99	0	1.89
Non-institutions	100	0	47.66

Source: Authors' calculations based on data from Prowess

is based on the concept of control rather than on cash flows. This is unique to India when compared to disclosure norms in other nations where concentrated ownership exists. Another area of concern is that it is sometimes even difficult to identify the insider group due to cross holding of shares. Further, although some of them may have professional management the family or promoter group may continue to play an important role in governance.

Concentrated ownership magnifies Type II agency problem. In such a situation the risks that non-promoters or non-controlling shareholders face is that the promoter group or controlling shareholders may use their position to deprive the former of any influence or participation in the process of decision making. Many of these firms have varied financial stakeholders (equity and/or creditors). In this regard it is pertinent to note that the effect of internal CG mechanisms, such as ownership and compensation, is also influenced by how the firm is financed. We observe that they predominantly rely on the family or promoters for funding expansion and growth. They sparsely avail bank financing because of the high risk they present to the lender in the credit risk and lack of collaterals. Structural barriers also act an impediment to bank lending, and includes, high search and transaction costs associated with such lending.

Concentrated ownership and control structures existed in India since the beginning of the country's industrialisation in the colonial period and it continued in the post-independence period despite significant shifts in the institutional environment, from a regulated economy between the early nineteen fifties to the early nineties, to the increasingly liberalised environment since then (Khanna and Palepu, 2005; Sarkar and Sarkar, 2009). However, this problem of concentrated ownership affected this sector also which has gained momentum only in the post liberalisation period.

The profile of some of the sample firms show that they are large companies, with significant market presence, but they prefer to remain unlisted. The concern here is, unlike listed companies, they are not under the scrutiny of regulatory watchdogs (like, the Securities Exchange Board of India, stock exchanges, and rating agencies) that play an important role in both reducing information asymmetries and fraud detection. Further, other external CG mechanisms, like trust and reputation concerns are absent and these non-legal mechanisms tend to play a crucial role in preventing opportunism within firms. Further, the Companies Act, 2013, like in many other countries, has legislations that prevent the abuse of minority or non-controlling shareholders. As the Act minority

Sarkar, 2008 observed, "laws in the books" both with respect to shareholders and investor rights are possibly at par with international best practices, but the "laws on the ground" that are not effectively implemented. Practically, since the company continues to be managed by the controlling shareholders, the minority shareholders may not be able to obtain sufficient information or records to substantiate their claim for a wrong-doing. Further, the efficacy of remedies under the Companies Act, 2013 remains to be legally tested. Traditionally, litigation based remedies have proven to be a long drawn process and expensive. Additionally, the entire cost of the litigation has to be borne by the aggrieved shareholder who files the claim, but the shareholder only gets a proportionate indirect benefit of a successful claim[6]

Conclusions

The significance of the agriculture and allied sector for wealth creation is widely recognised. In order to reduce poverty and promote sustainable growth and development, transformation of the agrarian economy is a necessity. In this regard it is imperative that steps be taken to increase the economic value of agricultural produce and generate employment opportunities in areas such as food processing and the allied sectors (like, logistics, marketing).

Across the agribusiness value chain, the main participants are farmers, suppliers (of seeds, fertilizers, and pesticides), utility companies (like, transporters and processors), and technology and finance providers. For the effective utilisation of the production factors (like, land, labour and technology) and resource endowments a coordinated mobilisation of resources is the need of the hour. This involves enhancing skills sets and know-how in areas such as management and marketing; capital through finance; adoption of quality control measures; and emerging technologies. In order to achieve success in the agricultural and allied sector business, proper and adequate managerial decisions must be made from the inception of the firm. It must be remembered that entrepreneurship in this sector shares the features of "generic" entrepreneurship, but with distinct characteristics specific to this sector. Thus, entrepreneurs must decide what will be the firm structure or business form, type of financing to be used, and how the business will be run as a going concern.Whatever is the form of business, the need for effective CG seems to be embedded in the process, whether it is for an existing firm or for a new venture. Additionally, majority of the resources in this sector are in the hands of the private sector. The challenge seems to be the fact that the sector is dominated by unlisted firms with a high degree of

In this research we looked at the opportunities and challenges in CG faced by unlisted companies operating in the agricultural and allied sector in India. In the context of CG, we have reviewed the research and theory on firm ownership and studies that foster a better understanding of the relationships between a firm's ownership structure and how they affect the firm growth and sustainability. We attempted to distil lessons from the ownership structures of unlisted companies. In order to prevent dilution of the promoter group's controlling stake, unlisted companies tend to use bank finance as the last resort when they are in the need of finances ignoring leverage benefits. Further, including debt in the financing structure of unlisted companies can bring in major benefits as the strategic use of debt acts as a disciplining mechanism for reducing agency costs by aligning the interests of various stakeholders. CG literature also suggests, debt offers the firm a strong incentive to ensure its success but with a rider that has policy implication, to guarantee strong creditor rights. Additionally, lending institutions and credit rating agencies insist on good CG by demanding that unlisted companies comply with best practices as part of their risk assessment process. In this area there is a need for innovative structured products from equity to debt, catering to the varying risk appetite of investors, from small enterprises to large businesses. Another area of concern seems to be the implementation of succession planning and the need to develop an efficient alternative dispute resolution mechanism to solve conflicts within family businesses.

The way forward seems to be the need for the legal framework to define and determine the internal and external CG mechanisms. Internal mechanisms for enhancing CG in unlisted companies should address improving transparency in the decision-making processes as well as on training and education of managers and shareholders with greater emphasis on succession planning. External mechanisms include a proper legal framework that can induce desired managers' and shareholders' behaviour. Additionally, policy initiatives both at the Central and State level will ensure that measures are taken to boost farm management services, investments are made in supply chain infrastructure and encouragement is offered to contract farming. This sector has massive scope for employment generation and India has the potential of being a global outsourcing hub. Tax incentives and other sops maybe extended to the enterprises and emphasis placed on research and development and modernisation. Agriculture must be viewed as a modern industry with distinctive scientific, technological and management inputs. The focus of the government should be on growth and

References

Berle, A., & G. Means. (1932). "The modern corporation and private property" in Thomas Clarke (ed.) Corporate Governance: Critical Perspectives on Business and Management, Routledge: London and New York, pp.173-189.

Bozec, Y. and Bozec, R. (2007), Ownership concentration and corporate governance practices: substitution or expropriation effects? Canadian Journal of Administrative Science, vol. 24: pp. 182-195. doi:10.1002/cjas.23

Dalton, D., Hitt, M. A., Certo, S. T. and Dalton, C. M. (2007). 'The fundamental agency problem and its mitigation: independence, equity, and the market for corporate control'. Academy of Management Annual Reviews, 1, 1–64.

Ghoshal, S. (2005). 'Bad management theories are destroying good management practices. Academy of Management Learning and Education, 33, 79–95.

Gopalan, R., Nanda, V., Seru, A., (2007). Affiliated firms and financial support: Evidence from Indian business groups. Journal of Financial Economics 86, 759–795

Hansmann, H. (1996), The Ownership of Enterprise, Cambridge: The Belknap Press of Harvard University Press, pp 12-14.

Jensen, C. and W.H. Meckling (1976), Theory of the Firm: Managerial Behavior, Agency Costs and Ownership Structure, Journal of Financial Economics 3: 305-360.

Khanna, T., & K. Palepu. (2005). "The evolution of concentrated ownership in India: Broad patterns and a history of the Indian software industry". In R. Morck (Ed.) A history of corporate governance around the world: Family business groups to professional managers, Chicago and London: The University of Chicago Press, pp. 283 - 324

Khanna, Tarun and Krishna Palepu (2000), "Is Group Affiliation Profitable in Emerging Markets? An Analysis of Diversified Indian Business Groups", Journal of Finance, 55 (2): 867-91.

La Porta, Rafael, Florencio, Lopez-de-Silanes and Andrei Shliefer (1999), "Corporate Ownership Around the World", Journal of Finance, 54(2): 471-517.

Morck, R., A. Shleifer, & R. Vishny. (1988). "Management ownership and market valuation: An empirical analysis". Journal of Financial Economics, 20, pp. 293–315.

Sarkar, Jayati and Subrata Sarkar (2008), "Debt and Corporate Governance in Emerging Economies: Evidence from India", Economics of Transition, 16(2):293-334.

Sarkar, Jayati and Subrata Sarkar (2009), "Multiple Board Appointments and Firm Performance in Emerging Economies: Evidence from India", Pacific Basin Finance Journal, 17:271-93.

Shleifer, A., & R. Vishny. (1997). "A survey of corporate governance". The Journal of Finance, 52(2), pp. 737–783.

Endnotes

[1]Agriculture and Allied Industries, Indian Brand Equity Foundation (available at www.ibef.org)

[2]Agriculture and Allied Industries, Indian Brand Equity Foundation (available at www.ibef.org)

[3]Agriculture and Allied Industries, Indian Brand Equity Foundation (available at www.ibef.org)

[4]The Prowess database distinguishes between: (i) independent private domestic owned firms not affiliated to business groups, (ii) firms affiliated with domestic business group, (iii) public sector enterprises, (iv) independent foreign firms and (v) group-affiliated foreign firms. This classification of firms is based on continuous monitoring of company announce-

https://www.sebi.gov.in/legal/regulations/apr-2017/sebi-substantial-acquisition-of-shares-and-takeovers-regulations-2011-last-amended-on-march-6-2017-_34693.html)

[6]Challenges In Protecting The Rights Of Minority Shareholders by Puneet Rathsharma and Kunal Mehta, Business World (dated 2 January, 2018) (accessed on 24 April, 2019, available at http://www.businessworld.in/article/Challenges-In-Protecting-The-Rights-Of-Minority-Shareholders/02-01-2018-136149/)

11

Entrepreneurial Opportunity in Organic Farming

Ayesha Afreen

Abstract

This paper is rooted in the issue of the failure of Green Revolution which was intended to achieve self-sufficiency in the agriculturally dominant country of India, following its independence. However five decades later, the current focus of the country is on engaging in a sustainable and economically feasible agricultural practice using principles of agro ecology. This paper tries to explore the potential of application of organic farming in a vast country like India. The author posits that organic farming can help India reverse the damage caused by Green Revolution by allowing for natural methods of agriculture rather than a severely mechanical form. This paper focuses on the modern concept of organic farming combining tradition, science and innovation, and the debatable issues surrounding organic farming particularly dealing with its economic feasibility and sustainability prospects. It is acknowledged that for the successful implementation of organic farming there has to be appropriate matching of the supply and demands the organic products. However, there is a need to address the challenge of adoption of organic farming in a diverse country like India because of its huge variance in education, income, living standards and health of the existing and potential consumers. The prospect of organic farming is discussed from the perspective of consumer awareness and state initiatives, in this paper.

Keywords: Green Revolution, Organic Farming, Sustainability, Food Security

The Green Revolution in India refers to a period when India adopted modern methods and technology such as the use of high yielding variety (HYV) seeds, tractors, pesticides, fertilizers and irrigation facilities with an aim to achieve self-sufficiency in the production of food grain. While it achieved dramatic increase in the technological transformation in the early stages, the success was highly selective in both aspects; the places in which Green Revolution created impact and the crops which were subject to the new technology. Over the years not only did the productivity fall but also the fertility of the soil degraded due to overuse of fertilizers and pesticides that accumulated over the years and also caused water salinisation and contamination of ground water. As a result 6% of India's land has been rendered useless (Rosset et al., 2000). The goal of this paper is to assess the present situation of the country and focus on the possible opportunities for achieving sustainable agricultural output. The author argues that organic farming is a method of farming that works at the grass-root level by preserving and regenerating the capacity of the soil with sound soil management, providing it with ample plant nutrition while producing nutritious food rich in vitality which has resistance to diseases.

According to International Federation of Organic Agriculture Movement, 'organic agriculture' is a production system that sustains the health of soils, eco systems and people. It relies on ecological processes, biodiversity and cycles adapted to local conditions, rather than the use of inputs with adverse effects. Organic agriculture combines tradition, innovation and science to benefit the shared environment and promote fair relationships and a good quality of life for all involved.

The paper substantiates its claim with a brief review of evolution in Indian agricultural scenario. Moving forward the author brings in the potential of organic farming as an alternate to industrialised farming and analyses how this may be considered an exciting opportunity for entrepreneurs. Some significant observations have been collated to set the background for the proposal laid down by the author.

The state of Indian agriculture has crossed many stages since the time of independence and to the current day it is undergoing transition and evolving as a new form of agriculture that is not only restricted to farmers but entrepreneurs, researchers and agriculture scientists. The state of Indian agriculture can be divided into three stages.

The state of traditional agriculture, that was prevalent under the British rule, were imported. This dependence worsened during the 1960's following two years of severe droughts which led to an increase in the price of food grains imported. In 1966 India had to import more than 10 million tonnes of food grains as against a domestic production of 72 million tons (Mooij, 1998).

Indian agriculture entered its phase two in the mid-1960s after the adoption of the high yield variety seeds. This phase was characterised by application of science and technology and subsequently led to a large proportionate increase with small additions in the form of fertilizers, pesticides and improved seeds. The stagnancy of Indian agriculture had been largely overcome in this phase. The major benefits of the Green Revolution were experienced mainly in northern and northwestern India between 1965 and the early 1980s; the program resulted in a substantial increase in the production of food grains.

Over time, Green Revolution led to reduced genetic diversity, increased vulnerability to pests, water shortages, soil erosion, reduced soil fertility, impoverishment and displacement of vast number of small farmers. Gradually Green Revolution presented itself with the paradox of more food yet more hunger. Green revolution failed to alleviate hunger and showed the irony of 'hunger amidst mass production'. The degradation of environment caused due to unchecked usage of fertilizers and pesticides was one of the major concerns of agriculture (Rosset et al., 2000).

India's need for an alternative sustainable farming practice has led to much literature which proposes organic farming. The role of organic farming in India rural economy can be leveraged to mitigate the ever-increasing problem of food security in India. With rapid industrialisation of rural states of India, there has been a crunch for farmland. Further, with the exponential population growth of India, the need for food sufficiency has become the need of the hour. Organic farming has the capability to take care of each of these problems. Besides the obvious immediate and positive effects organic or natural farming has on the environment and quality of food, it also greatly helps a farmer to become self-sufficient in his requirements for agro-inputs and reduce his costs (Chandrashekar, 2009).

There are certain constraints faced by the organic farming in India. Organic farming in India needs both technical and institutional support. Systematic training of farmers for gradual conversion to organic is the way to move forward. Low cost and hassle-free certification need to be put in place. Even group certification can be encouraged through cooperatives and self-help groups. Well-developed organic farming not simply as a source of export revenue but as an alternative model of agricultural development (Hans and Rao, 2018).

Objectives

The objectives of this paper are as follows:

- To understand the historical perspective and the consequences of green revolution as a medium to achieve self sufficiency and food security in India.
- To identify the possibility of introducing organic farming as a vehicle of sustainable food production.
- To interpret the role of government bodies to mitigate the gaps and enhance both mass consumption and mass production of organic products.
- To highlight the status of organic agriculture in India.

Research Methodology

This paper is based on secondary data, official reports and previous studies relating to the Green Revolution and organic farming. The data from Agricultural & Processed Food Products Export Development Authority (APEDA) 2018 is used to ascertain the status of organic farming in India and particularly in West Bengal. The official definitions have been sourced from the official Ministries of the Government of India. A more informed role of the government is assumed from the data and readings collected.

Discussion

Green Revolution and its impact on Indian economy

Agriculture is the backbone of Indian economy but colonialism became a fetter on India's agriculture. Agriculture not only stagnated but also deteriorated over the years under British rule. Post-independence, due to the inward looking policies of the country and the focus on strengthening the secondary and tertiary sectors of the economy, the primary sector was overlooked (Dantwala, 1976). The sector in which the majority of the population was engaged became the secondary objective of the government. Food security in India was a far-fetched concept and there was a huge quantity of food grain imported. This adversely affected India's balance of payments and a new breakthrough in agriculture was the

the agriculture to a modern industrial system adopting modern means of technology such as the bio-engineered high yielding variety seeds, tractors, heavy irrigation facilities, fertilizers and pesticides. With time, chemical factories were established to cater to the ever-increasing demands of the chemical inputs applied to the modern method of agriculture. In the mid twentieth century there was a spurt of agricultural growth driven by Green Revolution. India's production increased so much that it became an exporter of food grains in the course of time.

However, as the consequence of high agricultural productivity, the negative impacts of Green Revolution began to kick in. India started facing new challenges in the terms of sustainability of resource use. Green Revolution created spatial and social disparities. The rich farmers who could afford the heavy modern technology greatly benefitted from the Green Revolution primarily because they had the capital to invest and had large landholdings in which Green Revolution turned to be most successful. The poor and small marginal farmers lacked the availability and accessibility of land and resources and affordability of costly inputs. Also the regions where initially Green Revolution was started like Punjab, Haryana, Uttar Pradesh, etc., because of its extensively developed irrigation canals and home to wealthy farmers with huge landholdings, advanced economically leaving the other states agriculturally backward. Major crops like wheat, maize, paddy were the only selective crops in which the new technology was applied. Thus Green Revolution was highly selective both in terms of selective regional and crop influence (Fujita, 2009). Green Revolution brought about a change in pattern from traditional sustainable methods of agriculture to mono cropping and unsustainable practices. There grew a sense of discontentment within the community of small farmers due to their loss of landholdings in the absence of proper land reform measures. Subsidies too were favoured towards the commercial farmers which decreased their risk aversion and helped them to increase production with more intensive use of chemical inputs and modern seeds (Sebby, 2010).

Green Revolution created the issues of concentration of economic power by limiting the access of land and resources to the wealthy and socially affluent commercial farmers. Hunger too could not be alleviated since Green Revolution failed to redistribute purchasing power and resources towards those who were undernourished. The basic intuition behind this was that if people lacked basic affordability, increased food production would be of no use to them. Thus Green Revolution was a paradox of more hunger amidst more food production (Rosset

The Challenges of Green Revolution: Opportunities for Organic Farming

Since Green Revolution technology was selective in terms of the crops it could be applied to, like wheat, maize, paddy, it led to skewed distribution of high growth of certain crops only. The Green Revolution package has reduced genetic diversity at two levels. First, it replaced mixtures and rotations of crops like wheat, maize, millets, pulses and oil seeds with monocultures of wheat and rice. Second, the introduced wheat and rice varieties came from a very narrow genetic base. This resulted in nutritional disbalance. The alternative of organic food production is known for its huge variety. India produced around 1.70 million MT (2017-18) of certified organic products which includes all varieties of food products namely oil seeds, sugar cane, cereals & millets, cotton, pulses, medicinal plants, tea, fruits, spices, dry fruits, vegetables, coffee etc. The production is not limited to the edible sector but also produces organic cotton fibre, functional food products, etc. (APEDA, 2018).

Increased usage of the chemical fertilizers and pesticides over the years has led to the degradation in the quality of land and hence quality of food produced in such land is inferior and harmful to the health of consumers. This paper discusses the alternatives to the chemical inputs being bio fertilizers and pesticides, which do not harm or compromise with the quality of the land and the produce. Organic farming is a system which avoids or largely excludes the use of chemical inputs (such as fertilizers, pesticides, hormones, feed additives, etc.) and instead to the maximum extent relies upon crop rotations, animal manures, off-farm organic waste, etc. Sufficient quantities of biodegradable material of microbial, plant or animal origin produced on organic farms shall form the basis of the nutrient management programme to increase or at least maintain its fertility and the biological activity within it. Fertilisation management should minimise nutrient losses. As an impact of organic farming, accumulation of heavy metals and other pollutants shall be prevented. Non-synthetic mineral fertilizers and brought-in bio fertilizers (biological origin) shall be regarded as supplementary and not as a replacement for nutrient recycling [National Programme for Organic Production (NPOP), 2018].

In the Green Revolution period, due to high costs of inputs, only rich farmers with large land holdings were able to apply the modalities. This resulted in widening of the social gap between the farmers who could afford these inputs and farmers who could not. Organic farming largely helps to reduce costs by transgenic plants or plant material is prohibited. This makes organic farming practices affordable and economically feasible to farmers.

Green Revolution required huge fertile lands which had proper irrigation facilities. Hence it was primarily applied to states like Haryana, Punjab, Western Uttar Pradesh, etc. These states moved on to have a comparative advantage over the other states and thus Green Revolution created spatial disparities too. Farming practices that can draw from local resources and adapt to the regional conditions and allow for the production of the best suited crop in that region will help to remove the spatial disparity. Organic agriculture is an ecological production management system that promotes and enhances biodiversity, biological cycles and soil biological activity. This ensures that the soil is allowed to regain its fertility over a course of production cycle. It takes into account the regional conditions and the locally adapted systems, hence helping to maximise production given its geographical constraints. Soil fertility shall be maintained through, among other things, the cultivation of legumes or deep-rooted plants and the use of green manures, along with the establishment of a programme of crop rotation several times a year and fertilisation with organic inputs. Desired pH levels shall be maintained in the soil by the producer (NPOP, 2018).

The excessive usage of chemical inputs in Green Revolution resulted over time in environmental damage such as soil, water, air pollution, eutrophication of groundwater, etc. The usage of eco friendly inputs can allow for the conservation of the environment and help to restore the disbalance caused by Green Revolution. The use of bio fertilizers and manures ensures the preservation of the quality of the surrounding environment and helps to restore the ecological balance. Participatory Guarantee System for India (PGS-India) is a decentralised organic farming certification system. The system certifies organic products maintaining the requisite quality standards, including ensuring that the cultivation and production process is done in compliance with the standards laid down for organic products. The products are certified as organic in the form of a documented logo or a statement (Indian Council of Food and Agriculture, 2018).

Organic Farming as a Vehicle to Sustainable Food Production

Organic farming, as a mode of sustainable agriculture can be defined as one which protects the environmental health, promotes economic profitability and

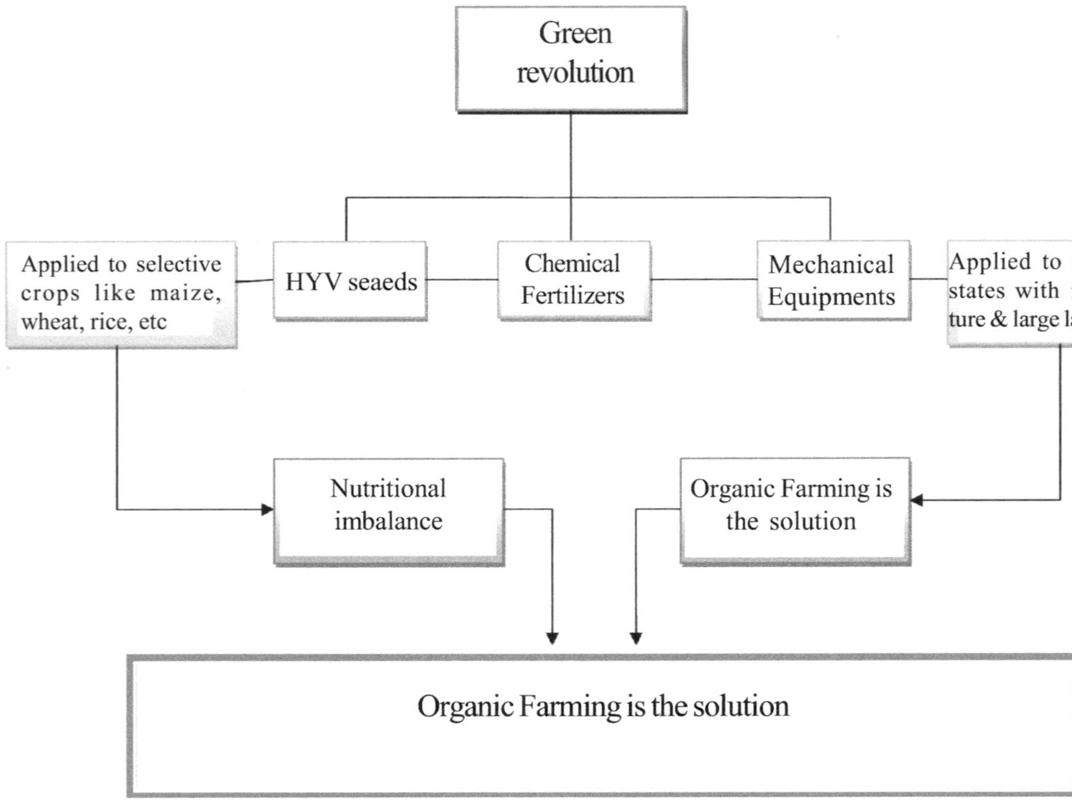

Fig. 1: The Evolution of Indian Agriculture Organic farming and way forward
Environmental degradation
Source: Author's own

It is in this context that India has slowly but steadily taken the road for transition from the practice of unsustainable chemical intensive agriculture to a sustainable and labor intensive organic agriculture. The word "organic" can be defined as an ecological management production system that promotes and enhances bio-diversity, biological cycles and soil biological activity. It is based on the minimal use of off-farm inputs and on management practices that restore, maintain and enhance 'ecological harmony' (National Organic Standards Board of the US Department of Agriculture, 2018). Organic farming thus consists of a holistic production method and it enhances agro-ecosystem health, including biodiversity, biological cycles and soil fertility. It emphasises the use of management practices in preference to the use of off-farm inputs, taking into account that regional conditions require locally adapted systems. In the production and marketing of organically produced agricultural goods, the focus is on the process of production rather than the product. Strict adherence to quality standards is a unique feature of organic production. Organic farming helps farmers to not only become self-sufficient in matters of inputs but also provides them with the incentives of low investment and high premium. Since the pesticides and bio fertilizers are locally produced and the primary source of irrigation in organic farming is rainfall, it helps to bring down the input costs of the farmers sufficiently and hence it provides them a higher margin of profit. Also organic products are generally priced higher than the inorganic products and the export market for organic products is so vast that it offers a producer high premiums to make the transition to organic farming. India has a natural varied agro-climatic region which is an added advantage which makes the country suitable for organic agriculture. These conditions make it promising for the producers to tap the organic domestic and export market.

Role of State as the Facilitator of Organic Agriculture in India

In India, the transition to a chemical-free farming is still at its nascent stage. There are various issues or shortcomings that have been found in the development of organic farms in India. Strong institutional and infrastructural support is required to further push the organic farming from a small niche market to mainstream agriculture. Marketing costs are very high due to limited market access and the majority of consumers belong to metros. One of the most important prerequisite of marketing an organic product is its authenticity certification. Faster, smoother and transparent mechanisms for certification of organic products are required to ensure credibility to organic products. Certification of from the farm to the market. The label of organic authenticity hence offers a claim on quality. Only products legally certified by accredited bodies conforming to national organic standards can be marketed as organic in India (Food and Agriculture Organizations of the United Nations, 2018).

The first institution for organic farmers was driven by a collection of farmers and traders who formed associations to advocate their cause. Many of these small institutions came together in 1972 to form the International Federation of Organic Agriculture Movements (IFOAM) giving the organic farmers an international platform to voice their opinions and concerns. Today IFOAM operates in 108 countries covering more than 750 organisations in them. The goal of IFOAM is to ensure adoption of ecological, social and economical sound systems based on the principles of organic farming.

In India for organic farming, the government established APEDA under the Agricultural and Processed Food Products Export Development Authority Act in 1985. At the time of its establishment, its main goals were to promote the export-oriented production and development of specified products, maintaining specified standards for export, carrying out inspection of meat and meat products for quality.

The Ministry of Commerce and Industry of India launched the National Programme on Organic Products in 2000. The main objectives of NPOP are as follows:

- To provide means of evaluation of certification of organic products.
- To accredit certification programmes.

  To facilitate certification in conformity with National Standards for Organic Products.
- To promote development of organic agriculture.

There has been introduction of organic contract farming in which specific supply chains are integrated so that organic products reach a larger segment of the market. Simultaneously, the government needs to take initiatives to spread awareness about the health and environmental benefits of organic consumption. Subsidies to the organic agriculturists will help to substantially lower costs of organic produce in the market as well as attract producers to shift to organic farming.

Organic Agriculture (FIBL) & IFOAM Year Book, 2018]. As on 31st March 2018, total area under organic certification process (registered under National Programme for Organic Production) is 3.56 million hectares (2017-18). This includes 1.78 million hectare (50%) cultivable area and another 1.78 million hectare (50%) for wild harvest collection. In 2017-18, India's total organic farm production was 17, 03,111 tons of which 98% came from farm production and 2% from wild harvest production. There are a total of 1million 91 thousand farmers engaged in organic farming and the total value for exports was 34,534.8 million INR. The highest organic production in 2017-18 came from Madhya Pradesh (5,79,764.129 tons) while Bihar has the lowest organic production with only 12.15 tons. Madhya Pradesh has the largest area (11,56,881.414 hectares) of organic farms under certification followed by Rajasthan, Madhya Pradesh and Uttar Pradesh while Pondicherry has the lowest area of organic farming cultivation (2.835 hectares). Sikkim has shown remarkable growth in the organic agriculture. In 2016 it declared itself as an 'organic state' for converting 100% of its cultivable land under organic certification (NPOP, 2017).

In 2003, Sikkim officially adopted organic farming as a part of the state policy to maintain ecological balance and eradicate the woes of chemical fertilizers, which will ensure long term sustenance. As a part of the implementation process, Sikkim imposed a ban on import and use of chemical fertilizers and pesticides in the state and moved towards adoption of traditional use of organic manure, thereby securing the title of the first organic state in the world. In 2018, Sikkim won the "Oscar for best policies" that was conferred by Food and Agriculture Organisation for the world's best policies promoting agroecological and sustainable food systems (FAO, 2018).

Even though there are programmes promoting organic cultivation in the centre, the programs are not very effective at the state level. Some states like West Bengal need to take active participation in the expansion of organic farming. At the farm level profits of the farmers can be increased by introducing cheaper methods of certification or with financial schemes such as Paramparagat Krishi Vikas Yojana which assists farmers to achieve certification. The policy of Participatory Guarantee System which promotes organic farming growth in India by providing easy, hassle-free cost effective access to certification and also provides training in the legal processes of the certification is not widespread and needs to be properly implemented in various parts of the country in order to successfully complete India's journey to becoming an organic country at large.

this increased consciousness has caused a spurt of growth in demand of food that is more nutritious and free from toxic chemicals and causes no damage to the natural resources of the country. This has led to recourse to organic methods of farming with a sense of protection of the environment and awareness of modern technology leading to a growing demand for organic producers. Currently organic produce market in India is very small and organic produce is mainly targeted for export purposes. In order to expand its base in the domestic market certain steps have to be taken by the public and private initiatives. The most prominent challenge is to be able to tackle the problem of food security in India in an organic manner. India is far from that lofty yet noble goal. Appropriate policy formulation and implementation mechanisms are required at each level to ensure expansion of organic products.

Organic farming has taken a rebirth in India with a more modern technology and a new objective. It is now a means to achieve food security in India as well as maintain ecological, social and economic sustainability. This implies that India has to look at agriculture with a more sustainable outlook and combine it with the latest technology to yield the highest best productivity. This paves the way forward for organic agri-entrepreneurship. Agri-entrepreneurship is defined as the ability to exploit the existing opportunities in agriculture and to broaden the horizon of traditional agricultural practices by combining it with science, innovation and tradition (Lans, et al., 2013). The coming of age agricultural entrepreneurs is as invested in maximising profits as achieving their objective in a sustainable manner. Over the years agriculture has been looked upon as backward and low-tech with limited dynamics for expansion. However, now that the agriculture sector is going through a transition, it is more than just crop cultivation or animal husbandry. Agriculture is now engaged in diversification, value addition, precision farming, high-tech agriculture, agri-entrepreneurship, global marketing, organic farming etc. and is gradually getting due attention of the people involved in redefining agriculture (Ahmed & Haneef, 2011). Thus agri entrepreneurship can help India with the transition from Green Revolution to an 'Evergreen' Revolution following the organic vehicle.

References

Ahmed, T., Hasan, S. and Haneef, R. (2011). Entrepreneurial characteristics of the agripreneurs under the Scheme of Agriclinics & Agri-buisness Centres. Journal of Community Mobilization and Sustainable Development, 6(2), 145-149.

APEDA. Organic Products. (2018). http://apeda.gov.in/apedawebsite/organic/Organic_Products.htm Codex Alimentarius Commission 1999 (FAO and WHO).

Dantwala, M. L. (1976). Agricultural policy in India since independence. Indian Journal of Agricultural Economics, 31(902-2018-1319), 31.

Fujita, K. (2009). Green revolution in India and its significance in economic development: implications for Sub-Saharan Africa. JICA-IR Working Paper.

Indian Council of Food and Agriculture (ICFA) http://icfa.org.in/assets/doc/reports/Organic_Farming.pdf

Lans, Thomas & Seuneke, Pieter & Klerkx, Laurens. (2013). Agricultural Entrepreneurship. 10.1007/978-1-4614-3858-8_496.

Manaloor, Varghese & Srivastava, Divyanshu & Islam, Shahidul. (2016). Growth of Organic Food Industry in India. Agro for International Journal. 1: 69-76.

National Programme for Organic Production (NPOP) http://apeda.gov.in/apedawebsite/organic/data.htm

National Standard Boards of US Department of Agriculture https://www.ams.usda.gov/rules-regulations/organic/nosb

PKVY Manual, (2017) https://darpg.gov.in/sites/default/files/Paramparagat % 20Krishi% 20Vikas%20Yojana.pdf

Rosset, Collins, Lapp. (2000). Lesson from Green Revolution: Do we need technology to end hunger? Tikkun Magazine, Vol 15 pp 52-56.

Sebby, Katheryn, (2010). The Green Revolution of the 1960's and Its Impact on Small Farmers in India Environmental Studies Undergraduate Student Theses.

The International Federation of Organic Agriculture Movements (IFOAM - Organics International)https://www.ifoam.bio/ 1-19.

12

Initiatives of Government of India in Transforming Women Farmers to Women Entrepreneurs: A Case Study

Sneha Km Pandey, Pritha Chanda and Anisha Pandey

Abstract

Agriculture is the backbone of India's economic development and has experienced immense growth in the past few decades. Agriculture not only involves the participation of male workers but also experiences active participation of all family members, as well. Women, as part of the family, take up agricultural activities as an extension to their household chores. The Government and voluntary agencies have also recognised the need for women in the farming community to become self-reliant and active participants in the agricultural sector. Increasing awareness and educating themselves with the passage of time, farmers have made themselves aware of new techniques of farming and growing and established themselves as agricultural entrepreneurs in the long run. Many initiatives supporting women entrepreneurs and creating a supportive ecosystem for women to become agricultural entrepreneurs have been initiated by the state. The case of Anita Devi popularly known as the Mushroom Lady of Bihar has been taken up in this paper to substantiate with evidence how government initiatives have helped her gain success and grow as an agricultural entrepreneur. This study aims at disseminating how such initiatives help in creating an ecosystem that motivates agricultural entrepreneurs in general and women in particular.

Keywords: Agriculture, Women, Agricultural Entrepreneurs, Women Entrepreneurs, Government Initiatives.

Introduction

Agriculture is the backbone of Indian economic development. According to the Central Intelligence Agency fact book, agriculture accounted for around 15.4% of India's GDP in 2017.India is the second largest producer of agricultural products and accounts for 7.39% of total global agricultural output. This in turn makes the contribution of the agricultural sector to the Indian economy much higher than the world's average (Ministry of Statistics and Programme Implementation, 2018-19). Indian agriculture has experienced immense growth over last few decades providing employment to 60% of the population which accounts for almost 52% of the total number of jobs in India (Arjun, 2013). Agriculture is one of the main sectors in India with 90.2 million agricultural households in rural India which is almost 57.8% of the total estimated rural households in the country (NSSO 70th Round, July 2012-July13). Agriculture is a labour intensive industry where both men and women are active participants but women's participation in agricultural work is not recognised. Due to this they end up being referred to as unpaid subsistence labourers and not farmers, thereby denying their access to credits and government benefits (Pandey, 2018). India continues to absorb and employ two-third of the female workforce but fails to provide them with the recognition of employed labour. The female work force still faces many problems and is still oppressed, even though they are hugely productive in agriculture. Their needs and problems are ignored by government and rural development initiatives are not designed to suit their needs (Ghosh & Ghosh, 2014).

According to Singh and Vinay (2012) even though female labour participation is significant in agriculture and allied activities like sowing, transplanting and post-harvest operations, their role in agriculture is not highlighted enough, making them 'invisible workers'. Approximately 45.3% of the total workforce in the agricultural sector consists of women labourers but their economic contribution is meagre. According to study by Damisa et al. (2007) despite various constraints and lack of decision making power, women still have a high level of participation and are committed to agricultural activity.Unati et al. (2010) and Bala (2011) stated in their study that there is discrimination in terms of women engaged in agricultural activities even though they do the same type of work as their male counterparts. Their role in farms' decision making activities is also negligible. Therefore active women participation can only be ensured if they acquire knowledge and have access to information (Ghosh and Ghosh, 2014).

(Pandey, 2018). As per Census 2011, 65% of the total female workers in India are engaged in agriculture. Out of the total cultivators 30.3% were female. Rural women engaged in agriculture form 78% of all women in regular work but despite their engagement and participation, their contribution remains unrecognised. The women in agricultural households are often found to be the worst sufferers of challenges of farming as a livelihood. It is the intersectionality of women in farming household that makes their position most critical.

According to a feature story by The World Bank in 2012, certain challenges that were faced by the agriculture sector in India were highlighted, overcoming which is important for India's overall development. The challenges involved the lack of cultivable land, limited water resources for irrigation and lack of knowledge of the farmers about the ways to increase productivity. The National Service Scheme 2003 Farmers' Survey brought to light some issues faced by small and marginal farmers which involved imperfect market for inputs/produce, low access to credit markets or imperfect credit markets, lack of trained human resources, low access to major infrastructural facilities like public irrigation, electricity grids and information regarding consequences of poor quality land and water management and contingency situations. The Farm Guide, 2017 India also recognised challenges like reduced role of women, credit facilities and climatic changes which affect the agricultural sector as a whole.

These challenges faced by the agricultural sector have adverse effects on the agricultural households in general and the women folk in particular. Some of those impacts may be reduced productivity due to smaller land holdings, lack of proper irrigation and infrastructural facilities. The imperfect markets dominated by middle-men and agents lead to smaller value realisations by the farmers along with low access to credit markets which restricts them from buying required inputs and lead to sub-optimal input decisions (NSS 2003 Farmer's survey). Moreover the social constructs and cultural barriers prevent rural women from being recognised as farmers, resulting in reduced participation of women in agriculture. Even if women actively participate in agriculture, they are not recognised as farmers (Pandey, 2018).

The Government of India had taken some measures to specifically address the challenges faced by women in the agricultural sector and improve the state of these women and motivate them to become entrepreneurs. Some of the measures are as follows:

i. **Support to States Extension Programme for Extension Reforms** functionaries. The scheme also provides for the representation of women in the Farmers' Advisory Committee at Block, District and State levels encouraging women farmers' to participate in the planning and decision making process.

ii. **National Mission on Oilseeds and Oil Palm (NMOOP)** ensures 30% of budgetary allocation for women farmers. The implementation of the allocation of resources for SC/ST/Women beneficiaries and maintenance of a database for the same is monitored by the concerned implementing agencies.

iii. **Sub-Mission for Seed and Planting Material (SMSP)** provides training under the components of the Scheme Seed Village Programme and Quality Control Arrangement of Seeds to both men and women farmers benefitting the women farmers equally. It also advises the State Governments to allocate adequate funds to women farmers.

iv. **National Food Security Mission (NFSM)** states that 30% of funds to be allocated must be earmarked for women farmers. It also includes an intervention which creates awareness about new technology amongst the SC; ST and women farmers by providing cropping system based training, so that the production and productivity of crops increase.

v. **National Horticulture Mission** helps women farmers to become self-reliant by organising Self Help Groups and by providing them with farm inputs and technological & extension supports.

vi. **Sub-Mission on Agricultural Mechanization (SMAM)** provides women in agriculture with 31 labour reducing technologies developed by The Indian Council of Agricultural Research (ICAR) which are promoted through training, demonstration and financial assistance. It also provides women farmers with 10% additional financial assistance for purchasing various agricultural machines and equipment. Farm Machinery Training and Testing Institutes provide women farmers with training on Agricultural Mechanisation on continual basis.

vii. **Indian Council of Agricultural Research (ICAR)** has a network of Krishi Vigyan Kendras (KVKs) in the country which assesses and demonstrates technologies/products and disseminates it through training programmes for farmers, updating their knowledge and skill. These in turn benefit farmers in terms of crop production and improved farm

viii. **Central Institute for Women in Agriculture** (ICAR-CIWA established National Research Centre for Women in Agriculture at Bhubaneswar in 1996) undertakes research on issues that affect the women in agriculture. Some of the major areas in which the research is being done include suitability of technologies and equipment for women, women friendly tools and equipment which reduce their hard work and enhance their accessibility to critical resources, and programmes and services which are important for women's empowerment in agriculture.

ix. **Support to Training and Employment Programme for Women (STEP)** was launched by Government of India's Ministry of Women and Child Development in 1986-87 for training women with no accessibility to formal skill training facilities in rural areas. It provides training to women in several sectors such as agriculture, horticulture, food processing, handlooms, traditional crafts like embroidery, travel and tourism, hospitality, computer and IT services.

x. **Grameen Bhandaran Yojana (GBY) or Rural Godown Scheme (RGS)**- This scheme met various requirements of the farmers for storing their farm produce, processing farm produce, agricultural inputs etc., by creating scientific storage capacity with allied facilities in rural areas, and preventing distressed sale.

The status of women and their position in any society is an index of its development. Women are the axis of the economy and their standards govern the rural market. No country can achieve its potential without adequately developing women's capabilities. In light of these initiatives by the government the objective of the article has been framed.

Objectives

- The study explores the impact of government initiatives targeted on women in agriculture by way of a case study.
- The case of Anita Devi- Mushroom lady of Bihar has been discussed to find out how government initiatives have helped her gain success and grow as an agricultural entrepreneur, along with recognising the initiatives which could have made the road to success easier.
- It also explores the constraints which have prevented women from not advancing as agricultural entrepreneurs.

Case Study: Anita Devi- Mushroom Lady of Bihar, Founder - Madhopur Farmers Producer Company Limited

About the Organisation

Anita Devi also known as Mushroom Lady of Bihar belongs to Anantpur in Nalanda and has studied Home Science. In college it was her urge to learn something that she could translate into an income-generating activity that led her to Krishi Vigyan Kendra in her district. Krishi Vigyan Kendra (KVK) was developed over various areas in different states by the ICAR under the Department of Agricultural Research and Education (DARE), Ministry of Agriculture and Farmers Welfare, Government of India. These KVKs help in coordinating, guiding and managing research and education in agriculture including horticulture, fisheries and animal sciences in the entire country and play a major role in promoting excellence in higher education in agriculture. In this case, KVK guided Anita Devi on which food crop she must plant and which could benefit her in the long run. The officials of KVK advised her to grow mushrooms and from there the journey of Anita Devi's success has started. Anita Devi's will to generate income, be self-sufficient and independent not only improved her life but also changed the fortunes of millions of women in her village. She started farming mushrooms in the year 2010 after getting trained at Dr. Rajendra Prasad Central Agriculture University, Bihar, and GB Pant University of Agriculture and Technology, Uttarakhand.

Organic mushroom farming has given a boost to the rural economy. Her success story encouraged and motivated dozens of women from her village to start mushroom farming. In 2012, the Bihar's agriculture department declared her village as Mushroom Village. Villagers now call her Mushroom Lady following her success in making mushroom cultivation so popular. As mushrooms can be cultivated easily in houses without much investment, this has become an easy, simple, viable and profitable venture for the village women. They have successfully changed their status from poverty-stricken to wealthy. Anita Devi had realised that as more and more women had started taking up mushroom farming, there was a vast demand for seeds which were not locally available. So she opted for diversification in her work.

Two years ago in 2015 Anita Devi established a high-tech laboratory for mushroom seed production after getting financial help under the **National Horticulture Mission**. The National Horticulture Mission helps women from The National Horticulture Mission which motivated her to form a high tech laboratory which could further take up research about mushroom plantations and become self-reliant. Along with education in agricultural techniques she also obtained knowledge about the various networks that could help her and other women in her community in marketing her products directly to the government agencies and NGOs. The National Horticulture Mission hence acted as a model for Anita Devi to directly sell their produce to the government agencies and NGOs. Anita Devi now sells mushroom seeds to small-scale farmers, mostly women, NGOs and also to government agencies. Her effort helped hundreds of women of her village to pull themselves out of poverty. She has now become an icon of mushroom growing in Nalanda, the mushroom farm of Bihar. Presently there are around 250 women attached with her organisation. These women have been linked to Self Help Groups formed under **Jeevika,** a rural livelihood program of Bihar government. Jeevika, is about mobilising women from impoverished, socially marginalised households into Self Help Groups. This programme focuses on building SHG of marginalised women.

Apart from mushroom farming her company 'Madhopur Farmers Producer Company Limited' is used as a common facility center in Ananthpur village supported by National Bank for Agriculture & Rural Development (NABARD's) Livelihood & Enterprise Development Program (LEDP). Around 150 SHG members were trained in making *jatasattu* (flour out of roasted gram) at 'Madhopur Farmers Producer Company Limited'.

Recommendations

Women's participation in family farms is not considered as an income generating activity- it is under most cases, another form of unpaid household work. With increasing awareness and spread of education, Indian women have started engaging in professional income earning occupations. Nowadays women have attained substantial success in every field, be itpolitics, academic, administration, industry, etc. Thereby it is the responsibility of the government and voluntary agencies to tap the previously unrecognised and unaccounted strength of women in agriculture and integrate them in the course of industrial development, particularly in small-scale industrial development of the country. A multi-branched approach is to be adopted to encourage the women to practise entrepreneurial activities. Intensive effort is required to develop soft skills and skills related to employability of women to make them established entrepreneurs. Government

The case in the study gives us an example of the Government's initiatives that play a major role in helping women to become successful entrepreneurs. Moreover it provides them with an opportunity to become self-reliant and motivated. Not only do the women achieve self-reliance but they also work for the greater good of the society, by helping and motivating other women to become financially independent. The ability of women to work hard, can lead to more economically beneficial activities, provided they have access to necessary information and resources.

Anita Devi motivated women in the villages to form SHGs which increased the scope of these women to access markets more easily and get information about training, how to access the financial support and low interest loans provided by the Government. This not only helped women become self-reliant but also motivated them to learn more about agriculture and encouraged them to become agricultural entrepreneurs. Also in the case of Anita Devi we observe that she did have the urge to become self-dependent from her youth and it is only through proper education and training that she has been able to start a business of her own and also motivated other women in her village and neighbouring areas as well. With the help of her training and necessary financial support from the Horticulture Mission she has been able to become an icon for the country.

Thus it can be said that it is only proper dissemination of information and awareness about these government initiatives and reforms which will empower women involved in agriculture. Proper education and awareness amongst the women in rural areas dealing with agricultural products may give rise to more strategically conscious agricultural entrepreneurs and more self-reliant women like Anita Devi in the near future. So the role of government cannot be overemphasised only in forming and implementing new initiatives beneficial for women but also in spreading awareness of the same, which in the long run could be very helpful in growth and development of the agricultural sector and particularly the women entrepreneurs. So the focus of the government should be on increasing awareness about the government initiatives among the rural agriculturalists. Moreover SHGs should be formed to transform the situation of marginalised women, to make them independent and self-sufficient economically.

References

All India Report of Sixth Economic Census (March 2016). Government of India: Ministry of Statistics &Programme Implementation, www.mospi.gov.in

Arjun, K.M., 2013, Indian Agriculture- Status, Importance and Role in Indian Economy,

Ashish, Mathur. 2011. "Women Entrepreneurs in the Indian Agricultural Sector." ZENITH International Journal of Business Economics & Management Research 1.2http://zenithresearch.org.in/

Clarence, H. Danhof. (1949) Observations of Entrepreneurship in Agriculture and the Entrepreneurs. Harvard University Press: Boston, Massachusetts, p.35.

DC-MSME Scheme, Development Commissioner Ministry of Micro, Small & Medium Enterprises, Retrieved from http://www.dcmsme.gov.in

Directorate of Marketing & Inspection, Ministry of Agriculture & Farmers Welfare, Government of India , http://dmi.gov.in/Schemeisam.aspx

E-NAM (June, 2017), Retrieved from https://en.wikipedia.org/wiki/E-NAMhttps://www.villagesquare.in/2017/12/01/anita-devi-anantpur-works-magic-mushrooms/ sangita-mhatre-woman-farmer

Farm Guide, Small and Marginal Land Holdings- Farmer Challenges, Retrieved from https://blog.farmguide.in/small-and-marginal-land-holdings-farmer-challenges-issues-role-in-indian-agriculture-c59b82661470

Ghosh M. & Ghosh A. (2014, May). Analysis of Women Participation in Indian Agriculture. IOSR Journal of Humanities And Social Science (IOSR-JHSS),Volume 19, Issue 5,e-ISSN: 2279-0837, p-ISSN: 2279-0845. Retrieved from www.iosrjournals.org

Global Entrepreneurship Summit (2017). Government of India Support for Innovation &Entrepreneurship in India. Retrieved from https://www.ges2017.org/govt-of-india-support-forentrepreneurs/

ICAR-Central Institute for Women in Agriculture, http://icar-ciwa.org.in/index.php/about-us

Measures Taken By Government of India for the Upliftment of Women in Agriculture Sector, Ministry of Agriculture and Farmers Welfare, Press Information Bureau, Government of India, Retrieved form http://pib.nic.in/newsite/PrintRelease.aspx?relid=148196

NSS 70thRound (2014, December). Key Indicators of Situations of Agricultural Households in Indian, Ministry of Statistics and Programme Implementation, Government of India

Overview in Agriculture Marketing (2013 March), http://vikaspedia.in/agriculture/womenand-agriculture/special-provisions-for-women-farmers-in-national-schemes

Pandey K. (September, 2018). Hard work, but low wages for women farmers, Down to Earth, Retrieved from https://www.downtoearth.org.in/news/agriculture/hard-work-but-low-wages-for-women-farmers-61656

Schaper, Michael (2002). The Essence of Ecopreneurship. Greener Management International, Vol. 38, pp. 26-30. in press.

The World Bank, India: Issues and Priorities for Agriculture (May, 2012), Retrieved from http://www.worldbank.org/en/news/feature/2012/05/17/india-agriculture-issues-priorities

Women Entrepreneurship, Promoting Youth Entrepreneurship a SIDBI Initiative (Policies/ Schemes), Retrieved from https://smallb.sidbi.in/

Part-III: Farmers' Development and Welfare through Agriculture

13

Infrastructure Investment and Rural Entrepreneurship in India: An Empirical Study

Biswajit Paul and Ashish Kumar Sana

Abstract

Out of 1.37 billion populationof India 67 % lives in rural areas whose major source of income is agriculture and allied activities (World Population Review, 2019). In simple words, the livelihood of this vast majority is closely related to rural enterprises. Fostering rural entrepreneurship may be affected by several issues, infrastructure being one of them. This paper attempts to examine the relationship between infrastructure investment by the state and rural entrepreneurship in India, with 'Gross Fixed Capital Formation' and 'Agriculture, Forestry, and Fishing, Value Added' considered as proxy variables. Time series econometrics is compiled with the data collected from World Bank Database for the period of 1961-2017. The study has established evidence in support of greater investment in infrastructure enhancing rural entrepreneurial opportunities in India.

Keywords: Rural Entrepreneurship; Infrastructure Investment; Time Series Econometrics.

Introduction

India has already marked its presence as one of the fastest growing economies of the world, in spite of being a majority rural economy. Rural entrepreneurship is therefore a buzz word that has significant relevance for the country. In simple

Today, entrepreneurship as well as rural entrepreneurship both has emerged as dynamic concepts. In general parlance, rural entrepreneurship is defined as 'entrepreneurship emerging at village level which can take place in a variety of fields of endeavour such as industry, business, agriculture and act as a potent factor for overall economic development'. (Das, 2014)

From the viewpoint of localisation, rural entrepreneurship is different from the general concept of entrepreneurship. The entrepreneurs may be based anywhere, but their enterprises have to be located in a rural area using mainly local resources, both material as well as human. Also, the enterprises may be located in a rural area though it need not be actually using 100% local material and human resources. Some amount of material and some people may be from urban centres.

The policy for rural entrepreneurship development is expected to address the problems of rural development by providing alternative occupational options to the rural youths. Entrepreneurship is one such viable option. But for the purpose of rural entrepreneurship, some basic infrastructural facilities like rural road, transport, storehouses, irrigation, housing, water supply, electrification, telecommunication etc. are absolutely essential.

At present, the Government of India is giving more emphasis on the development and expansion of rural entrepreneurship. The Government of India has allocated Rs. 187,223 crore (US$ 28.08 billion) towards rural, agriculture and allied sectors in its Union Budget 2017-18. India's per capita Gross Domestic Product (GDP) in rural regions has grown at a Compound Annual Growth Rate (CAGR) of 6.2% since 2000 (IBEF Report, 2017), whereas the CAGR of GDP of last five years is 7.3% for our country as a whole (Central Statistics Office, Ministry of Statistics and Programme Implementation, Government of India, 2018). This leads the authors to argue that there is serious need for development of the rural communities wherein entrepreneurship is one of the most attractive vehicles.

On the other hand, infrastructure investment's overall impact on economic output largely depends on how effective the investments are increasing productivity - in other words, how helpful they are in the production of goods and services. Infrastructure is a heterogeneous term, including physical structures of various types used by many industries as inputs to the production of goods and services (Chan et al., 2009). This description encompasses "social infrastructure" (such as schools and hospitals) and "economic infrastructure" (such as transport which is having a direct relationship with the productivity of the country. On the other side, social infrastructure contributes to the production process from outside the system by providing Education, Health, Training, Housing etc. related services. But in this study, a macroeconomic indicator of infrastructure investment i.e. 'Gross Fixed Capital Formation' is used as a proxy of infrastructure (OECD, *UK Economic Survey, 2015)*. The premise on which this indicator is chosen is that a rural entrepreneur can be a proactive contributor to capital formation and infrastructure development of his immediate community by improving the land (fences, ditches, drains, and so on), using plant and machinery, purchasing small necessary equipments etc. (which are all included in the World Bank Definition cited later on in this paper).

Literature Review

So far, very few studies on the relationship between infrastructure investment and rural entrepreneurship have been conducted in India as well as at the international level. To identify the research gap of the study, an attempt has been made to review some of them.

Andersen and Shimokawa (2006) showed in their study that a massive investment campaign for the construction of new rural infrastructure and maintenance of existing infrastructure in low-income developing countries is long overdue. They also mentioned that the potential benefits embodied in globalisation are not likely to be captured by low-income developing countries and their poor people. They also tried to analyse the importance of physical infrastructures such as roads, electricity generation, irrigation facilities and telecommunications in rural development.

Kigoni and Ervin (2010) studied information and communication technology solution and its objective for sustainable development to reach rural, remote, and isolated communities across the African continent. They highlighted in their study that nothing happens in a vacuum Intersat Africa and Voices of Africa for Sustainable Development are raising to the challenge to meet the information and communications needs of rural communities, using a multi-sectoral social business approach to achieve universal, affordable and equitable access through the implementation of the Rural Internet Kiosk.

Sharma et al. (2013) identified and examined the challenges observed for entrepreneurial activities in rural regions in developing countries such as that of India and the problems faced by the rural entrepreneurs for setting up of an

Patel and Chavda (2013) explained how rural entrepreneurship is nowadays a major opportunity for the people who migrate from rural areas or semi-urban areas to urban areas. They found out that the majority of rural entrepreneurs are facing many problems due to non- availability of primary amenities in rural areas of developing countries like India and with lack of education, financial problems, insufficient technical and conceptual ability, it is too difficult for the rural entrepreneurs to establish industries in the rural areas. They tried to find out the problems and challenges for the potentiality of rural entrepreneurship.

Paul and Sharma (2013) described through their study the rural people in two districts of Bihar, studying the usability of the innovations and impact of the innovations in the lifestyle of rural people. They focused on how entrepreneurship and its trails are found in rural people and they solved their issues with its help. They concluded that maximum innovations are in the field of agriculture and rural energy and are technology-based. So far the local area is benefiting from the technology and innovation, not much support is there from the government to promote.

Lavanya et al. (2014) highlighted insights into the present scenario of rural entrepreneurship – its advantages, opportunities, challenges faced by the entrepreneur, institutions promoting rural entrepreneurship and their roles in developing and fostering rural enterprises. They concluded very lucidly that rural entrepreneurship plays an important role for economic development in developing countries such as India, where it is still underdeveloped, and to bring a change the institutions need to focus on synergies between Education (including modern vocational education training/skill development), Innovation (converting ideas into wealth and employment) and Entrepreneurship.

Samanta (2015) stated that importance should be given to the development of rural roads as part of the overall development of the country. He suggested that public investment in infrastructure, specifically in the rehabilitation of rural roads, improves the local community and market development. This study also analysed some past trends and present practices related to rural transport in India. The study examined the impact of rural road infrastructure development on socio-economic conditions of the rural population, including the overall contribution to the nation. He concluded that rural roads are the wealth of a nation, a tool for social inclusion, economic development and environmental sustainability and rural roads link communities and their agricultural fields to the main transport system and markets. He also concluded that improving rural roads reduces viability of nations and it is essential for poverty eradication since global poverty is overwhelmingly rural.

Jayadatta (2017) pointed out some obstacles or challenges to overcome by looking forward to the prospects to be a successful entrepreneur. This study attempted to find out the challenges and problems for the potentiality of rural entrepreneurship and major problems faced by entrepreneurs especially in the field of marketing of products, other primary amenities like water supply, availability of electricity, transport facilities, required energy and financial amenities.

Meera (2017) tried to know who takes up entrepreneurial activities in rural areas and their social background. This was an empirical study based on data collected from rural entrepreneurs located in Bangalore rural district, Devanahally taluk, on survey method. The study found that the education of rural entrepreneurs was very less, middle-aged entrepreneurs and male-dominated entrepreneurs were more and the majority of the rural entrepreneurs were running the business with the help of family members. The researcher concluded that a person with little education, either male or female, in early age or in middle age and with or without the support of family members, can start a business and can become rural entrepreneurs.

Manggat et al. (2018) tried to investigate the impact of infrastructural development on rural communities and the role played by the social workers. They also mentioned that it is important to understand the needs and wants of the rural communities from the communities' perspective. This study contributed ideas on issues related to the impact of infrastructural development on Malaysian rural communities.

An extensive review of the literature has been done for this study. It can be said that no comprehensive research work has been done on the relationship between infrastructure investment and rural entrepreneurship as a whole in our country. So, an attempt has been made by the researchers to identify the gap and examine whether any relationship exists between them or not.

Objectives

The specific objectives of the study include:

- To investigate the long-run relationship between infrastructure investment and rural entrepreneurship in India during the period of 1961 to

Methodology

Two macroeconomic variables i.e. 'Gross Fixed Capital Formation' and 'Agriculture, Forestry, and Fishing, Value Added' have been considered mainly in this study. Gross Fixed Capital Formation has been considered as a proxy variable for overall infrastructure investment and an assumption has been made that the increase of gross fixed capital formation implies the increase of infrastructure investment throughout the country. In case of infrastructure investment, there is no demarcation of rural and urban areas because macroeconomic time series data for Gross Fixed Capital Formation (GFCF), transformed in real terms by dividing the variables with the CPI base in 2010* has been used to analyse the trends in infrastructure investment activity over the time for the whole country irrespective of rural and urban areas. (The author follows World Bank Database, base period is considered as 2010. The Laspeyres formula is generally used and data are period averages).

On the other hand, 'Agriculture, Forestry, and Fishing, Value Added' has been considered as a proxy variable for rural entrepreneurship and it is assumed that enhancement of activities like forestry, hunting and fishing, as well as cultivation of crops and livestock production etc., propels rural people to enter into the business by using the end-products of those activities. For that reason, this variable has been considered as a proxy variable for the development of rural entrepreneurship.

To investigate the relationship empirically between infrastructure investment and rural entrepreneurship in India, secondary data has been collected from the World Bank Database (WDI) for the period from 1961 to 2017 (Appendix - 1). For theoretical discussion, different books, journals, conference proceedings, government reports newspapers, magazines and websites have been consulted. The variables and their representations are being portrayed in Table 1.

Two functional regression equations have been formulated for the purpose of analysing the dynamics of the relationship between infrastructure investment and rural entrepreneurship by taking the above-mentioned variables. In the first model, 'Gross Fixed Capital Formation' has been considered as the dependent variable to examine the influence of rural entrepreneurship on infrastructure investment and in the second model, 'Agriculture, Forestry, And Fishing, A Value-Added' variable has been considered as the dependent variable to investigate the influence of infrastructure investment on rural entrepreneurship. In both the cases, the Crop Production Index has been used as a control variable

Variables and their Representations

Representation	Explanation	Source	Purpose of use
Capital _GCFL)	'Gross Fixed Capital Formation' (formerly gross domestic fixed investment) includes land improvements (fences, ditches, drains, and so on); plant, machinery, and equipment purchases; and the construction of roads, railways, and the like, including schools, offices, hospitals, private residential dwellings, and commercial and industrial buildings. According to the 1993 SNA, net acquisitions of valuables are also considered capital formation.	World Bank (World Development Indicators/WDI)	Proxy variable for Infrastructure Investment
Forestry, (AFFV)	'Agriculture, Forestry, and Fishing, Value Added' includes forestry, hunting, and fishing, as well as cultivation of crops and livestock production. Value added is the net output of a sector after adding up all outputs and subtracting intermediate inputs. It is calculated without making deductions for depreciation of fabricated assets or depletion and degradation of natural resources. The origin of value added is determined by the International Standard Industrial Classification (ISIC)[1], revision 3 or 4.	World Bank(WDI)	Proxy variable for Rural Entrepreneurship
ion Index	'Crop Production Index' shows agricultural production for each year relative to the base period 2004-2006. It includes all crops except fodder crops. Crop Production Index (2004-2006 = 100)*	World Bank(WDI)	Control Variable

resentation made by Researchers. Note: *Crop production index shows agricultural production for each year relative to the base period These indexes are calculated from the underlying values in currency, normalised to the base period 2004-2006. This base period has been y World Bank. This index is calculated by the Laspeyres formula. Production quantities of each commodity are weighted by 2004-2006 national commodity prices and summed for each year. To obtain the index, the aggregate for a given year is divided by the average r the base period 2004-2006.*

ble 1: *The International Standard Industrial Classification (ISIC) of All Economic Activities is a United Nations industry classification system. been made of ISIC in classifying data according to kind of economic activity in the fields of employment and health data. It is maintained Nations Statistics Division (Source: Wikipedia).*

$$L\_GCFL_t = \alpha_0 + \alpha_1 L\_GCFL + \alpha_2 AFFV_t + \alpha_3 CPI_t + \quad \varepsilon_t \text{ - Model (1)}$$

$$AFFV_t = \alpha_0 + \alpha_1 AFFV + \alpha_2 L\_GCFL_t + \alpha_3 CPI_t + \quad \varepsilon_t \text{ - Model (2)}$$

As the data are time series in nature, so, time series econometric techniques have been used for the analysis of data. Before doing any estimation, the researchers have performed several transformations of data. First, 'Agriculture, Forestry, and Fishing, Value Added' and 'Gross Fixed Capital Formation' are transformed in real terms by dividing the variables with the CPI base in 2010. After that, the real term of 'Gross Fixed Capital Formation' is taken in natural logarithm. The real and only log values of the variables are renamed with an "L_" sign at the front respectively.

To substantiate the methodology of this study, methodology is divided into five sub-sections, which are included in Appendix II.

Findings and Discussions

Step-wise findings of analysis of data are discussed below:

Step -1: Unit Root Test

Tables 2 and 3 both show the results of unit root tests under Augmented Dickey-Fuller (ADF) and PP methodology. The results of Unit Root Test are as follows:

Table 2: Results of Augmented Dickey-Fuller (ADF) Unit Root Test

Variables and Specifications	Level		First Difference		Order of Integration
	Statistic	Prob.	Statistic	Prob.	
L_GCFL	1.084	0.999	-6.491	0.000	I(1)
AFFV	-0.161	0.936	-7.570	0.000	I(1)
CPI	1.673	0.999	-9.306	0.000	I(1)

Source: Researchers' own estimate by using E-Views Software.
Note: Test Critical Value has been checked at 1%, 5% and 10% level of significance respectively.

Table 3: Results of Phillips-Perron (PP) Unit Root Test

Variables and Specifications	Level		First Difference		Order of Integration
	Statistic	Prob.	Statistic	Prob.	
L_GCFL	0.951	0.995	-6.556	0.000	I(1)
AFFV	-0.354	0.909	-8.982	0.000	I(1)

Since, both tests have given the same results, the variables considered in this study are all in I (1) series. For this reason, the researchers have adopted the Autoregressive Distributed Lag (ARDL) modeling approach for co-integration analysis to identify the long-run relationships between the above-mentioned sets of variables.

Step -2: ARDL Bounds Test for Co-integration

The results of the bound test of model (1) and (2) are as follows:

Table 4: Result of Autoregressive Distributed Lag Bound Test
(Model 1: Dependent variable is L_GCFL)

DW-statistic 2.3248				
Testing for existence of a level relationship among the variables in the ARDL model				
F-statistic	95% Lower	95% Upper	90% Lower	90% Upper
4.2622	Bound 5.1884	Bound6.2614	Bound 4.3580	Bound 5.3144
W-statistic	95% Lower	95% Upper	90% Lower	90% Upper
12.7865	Bound15.5652	Bound18.7843	Bound13.0740	Bound15.9433

Source: Researchers' own estimate by using Microfit 5 Software.

Table 5: Result of Autoregressive Distributed Lag Bound Test
(Model 2: Dependent variable is AFFV)

DW-statistic 2.4507				
Testing for existence of a level relationship among the variables in the ARDL model				
F-statistic	95% Lower	95% Upper	90% Lower	90% Upper
8.3634	Bound4.9961	Bound5.1884	Bound6.2614	Bound5.3144
W-statistic	95% Lower	95% Upper	90% Lower	90% Upper
14.9884	Bound15.5652	Bound18.7843	Bound13.0740	Bound15.9433

Source: Researchers' own estimate by using Microfit 5 Software.

The results of the bound test indicate that the calculated F statistic is 4.2622 (Table 4) in the case of model (1) and 8.3634 (Table 5) in the case of model (2). In model 1, the value of the F statistic is below the lower bound, that means the null hypothesis of no level effect cannot be rejected which implies that there is no long-term equilibrium among the considered variables, in the examined period but in model 2, the value of F statistic is above the upper bound, the null hypothesis of no level effect is rejected which implies that there is co-integrating relationship among the considered variables, in the examined period.

Step -3: Short-Run Error Correction Model

Table 6: Short-Run Error Correction Elasticity Estimates
(ARDL (1,0,0) selected based on Schwarz Bayesian Criterion)

Model 1: Dependent variable is L_GCFL		
Regressor	Coefficient	T-Ratio[Prob]
ECM(-1)	-.05440	-.80313[.426]

Source: Researchers' own estimate by using Microfit 5 Software.

Table 7: Short-Run Error Correction Elasticity Estimates
(ARDL (1,0,0) selected based on Schwarz Bayesian Criterion)

Model 2: Dependent variable is AFFV		
Regressor	Coefficient	T-Ratio[Prob]
ECM(-1)	-.40049	-3.7336[.000]

Source: Researchers' own estimate by using Microfit 5 Software.

Table 6 shows that the error correction coefficient for the model is negative (-.05440) but it is not statistically significant (.426), which demonstrates that there is no long-run relationship between the variables. As ECM is not working in model 1, the long run relationship must not be there, that means the variables are not moving towards equilibrium (as reflected in Table 8).

But model 2 gives the favourable result. Table 7 shows that the error correction coefficient for the model is negative (-.40049) and statistically significant (.000), which demonstrates the long-run relationships between the variables. This confirms once again, the existence of the co-integration relationship among the variables of model 2. This means that the adjustment takes place relatively quickly, i.e. the speed of adjustment is relatively high. The values indicate rapid adjustment processes, with almost the whole disequilibrium of the previous year's shock adjusting back to the long-run equilibrium in the current year.

Step -4: Estimated Long Run Coefficients

The necessary results of long-run estimations are being shown in the following two tables (Table 8 and Table 9):

Table 8: Estimated Long-Run Coefficients using the ARDL Approach (ARDL ((1,0,0)) selected based on Schwarz Bayesian Criterion)

Dependent variable is L_GCFL Testing for existence of a level relationship among the variables in the ARDL model				
F-statistic	95% Lower	95% Upper	90% Lower	90% Upper
4.2622	Bound5.1884	Bound6.2614	Bound4.3580	Bound5.3144
W-statistic	95% Lower	95% Upper	90% Lower	90% Upper
12.7865	Bound15.5652	Bound18.7843	Bound13.0740	Bound15.9433

Source: Researchers' own estimate by using Microfit 5 Software.

Table 9: Estimated Long-Run Coefficients using the ARDL Approach (ARDL (1,0,0) selected based on Schwarz Bayesian Criterion)

Dependent variable is AFFV Testing for existence of a level relationship among the variables in the ARDL model				
F-statistic	95% Lower	95% Upper	90% Lower	90% Upper
8.3634	Bound4.9961	Bound5.1884	Bound6.2614	Bound5.3144
W-statistic	95% Lower	95% Upper	90% Lower	90% Upper
14.9884	Bound15.5652	Bound18.7843	Bound13.0740	Bound15.9433

Source: Researchers' own estimate by using Microfit 5 Software.

In the case of the long-run estimation, as per expectation, only model 2 gives the favourable result. That means estimation result from model 2 reveals that infrastructure investment is having a long-run influence on rural entrepreneurship.

Step -5: Stability Tests

A graphical representation of Cumulative Sum Control Chart (CUSUM) and Cumulative Sum of Squares (CUSUMQ) statistics are shown in Figure 1 to 4.

It can be clearly stated from figures 1 and 2 that the plots of both the CUSUM and the CUSUMQ are within the boundaries and by that, these statistics confirm the long-run relationships among variables and it establishes the stability of the models 1. But for model 2, figures 3 and 4 show that the plots of both the CUSUM and the CUSUMQ are not within the boundaries throughout the period which confirms that model 2 is not stable for the selected period.

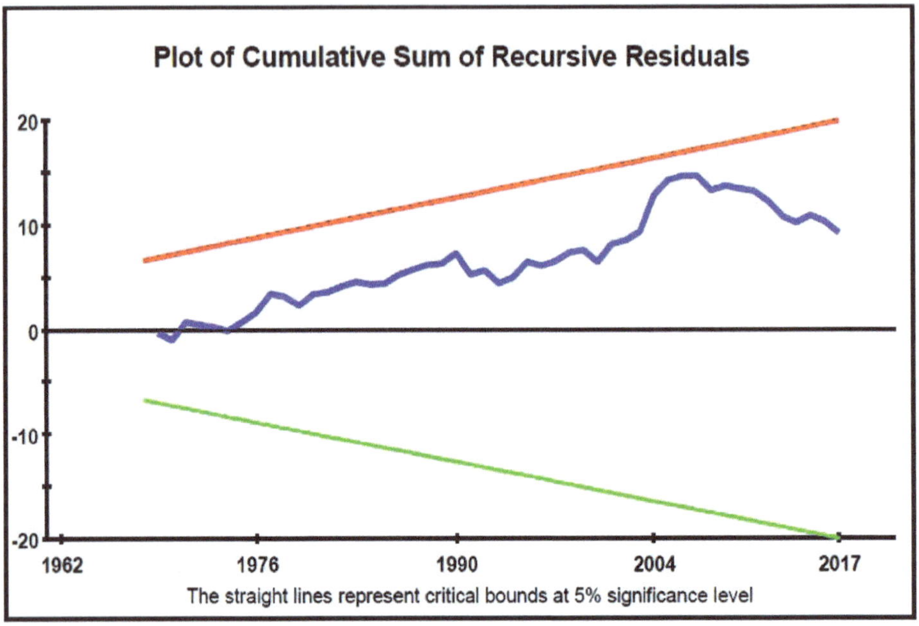

Fig. 1: Plot of Cumulative Sum of Recursive Residuals

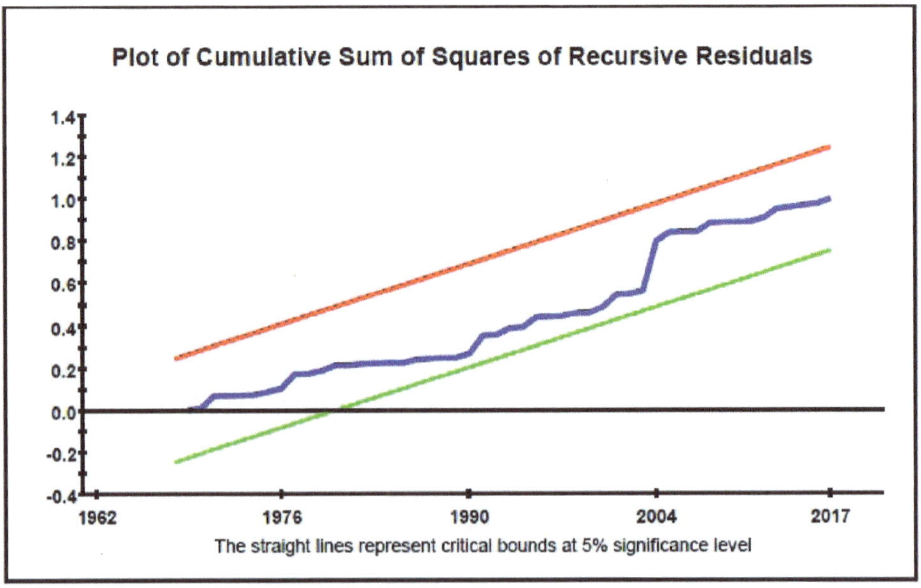

Fig. 2: Plot of Cumulative Sum of Recursive Residuals

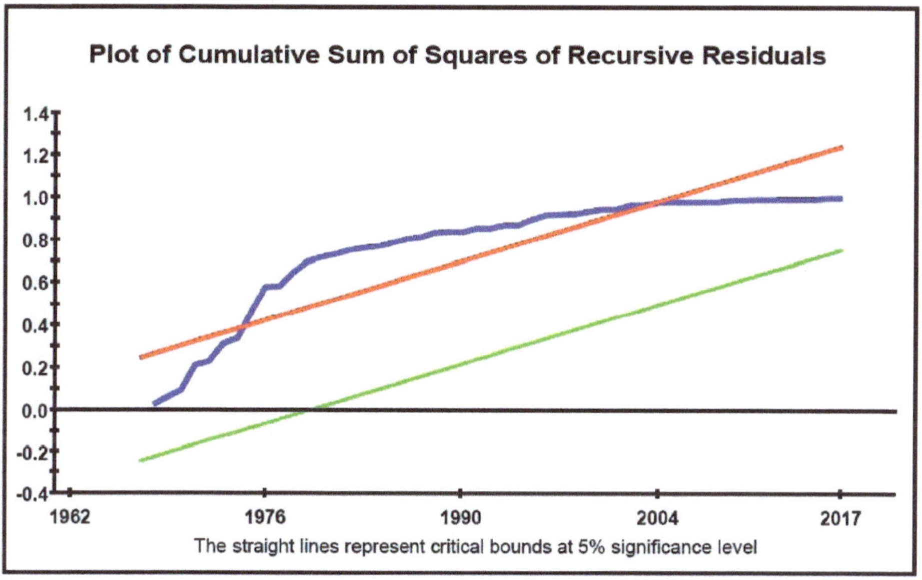

Fig. 3: Plot of Cumulative Sum of Residuals

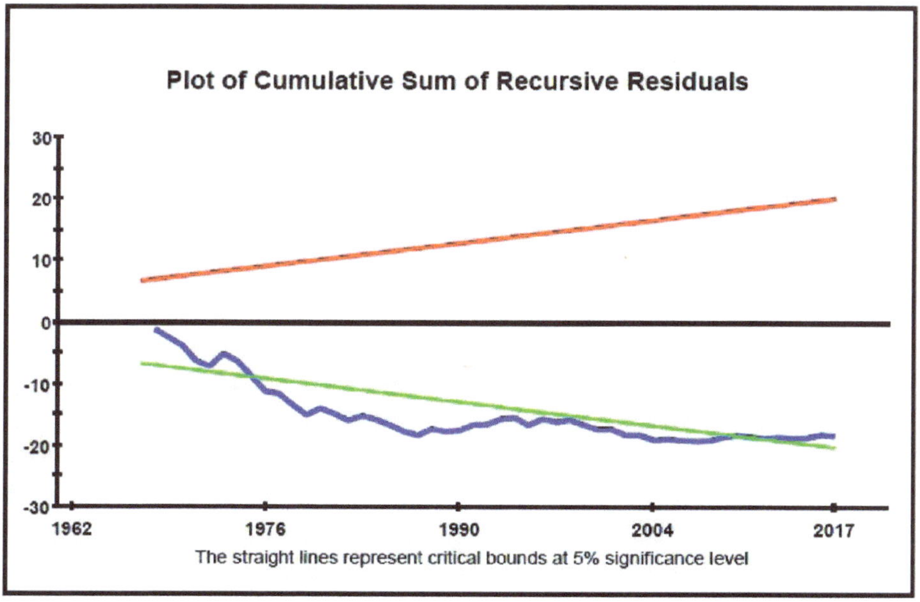

Fig. 4: Plot of Cumulative Sum of Recursive Residuals

Conclusion

The objective of this study was to investigate empirically the relationship between infrastructure investment and rural entrepreneurship in India. From the analysis it can be concluded that rural entrepreneurship does not have any influence on infrastructure investment but infrastructure investment has influence on rural entrepreneurship. It is revealed that more infrastructure would be required if entrepreneurial activities grow in rural areas but rural infrastructure alone does not ensure more entrepreneurial activities in those areas.

As a part of our country's policy implications, it may also be reviewed how the infrastructure can be used for the development of rural entrepreneurship in a better way. The Government of India and other State Governments have taken more initiatives to develop the rural economy. Since the rural economy is basically based on agriculture and rural entrepreneurship is usually agriculture based, it is necessary to promote sustainable, inclusive business opportunities for the rural poor through agri-business, which has been examined in the study. Further, more investment in infrastructure ensures more agri-entrepreneurship, thereby supporting creation, promotion and development of agri- entrepreneurship.

References

Andersen, Per Pinstrup. and Shimokawa, Satoru. (2006). Rural Infrastructure and Agricultural Development. Annual Bank Conference on Development Economics, Tokyo, Japan. May 29-30, 2006.

Banerjee, A., J. Dolado and R. Mestre, (1998). Error-correction mechanism tests for cointegration in the single equation framework. J. Time Series Analysis. 19: 267-83.

Das, Dilip Ch. (2014). Prospects and Challenges of Rural Entrepreneurship Development in NER-A Study. International Journal of Humanities & Social Science Studies. Volume-I. Issue-III. November 2014. pp. 178-182.

Dickey, D. A., Fuller, W. A. (1981). Likelihood Ratio Statistics for Autoregressive Time Series with a Unit Root. Econometrica. Vol. - 49. pp. 1057–72.

Dickey, D. A., Fuller, W. A. (1981). Likelihood Ratio Statistics for Autoregressive Time Series with a Unit Root. Econometrica. Vol. - 49, pp. 1057–72.

IBEF Report (2017)

India Rural Development Report, Economic Survey (1996-97)

Jayadatta, S. (2017). Major Challenges and Problems of Rural Entrepreneurship in India. IOSR Journal of Business and Management (IOSR-JBM). Volume – 19. Issue - 9. Ver. II. pp. 35-44.

Johansen, S. (1991). Estimation and Hypothesis Testing of Cointegration Vectors in Gaussian Vector Autoregressive Models. Econometrica. Vol. - 59. No. 6 (Nov., 1991). pp. 1551-1580.

Kigoni, Crystal Watley. and Ervin, Hilary. N. (2010). ICTs, Infrastructure and Entrepreneurship.

Meera, H. N. (2017). A Study on Impact of Social Background to Rural Entrepreneurship. International Journal of Research Culture Society. Volume – 1. Issue – 7. Sept – 2017.

OECD, UK Economic Survey. (2015). Improving Infrastructure. February 2015.cited in http://researchbriefings.files.parliament.uk/documents/SN06594/SN06594.pdf.

Patel, Brijesh. and Chavda, Kirit. (2013). Rural Entrepreneurship in India: Challenge and Problems. International Journal of Advance Research in Computer Science and Management Studies. Volume 1. Issue 2. July, 2013

Paul, Mansi. and Sharma, Achla. (2013). Entrepreneurship as a Tool for Rural Development. Global Journal of Management and Business Studies. Volume 3. No. 3 (2013). pp. 319-322.

Pesaran, H.M. and B. Pesaran, (1997). Working with Microfit 4.0: Interactive Econometric Analysis. Oxford University Press.

Pesaran, M. H. and Y. Shin. (1996). Cointegration and speed of convergence to equilibrium. Journal of Econometrics. 71: 117-43.

Pesaran, M.H., Y. Shin and R. Smith. (2001). Bounds testing approaches to the analysis of level relationships. J. Appl. Economy. 16: 289-326.

S. Moghana Lavanya, S. Hemalatha & V. M. Indumathi (2014). Perspectives of Rural Entrepreneurship in India. Samzodhana – Journal of Management. Vol. - 3. Issue – 1. October 2014.

SA, Shane. (2003). A General Theory of Entrepreneurship: The Individual-Opportunity Nexus. A General Theory of Entrepreneurship: The Individual-Opportunity Nexus. 1-327. 10.4337/9781781007990.00001.

Samanta, Pradeepta Kumar. (2015). Development of Rural Road Infrastructure in India. Pacific Business Review International. Volume 7. Issue 11. May, 2015.

Samreth, Sovannroeun (2008),. "Estimating Money Demand Function in Cambodia: ARDL Approach". MPRA. Paper No. 16274.

Sharma, Monika., Chaudhary, Vandana., Bala, Rajni., and Chauhan, Ranchan. (2013). Rural Entrepreneurship in Developing Countries: Challenges, Problems and Performance Appraisal. Global Journal of Management and Business Studies. Volume – 3- 9. pp. 1035-1040.

Vedanthadesikan, G. and Pathmanathan, P. (2016). Rural Entrepreneurship - An Indian Scenario. International Journal of Humanities & Social Science Studies (IJHSSS). Volume-III. Issue-II. September, 2016. pp. 88-95.

www.indiapopulation2019.in

www.worldpopulationreview.com

Appendix I

Appendix 1: Data for the Study

Year	Crop production index (CPI)	Agriculture, forestry, and fishing, value added (AFFV)	Gross fixed capital formation at constant LCU (GCFL)	Gross fixed capital formation at constant LCU (L_GCFL)
1961	34.95	40.85168	1103191398400	27.7292283664
1962	34.64	38.81244	1208386178100	27.8203068482
1963	35.66	39.77176	1369159952000	27.9452184940
1964	36.61	41.66122	1487283690700	28.0279725458
1965	34.47	39.39993	1536424672900	28.0604791922
1966	34.15	40.48557	1542992120700	28.0647445828
1967	36.78	43.25927	1619696719800	28.1132600376
1968	38.59	42.11216	1680546718100	28.1501402838
1969	39.94	41.83379	1685851231800	28.1532917342
1970	42.44	40.3868	1622735648900	28.1151345131
1971	43.02	38.53776	1795565087200	28.2163409001
1972	40.60	38.45476	1884848009900	28.2648683022
1973	44.16	41.63523	1856880646700	28.2499191241
1974	42.24	38.63883	1945795337000	28.2966919230
1975	47.05	35.67495	1941746060100	28.2946087152
1976	46.00	33.82742	2135356034600	28.3896545096
1977	50.24	35.34948	2393477370200	28.5037683910
1978	52.40	33.54124	2502463179700	28.5482966346
1979	48.82	31.64056	2491149533900	28.5437653801
1980	50.43	33.4375	2690255575600	28.6206573145
1981	54.02	32.07973	2797599891700	28.6597829840
1982	52.74	30.9219	2975022136400	28.7212725957
1983	59.44	31.68424	3165458640600	28.7833190712
1984	60.31	30.49335	3278670078900	28.8184589924
1985	61.21	28.96447	3458718785800	28.8719193433
1986	61.16	27.78453	3787751760600	28.9627937560
1987	59.85	27.19312	4014872456500	29.0210266961
1988	67.00	28.3039	4292428873600	29.0878738597
1989	71.58	27.22738	4622052102000	29.1618599003
1990	72.59	27.20563	5250603095900	29.2893640613
1991	73.68	27.64743	4958300191300	29.2320840946
1992	77.07	26.97636	5404453455400	29.3182444436
1993	79.74	27.19083	5354451270200	29.3089493440
1994	82.07	26.69197	5860884359700	29.3993216228
1995	83.68	24.738	6814326195400	29.5500483054
1996	87.07	25.70922	7021943192600	29.5800611037

2001	94.78	21.86905	10293151376900	29.9624998751
2002	84.74	19.76129	10248281158300	29.9581311156
2003	96.97	19.8057	11331247726400	30.0585853108
2004	94.12	18.01946	14048669654900	30.2735488207
2005	99.90	17.84226	16323618138500	30.4236341406
2006	105.98	17.39412	18579079608000	30.5530573114
2007	116.23	17.33146	21589404601200	30.7032237825
2008	117.28	17.3101	22346576806700	30.7376942622
2009	112.83	17.28273	24059706492500	30.8115596274
2010	124.91	17.51735	26705141831900	30.9158772408
2011	134.07	17.19197	29977328688700	31.0314625015
2012	136.19	16.84538	31457931948100	31.0796722755
2013	141.74	17.14842	31949243100300	31.0951696063
2014	144.36	16.79193	33021727508500	31.1281868701
2015	139.61	16.16799	35184458985200	31.1916255949
2016	142.83	16.28459	36020414632000	31.2151069668
2017	145.23	15.45026	36020414632000	31.2151069668

Source: World Development Indicators, World Bank.

Appendix II

1. Unit Root Test

A unit root test examines whether a time series variable is non-stationary and possesses a unit root. If the data series are non-stationary then time series modeling cannot be done. For that reason, at first, the researchers applied the unit root test. Dickey and Fuller (1979) and Phillips and Perron (1988) are two popular unit root tests which are employed in this study. In most literature, these tests have been used extensively in order to find out the order of integration i.e. stationarity at which level. To apply time series econometrics, the data series must be stationary. So, the stationarity of the variables is assessed by testing the presence of unit roots by using The Augmented Dickey-Fuller (1981; ADF, henceforth) and the Phillips and Perron (1988; PP, henceforth). The Augmented Dickey-Fuller (1981; ADF, henceforth) test used on the basis of the following regression:

$$\Delta Y_t = \alpha + \beta_t + \gamma_i Y_{t-1} + \Sigma^n_{i=1} \lambda_i \Delta Y_{t-1} + \varepsilon_t$$

Where Y_t is the variable under consideration, Δ is the first difference operator and α, β, γ, λ are the parameters to be estimated. The test of unit root involves testing $\lambda = 0$. The null hypothesis is that the variables have a unit root. Analysing the result of ADF and the PP test of stationarity, the test reveals that the selected variables are stationary at I (1) order of integration.

2. Autoregressive Distributed Lag' or ARDL Bounds Test for Co-integration

After unit root test, to examine the short-run as well as the long-run relationship between infrastructure investment and rural entrepreneurship in India, the researchers have used the already well-known though relatively new co-integration techniques of ARDL. Co-integration is the existence of long-run relationship between two or more variables.

A team of work led by Pesaran and Shin (1996), Pesaran and Pesaran (1997) and Pesaran et al. (2001) introduced an alternative co-integration technique known as the 'Autoregressive Distributed Lag' or ARDL bound test. It is argued that ARDL has a number of advantages over conventional Johansen co-integration techniques. To start with, the ARDL is a more statistically significant approach for determining co-integrating relationships in small samples (Ghatak and Siddiki, 2001), while the Johansen co-integration techniques still require large data samples for the purposes of validity. As stated above, a further advantage of the ARDL is that while other co-integration techniques require all of the regress to be integrated of the same order, the ARDL can be applied whether the regressors are I (1) and/or I (0). This means that it avoids the pre-testing problems associated with standard co-integration, which requires that variables are already classified I (1) or I (0) (Pesaran et al., 2001).

In this study, to assess the presence of long-run relationship among the selected variables and their dynamics methodology suggests to apply the ARDL bound test approach of co-integration followed by the ECM-ARDL model, which is introduced by Peasran, Shine, and Smith (2001). The estimable form of ECM-ARDL model is stated below:

$$\Delta L\_GCFL_t = \alpha + \Sigma^n_{i=0}\, \beta_i \Delta L\_GCFL_{t-i} + \Sigma^n_{i=0}\, \gamma_i \Delta AFFV_{t-i} + \Sigma^n_{i=0}\, \theta_i \Delta CPI_{t-i} + \mu_1\, L\_GCFL_t + \mu_2\, AFFV_t + \mu_3\, CPI_t + \lambda\, ecm_{t-1} + \varepsilon_t$$

$$\Delta\, AFFV_t = \alpha + \Sigma^n_{i=0}\, \beta_i \Delta\, AFFV_{t-i} + \Sigma^n_{i=0}\, \gamma_i \Delta L\_GCFL_{t-i} + \Sigma^n_{i=0}\, \theta_i \Delta CPI_{t-i} + \mu_1\, AFFV_t + \mu_2\, L\_GCFL_t + \mu_3\, CPI_t + \lambda\, ecm_{t-1} + \varepsilon_t$$

Where the parameter λ indicates error correction term or speed of adjustment to restore equilibrium, and 'n' is the optimum lag-length(s) chosen for the estimation. The parameters β_i, γ_i, and θ_i and indicate short-run multiplier, while parameters μ_1, μ_2, and μ_3 stand for the long-run multiplier. In this model, the null hypothesis of no co-integration implies $\mu_1 = \mu_2 = \mu_3 = 0$ and the alternative hypothesis of existing co-integrating relation implies $\mu \neq \mu \neq \mu \neq 0$.

3. Short-Run Error Correction Model

As the bound test has given the favorable result to proceed with further analysis, the researchers have applied a short-run error correction mechanism or model (ECM) under the ARDL framework. The error correction term indicates the speed of the adjustment which restores equilibrium in the dynamic model. The ECM coefficient shows how quickly variables return to equilibrium and it should have a statistically significant coefficient with a negative sign. Bannerjee et al. (1998) holds that a highly significant error correction term is further proof of the existence of a stable long-term relationship. If ECM is working in any model, then the long run relationship in the said model must be there.

4. Estimated Long Run Coefficients

When ECM is found working, the long run equilibrium relationship has been estimated by long run coefficients between the variables for both the models.

5. Stability Tests

Lastly, to analyze the stability of the long-run coefficients (calculated) together with the short-run dynamics, the cumulative sum (CUSUM) and the cumulative sum of squares (CUSUM) are applied. CUSUM and CUSUMSQ test roughly support the stability of the estimated model (Samreth, 2008).

14

Entrepreneurship in Food Processing Industry in India

Alokananda Bhattacharya

Abstract

India is the second largest food producing country in the world. Food processing is one of the key industries in the country and a sector that has direct linkage between agriculture and industry. Being the second largest producer of fruits and vegetables along with its strategic geographic location and proximity to food importing nations, India is in an advantageous position in terms of exporting processed food. As per estimates, Indian food processing sector stood at USD258 billion in the financial year 2015. The growth and development of this industry have direct impact on the Indian economy. The aim of the present study is to discuss about the growth of the food processing industry, analyse its strengths and weaknesses and generate possibilities of entrepreneurial development towards the expansion of the sector. This study has been a secondary data analysis based on data collected from journals, magazines, web searches and reports from various government and private agencies.

The study has identified the main drivers aiding to the growth of the sector. It includes strong domestic demand, rising export opportunities; supply side advantages for exporters due to rising global demand and strong policy support from the Government. On the other hand, fragmented market, infrastructure support, namely cold chain, innovation and skill development are the major hurdles that have to be overcome. This article makes an attempt to explore entrepreneurial opportunities and few areas where new business could be initiated. The entrepreneurial opportunities highlighted in this paper are based on Drucker's opportunity construct that entrepreneurs have an eye more for possibilities created by change

Introduction

India with second largest arable land in the world and 127 agro-climatic zones (Ministry of Finance, 2015) has a large raw material base for food industry. India is the second largest producer of food in the world and is expected to double its food production in the next ten years.

At the same time, Food Processing Industry (FPI) is the bridge between two major pillars of the economy, agriculture sector and manufacturing sector. FPI termed as the 'Sunrise industry' in India, has undergone a significant transformation over the last decade. Abundant supply of raw materials, increased demand of processed food, policies and incentives offered by the Government, have resulted positive growth towards the FPI over the decades. During the four years ending 2015-16, this sector is growing at a faster rate on average compared to the agriculture sector. An average annual growth rate of around 2.88 percent was observed in the food processing sector compared to 1.88 percent in agriculture and 6.61 percent to manufacturing sector at 2011-12 prices (MoFPI Annual Report, 2017-18). With its immense potential to generate rural income and reduction of food wastage the industry has earned 'high priority' status from the Government of India. The Indian food processing industry accounts for 32 percent of the country's total food market, one of the largest industries in India and is ranked fifth in terms of production, consumption, export and expected growth. FPI contributes around 14 percent of manufacturing Gross Domestic Product (GDP), 13 percent of India's exports and six percent of total industrial investment (India Briefing, 2017).

In spite of strong growth in the sector, FPI in India is still facing few challenges. The growth is suffering mainly from the constraints like non-availability of adequate infrastructural facilities, lack of adequate quality control, testing infrastructure and applied research, inefficient supply chain, seasonality of raw material supply and inadequacy of cold chain systems. Considering these challenges and understanding the importance of food processing sector, Government of India aims to boost growth in the sector by adopting new policies and strategies. Leveraging reforms such as 100 percent Foreign Direct Investment (FDI) in marketing of food products and various incentives at central and state government level along with a strong focus on supply chain infrastructure are some of these initiatives. As per Department of Industrial Policies and Promotion (DIPP), the food processing sector in India has received around USD 7.54 billion worth of Foreign Direct Investment (FDI) during the and Industry of India (ASSOCHAM),Confederation of Indian Industry (CII), and Competition Commission of India (CCI) etc.

Food Processing Industry

Food processing is a technique of value addition to the agricultural, horticultural, dairy, poultry and marine produce in an effective manner with a view to enhance their shelf life; improve quality as well as make them functionally more useful. The food processing sector mainly comprises of two segments- primary processed food and secondary or value added food. Primary segment includes basic cleaning, grading and packaging as fruits & vegetables. The level of value additions is least. It comprises of packaged fruit and vegetables, milk, flour, rice, spices etc. and constitutes around 62 percent value in terms of the total processed foods. Value added segment includes alteration of the basic products to a value added product. It covers processing of fruits and vegetables, to make juices, jam and jelly etc. and holds around 38 percent share in the total processed food segment.

Advancement of food processing sector helps the growth of the economy by improving value addition, reducing the wastage, increasing employment and promoting higher export returns. The unorganised sector accounts for 42 percent of India's FPI. In fact, more than 75 percent of the processing units are unorganised or small-scale in nature. The organised sector has a larger share in the secondary processing units than the primary units with rice mills having largest share among the processing units in the organised sector.

Over the decades India has become a food surplus country with the success of Green Revolution. The estimated growth of Indian food and retail industry would be USD482 billion in 2020 from USD258 billion in 2015 (IBEF report, 2017). The sector has been growing at a faster rate than agriculture sector in 2015-16 in terms of 5 years annual average growth rate and the gross value addition (GVA) of food processing sector is 8.71 percent in agriculture and 10.04 percent in the manufacturing sector in 2015-16 at 2011-12 prices (MoFPI Annual Report, 2017-18).

At the same time, food processing sector is a highly labour intensive industry having key contribution in employment generation. In 2014-15, among all registered factories FPI generated 12.77 percent of employment. A steady growth is observed in the employment of registered food processing units since 2009-10 till 2014-15 (Annual Report 2017-18, MoFPI). As per National Sample

India's share in global agricultural export is 2.2 percent. The Agricultural & Processed Food Products Export Development Authority (APEDA) is a Government of India initiative that promotes exports oriented production and development of the scheduled products. The total exports of agricultural products during 2016-17 were over USD 30 billion. In this the share of APEDA products is valued at $ 16.25 billion which is about 49 percent of the total agricultural exports from India (APEDA report, 2017).

India has a locational advantage of being close to Middle Eastern countries which are key export destinations. Export scenario of the FPI also looks promising with 5 year average annual growth rate of 0.25 percent in total export of the processed food products from India as on year ending 2016-17. Although there was a slump in export value in the years 2013-14 and 2015-16, a positive growth was observed in 2016-17. The growth could be primarily accounted for several Government initiatives along with successful export promotion strategies and rising global demand with the growth of the world economy.

Table 1: Export of Processed Food in India
Export of Processed food in India (in million USD)

Year	2011-12	2012-13	2013-14	2014-15	2015-16	2016-17	AAGR
FPI Exports	31459.58	35898.06	38051.43	36171.92	29672.37	30871.47	
0.25percent*							
e Growth (percent)		14.11	6	-4.94	-17.9	4.04	

*Source: MOFPI Annual Report, 2016-17 *Five Year Average Annual Growth Rate for year ending 2016-17*

Key Drivers of Growth of FPI

The growth of FPI in India was resulted from several natural, economic and strategic factors. India has got a natural advantage of diverse agro-climatic conditions, wide variety of crops and population growth. With urbanisation and increase in young and middle class population and rising disposable income strong domestic demand of processed food is climbing up. The consumption pattern of the population is driving towards convenience foods which led to a boost in the demand side of the food processing sector. India's integration into the global economy and surge in global demand along with its proximities to export destinations, the demand of Indian processed food in the export market is rising.

food processing was launched to promote post-harvest operations and setting up food processing industries in the country. As per latest revision of Goods and Service Tax (GST) rates, almost 66 percent of the food items are on lowest tax slabs (MoFPI annual report, 2017-18). Foreign Direct Investment (FDI) inflows for the sector have played a major role in the growth. These investments were used in setting up mega food parks help to achieve faster growth of FPI.

Entrepreneurial Opportunities in the Food Processing Industry

FPI in India with its unique positioning at the crossroads of agriculture, manufacturing and service industry has huge potential to contribute to the economy but is still at an early stage of development and suffers from few constraints. The challenges may be addressed as far as possible by suitably nurturing the innovative Star ups and small agro-entrepreneurs to strengthen the growth of the sector which has a great capability to dominate the global market. To foster development and growth of sector, identification of strengths, weaknesses, opportunities and threats (SWOT) of the industry is imperative. From various reports and research in this field the following points emerge.

Strengths

- Seasonal cultivation of fruits and vegetables ensure that demand for processed and preserved product is perennial.
- Acknowledgement from the Government of India as 'high priority' sector and related support
- Huge domestic market with world's second largest population base
- Demographic changes in domestic market creating demand for convenience of processed food

Weaknesses

- Low processing efficiency with traditional technologies in unorganised sector
- Unattractive hurdles of conversion compared to other professions
- Bureaucratic hurdles of conversion from unorganised to organised sector
- Inadequate linkage between research and development laboratories and

Opportunities

- Immense potential of agro processing activities being second largest food producing country
- Demographic and economic changes with urbanisation, change of lifestyle and growing disposable income increase the demand of processed food
- Global markets provide export market of processed food with India specialising on tropical fruits
- Generation of more employment and income with the development of agro- entrepreneurial opportunities

Threats

- Supply chain infrastructural gaps mainly because FPI needs special storage
- Lack of product development and innovation
- Seasonality and supply fluctuations of agricultural produce
- Competition from inorganic fruit substitutes
- Quality standards violation may bring loss of goodwill

This SWOT analysis of the FPI in India enables the author to posit the immense entrepreneurship potential that exists in the sector. The opportunities of domestic and global demand, substantiated by government lead initiatives are positive pathways for entrepreneurial activities. The challenges discussed in this paper are clean indication for forthcoming entrepreneurs who would match technology to solve the challenges of FPI.

Entrepreneurship becomes a crucial factor with more entrepreneur engagement and government initiatives to strengthen the vital linkage between the two pillars of the Indian economy namely agriculture and industry. The author posits that entrepreneurs identify business opportunities in the FPI sector to create and deliver value for stakeholders in prospective ventures. In opportunity based entrepreneurship, entrepreneurs do not cause change but exploit the opportunities that change creates (in technology, consumer preferences etc.) (Drucker, 1985). The entrepreneur searches for required change, respond to it, and exploit it as an opportunity". The entrepreneurial opportunities highlighted in this paper are based on Drucker's opportunity construct that entrepreneurs have an eye more

II and Tier III cities of India. More and more people are getting to learn about the benefits of packaged food with low-cost access to the internet.

One of the major challenges of the food processing sector is the mismanagement in the supply chain of fruits and vegetables and dairy products. Forward and backward integration gives the business a competitive edge which may be utilised by entrepreneurs. The establishment of value addition and preservation facilities for agricultural, horticultural, dairy, fish & marine, poultry & meat products by creating linkages from farm gate to the consumer, end to end, to reduce wastage through efficient storage, transportation and minimal processing could be seen as entrepreneurship development in this sector. To facilitate sustainable food processing, maximum utilization of all raw materials produced and integration of activities throughout all the production-to-consumption stages is required. New innovations and business ideas like mobile refrigeration, packaging, quality compliance check etc. could reduce postharvest losses and increase use of by-products.

Entrepreneurial endeavours may also use positive dynamics like supply side advantages, huge market base, rising export opportunities and government support. MSEs within this segment often lack managerial capacities and have insufficient knowledge of business and use of modern technologies as well as of operational and production cycles. Entrepreneurs in the field of human resource development are necessary to meet increasing demand for skilled manpower. Academia and government need hand holding for development of specialised institutes and courses for providing training on managerial, safety and enforcements, packaging and processing technology and production, warehousing and distribution aspects. Small-scale processing enterprises also find it difficult to deal with policy and regulatory challenges bureaucracy that impact the sector and thus, become competitive in domestic and international markets. Such challenges of the SME close off unusual entrepreneurial venture openings. Development of the supply-side of the unorganized sector through clustering and upgrading of micro and small enterprises (MSEs) and collective and individual actions to improve management, quality, safety, production and sustainability practices could push towards significant and healthy boost of the sector.

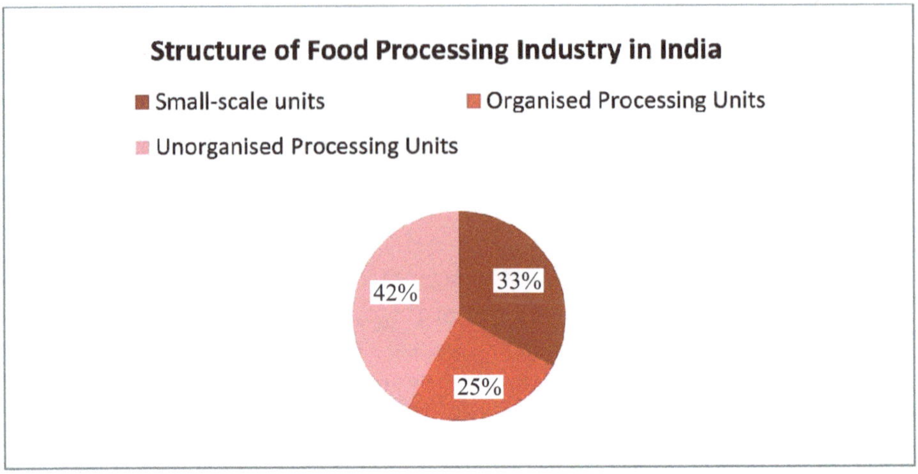

Fig. 1: Structure of Food Processing Industry in India
Source: Annual Report 2014-15 Ministry of Food Processing Industries

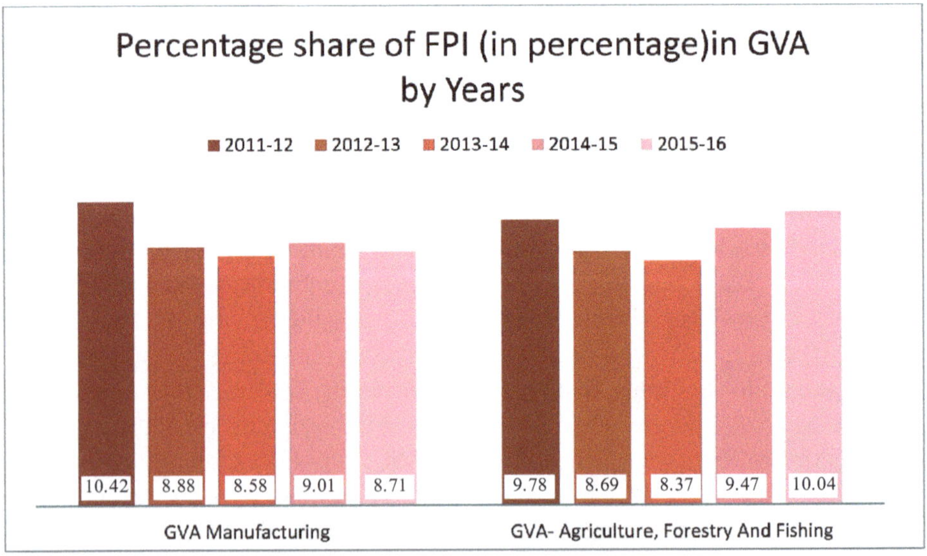

Fig. 2: Percentage Share of FPI in GVA
Source: Annual Report 2017-18 Ministry of Food Processing Industries

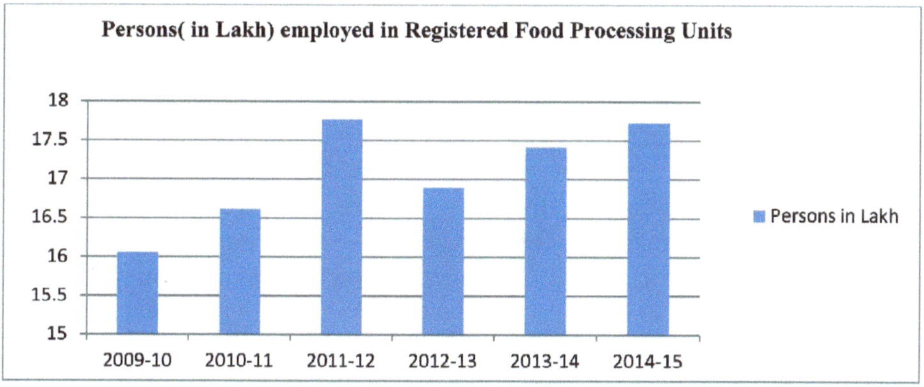

Fig. 3: Employment in Registered Food Processing Units
Source: Annual Report 2017-18 Ministry of Food Processing Industries

Conclusion

The Indian food processing industry has seen a drastic positive transformation in last decade driven by the rise in strong growth of demand growth for processed food with the growing young population, urbanisation and disposable income. The online food ordering and delivery business in recent years has taken the sector to a new height. Although in its early stages, the immense potential of the industry as a means of generating rural income and reducing food wastage has encouraged the Government of India to accord 'high priority' status to this sector. Several initiatives have been undertaken with the objective of promoting investments, innovation and bringing best practices. The Indian government has taken steps to boost the food industry by allowing the Indian food manufacturers to sell its products manufactured in India through wholesale and/or retail, including through e-commerce. Favourable supply side fundamentals (abundant raw materials supply, cost advantages) are also helping the country to become a potential global outsourcing hub in near future.

FPI in India, ranking fifth in industries having a considerable share in the manufacturing and agriculture sector, still could process only 2.2 percent of total food produce due to lack of improved technological and infrastructural framework. Only a handful of companies have full-fledged research and development centres to bring out innovative and quality conscious products. Demand-based innovation and effective technology transfer from research laboratory to food processing units is a major challenge faced by this sector.

Moving forward, good food safety and quality practices would enable adherence food testing infrastructure by upgrading its existing food testing laboratories and set up new mobile testing labs.

The study has indicated that vast opportunities exist to the entrepreneurs for development of FPI and reduce agro and horticulture produce wastages, value addition, generation of employment and increase of farmers' income. Technology has increased the awareness of the consumers and they are now conscious in including nutrition in their daily food intake. As a result, numerous new products like dietary supplements, weight management diet, probiotics, sports energy drinks etc. are coming to the market and are gaining prominence. Innovation of new products and efficient technology transfer will play vital role entrepreneurial growth in this sector. All initiatives when implemented in proper manner would lead to a well-developed food processing sector which will ensure reduction in food wastages, increase in value addition, more employment and export earnings and would make India a global outsourcing hub and thus strengthen the economy of the country.

References

APEDA. (2017). Export Promotion Strategy of APEDA products (Part 1). New Delhi http://apeda.gov.in/apedahindi/Announcements/FINALEXPORTSTRATEGY11.09.2017.pdf

Ardichvilia,A. Cardozob,R. Ray.S, (2003). A theory of entrepreneurial opportunity identification and development. Journal of Business Venturing 18 (2003) 105 – 123

ASSOCHAM. (2015). Make in India: Pressing the Pedal. New Delhi: Economics knowledge Banking, Yes Bank and Associated Chamber of Commerce and Industry in India.

DIPP, Ministry of Commerce. (2014). Make in India.

Drucker, P.F. (1985).Innovation and Entrepreneurship. New York: Harper & Row Publishers

FICCI. (2010). Bottlenecks in Indian Food Processing Industries.Federation of Indian Chambers of Commerce and Industry.

IBEF report (June,2017). www.ibef.org

Ministry of Finance. (2015). Economic Survey 2015-16. New Delhi: Ministry of Finance, Governmnet of India.

MOFPI, Government of India. (2017). Annual Report 2016-17. New Delhi: Ministry of Food Processing Industries, Government of India.

MOFPI, Government of India. (2018). Annual Report 2017-18. New Delhi: Ministry of Food Processing Industries, Government of India.

Negi, S. (2013). Food Processing Entrepreneurship for Rural Development: Drivers and Challenges. In IIM, SUSCON III Third International Conference on Sustainability: Ecology, Economy & Ethics (pp. 186-197). New Delhi: Tata McGraw Hill Education, ISBN-13978-1-25-905869-1.

Vasundhara Rastogi, 2017, The Food Processing Industry In India: Investment Prospects, India Briefing, India. www.india-briefing.com

15

Role of Marketing Intelligence in Agriculture as a Business

Tuhin Narayan Roy

Abstract

This paper studies the role and status of Indian Agricultural Market Intelligence System (IAMIS) in improving the economic returns of agri-sector in India. Marketing intelligence makes agricultural marketers, including agri-entrepreneurs, aware and updated and reduces risk in decision making. India produced 275.112 million tonnes of food grains in 2016-17 and the projected requirement is 311million tonnes in 2030. Income of farmers has increased at a CAGR of 10.61% and number of farmers has declined at a CAGR of -0.25% from 1993-94 to 2014-15. Acreage remains stagnant. Given this background, to exploit full potential of agricultural production, market intelligence has a great role. The DES and Department of Food with their 435 market information systems (MIS) units transmit daily information through public media. The essential pre-requisite of ensuring farmers' income is that they need credible information about "likely price situation". Agriculture Marketing Intelligence System (AMIS, 2011) has emerged with the aim to provide services in agriculture and allied sectors. ICAR (1991) took initiatives under World Bank to assist National Agricultural Innovation Project (NAIP) and Export Market Intelligence Cell (EMIC) was set up in Tamil Nadu with ten State Agricultural Universities. This paper uses globally available price forecasting models (ARIMA, GARCH, etc.)on 20 crops to provide an idea of the existing status and policies in agricultural market intelligence.

Keywords: Agriculture Market Intelligence (AMI), Role of government policies, Status of AMI, Limitation and Suggestion the existing status and anticipated effect of the market conditions such as price, demand, forecasting, etc. Market Intelligence is a process of probing insights into what would happen in the near future. This process starts from collecting market information, and then proceeds to using the information in the form of market intelligence to examine the possible conditions in the future market. (CIAMI, 2016).

In agriculture or agri-business, marketing is the key factor that determines the economic viability of farming. Price, volume, values, weather impacts, supply, demand and other economic factors surrounding it, can be complex to track and understand. From the smallest farmer to the largest grocery store chain, all of Indian agriculture is impacted by the trends and prices within the marketplace. To convert successfully any business idea into higher capital gains, it is important for farmers to understand and to determine the fair value of their investment (Zazaku, 2015). Market intelligence is able to provide timely and unbiased market insight that helps farmers and businesses understand these trends and make informed decisions about the marketing, sale and delivery of the products (supply chain) and keep competitive.

Demand for food grain production in 2030 will increase to 310.8 million tonnes from 272 million tonnes in 2016 (Kumar et al., 2016) while acreage of land is stagnant. Technology- oriented intensive agriculture may increase productivity. But Indian agriculture runs with a persistent situation of imperfect knowledge. Farmers are not benefitted from sophisticated facilities unless market intelligence is applied effectively. In view of approaching the target of doubling farmers' income within a stipulated time (Farmers' Income: Rationale, Strategy, Prospects and Action Plan, NITI Ayog, 2017) recent advances in information technology (IT) or market intelligence system may help farmers with feasible marketing information (mainly price). So, proper design and management of the system is needed. Agricultural market intelligence (AMI) requires some form of analysis from the piles of data and information. A lot of information is required about the complete cycle of cultivation, production, processing, consumption and commerce.AMI is crucial to enabling farmers and traders to make informed decisions about what to grow, when to harvest, where to markets the produce and whether to store it or not.

The importance of data and information management is beyond any doubt. According to Blumberg and Atre (2004), Gartner said that white-collar workers spent anywhere from 30 to 40 percent of their time in 2003 managing documents, workers. Blumberg and Atre (2004) also showed that according to market research from Outsell, Inc., office workers spend an average of 9.5 hours each week searching, gathering and analyzing information. Moreover, nearly 60 percent of that time, or 5.5 hours a week, is spent on the Internet, at an average cost of $13,182 per worker per year.

However, utility of data has been constrained due to low level of understanding and use of market intelligence. This is because of limited availability of market intelligence, poor access to relevant market information, limited dissemination of existing information to farmers and entrepreneurs, lack of price forecasting system and limited capacity to understand and use market intelligence.

In view of the above, an effort has been made in this paper to provide an overview of the existing status and government policies in agriculture market intelligence (AMI) in India.

Methodology

The paper is exclusively a review work in nature. Different sets of data and information have been collected from various secondary (published) sources like journals, books, periodicals, statistics, websites, etc. and analysis is made using this information only. Mainly tabular analysis has been made to discuss and interpret the findings.

Discussion

Self-sufficiency in food grains is the main outcome of India's agriculture. In 1950-51, India produced 50.825 million tonnes of food grains and the volume has reached at 275.112 million tonnes in 2016-17. It has been possible only due to the contribution of science & technology, infrastructure development, State support, extension mechanism, etc. Besides, it is pertinent to presume that dissemination of market information to all the stakeholders had catered a great role.

Operation of Agricultural Market Information System in India

The operation system of AMI has continued to be far from satisfactory. Farmers are mostly interested in market news. Market news of interest to farmers is collected/compiled by APMCs, SAMBs, and State Departments of Agricultural Marketing, field staff of Directorate of Economics and Statistics and Department of Food. There are 435 market information systems (MIS) centres in the country.

news is able to provide only a broad overview to the farmers. There is also a serious misconception about the buying and selling price. However, developments in information technology have opened new opportunities for real price information across the country. Agmark Net, a public portal connecting 2900 markets all over the country and displaying information of about 400 commodities on daily basis is the most successful intervention in this area. Following chart explains details of dissemination news on agricultural marketing through different sources.

Table 2: Dissemination Approach of Agriculture Market Information in India

A. Public	B. Private
NHB, APEDA, Spices Board/ Commodities Board, DGCIS/ NAFED, State Agricultural Marketing Board, KVK & Universities, V. Darpan, etc.	ITC,Cargil, Chambal Fert, Commodity World, Rallis, Haryali.com, EID-Parry, NCDEX, MCEX, nlogue, Tata Kisan Kendra, Agriwatch
C. NGOs	D. Others
M.S.S.R.F., Tarahat.com, Gram Haat, Drishti, Village KIOSK, Akshay, Bhoomi, Warna, e- seva, etc.	Electronic & Print Media, Mobile, Doordarshan, FM Channel, etc.

Source: Shodhganga Inflibnet (2018)

Trends of Farmers' Income

Trend of farmers' income shows that since 1993-94 to 2015-16, farm income per capita has increased by 10.61 percent (market price) and 3.13 percent (real price). This rate was highest during 2004-05 to 2011-12 with respective value being 17.17 percent and 7.46 percent (Table 3).

Table 3: Trend and Growth of Farmers' Income in India

Year	No. of Cultivators (in Millions)	Farm Income per Cultivator(Rs.)		Growth Rate of FarmIncome (%)	
		Market price	Real price	Marketprice	Real price
1993-94	143.9	12365	21110	7.04	1.96
1999-00	138.8	24188	26875		
2004-05	166.1	26146	26146	17.17	7.46
2011-12	146.2	79137	43258		
2012-13	143.6	91414	41553	11.01	0.44
2013-14	141.0	104763	42760		
2014-15	138.5	112507	43106		
2015-16	136.0	120193	44027		

The Ashok Dalwai Committee points out that real incomes of farmers need to register a compound annual growth rate of 10.4 percent for farmers' incomes to double by 2022. In 2017–18, agricultural growth is expected to slow to 2.1 percent, compared to 4.9 percent in the previous year, according to official forecasts (www.hindustantimes.com).

Indian Council of Agricultural Research (ICAR) states that "the Indian agriculture sector incurs 18 to 25 percent losses in the entire supply-chain (moving produce)," DFI report, (2018).

In view of the above, reform in marketing policy, in general, and AMI, in particular, assume much more importance. Policies have strong effect on farmers' income and create environment for harnessing opportunities and potential of technologies. A set of reforms has been identified, which include institutional measures to reform APMC Act in States and use of technology in marketing. (Ramakisen, 2007).

A new initiative namely e-NAM has been undertaken to encourage States to adopt e- trading platform for agricultural commodities. E-NAM is a National Agriculture Market to increase the income of farmers with incidental benefit of moderating price rise respectively. The scheme envisaged deployment of a common e-market platform in 585 selected regulated wholesale agriculture markets by March 2018. The common e-market portal is called e-NAM. E-NAM focuses on crop sectors and accordingly, a 13 percent raise in crop price translate into 9.1 percent increase in farmers' income (NITI Ayog, 2017).

Current Status of Agricultural Marketing Intelligence in India

In India, existing market information systems frequently fall short of the demand. Among all the information, information on price assume more important. Govt. has decided to provide price forecast before sowing of the crop or commodity. As a consequence, Agriculture Marketing Intelligence System (AMIS) was set up in 2011. The main focus of AMIS is to provide market intelligence services in the field of agriculture, horticulture and allied commodities including livestock and livestock product.

The Directorate of Economics and Statistics, Ministry of Agriculture (DESMOA) set up 14 Market Intelligence Units (MIU) in different States for helping DESMOA in the formulation, implementation and review of the agricultural price policy relating to procurement, marketing, storage, transportation, import, export and credit, etc. The units furnish regular reports on market arrivals, off-

Efficient market information can be shown to have positive benefit for farmers and traders. Very few farmers participate in commercial markets due to lack of access to market information. Furthermore, lack of access to market information is one of the contributing factors to the slow development of market opportunities.

Though the data to be supplied by the market intelligence units are of great utility, but the impact of this effort is yet to satisfy all the stakeholders. Deficiencies in working of MIU occur mainly due to a lack of proper direction and control of their activities. Over the years, the staff strength of the units has been considerably reduced, resulting in even worse performance.

The essential pre-requisite for effective implementation of the schemes i.e. Minimum support price (MSP), Market intervention scheme (MIS), Price stabilization fund (PSF) and Trade policy decisions ensuring farmers' income, is credible information about "likely price situation required" (Acharya, 2015). Realizing this, ICAR took initiatives under National Agricultural Research System (NARS) and World Bank assisted National Agricultural Innovation Project (NAIP). The specific objectives of the project are to provide price forecast before sowing and during harvesting of selected farm commodities; to make available product intelligence; to provide information on high price markets; to improve the dissemination of market intelligence; to increase the capacity to absorb and use such market intelligence by all stakeholders and to develop commodity market outlook along with NCAP-NAIP for selected commodities at state level besides providing commodity market research reports.

The project was started from August 2009. Under this scheme, Domestic and Export Market Intelligence Cell (DEMIC) was set up at Tamil Nadu Agricultural University (TNAU), Coimbatore with ten State agricultural universities (SAUs) being consortium partner.

Specific Jobs Done Under DEMIC

- In view of forecasting price accurately, it reviews globally available price forecasting Models.
- Results are circulated through print /electronic media and feedback are also taken.
- It creates demand for price forecasts.
- So far, it has published 42 reports covering 20 crops / commodities.

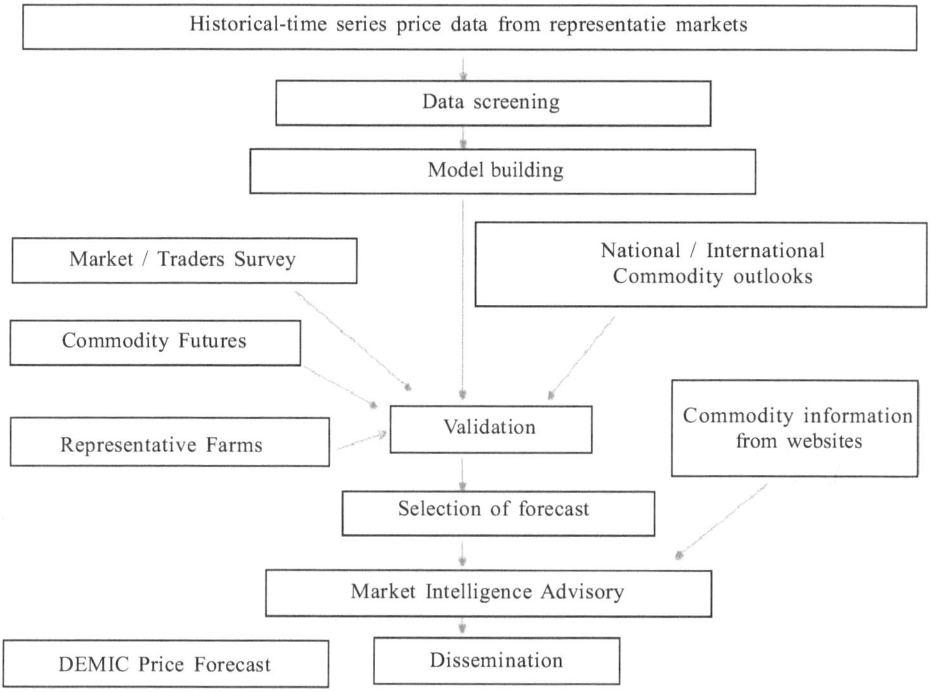

Fig. 1: Represents the system of DEMIC price forecasting with sketch.
Source: http://macp.gov.in

After NAIP, ICAR decided to further strengthen the programme by launching a network project with technical and human resource capacity for price forecasts (Saxena and Pavithra, 2016).

Followings are some important models used in price forecasting:

1. **Autoregressive Moving Average (ARMA)**:It assumes that time-series is stationary and the models are not conditionally heteroskedastic, that is, they don't take into account volatility clustering. These models will help us attempt to capture or "explain" more of the serial correlation present within an instrument. Ultimately they will provide us with a means of forecasting the future prices.

2. **Autoregressive Integrated Moving Average (ARIMA)**:It includes non-stationary data and is a univariate (single vector) forecasting model for future value of a time series. Application in the area of statistical forecasting requires at least 40 historical data points with stable or

used in finance due to effectiveness in modelling assets return and inflation. Aims at minimizing error or forecasting by accounting for error in prior forecasting and thereby enhancing the accuracy of on-going prediction.

4. **Autoregressive Fractionally Integrated Moving Average (ARFIMA):** Is a generalised ARIMA model by allowing non-integer values of the differencing parameter. These models are useful in modelling time series with long memory—that is, in which deviations from the long-run mean decay more slowly than an exponential decay.
5. **LARCH**: It is a Geographic Information System model based decision rule. When habitats are somehow connected, plants and animals can migrate better through the landscape. The model LARCH can be used to evaluate landscape connectivity for plant and animal species in a scattered landscape like the river Rhine delta. Models are used in relation to nature restoration plans, e.g. for the design of stepping stones, corridors or road overpasses for animals.
6. **Artificial Neural Networks (ANNs)**:These are biologically inspired computer programs designed to simulate the way in which the human brain processes information. ANNs gather their knowledge by detecting the patterns and relationships in data and learn (or are trained) through experience, not from programming.

Current Status of Government Efforts for AMIS

Seeking to build up a key decision-making institutional mechanism for helping farmers take right calls for sowing and marketing of particular crops in particular area, the Centre is working on a data-driven system of "Marketing Intelligence" for farm sector. It will take care of area, crop, demand, supply, price, etc. It will help them deal with the issue of "problem of plenty"– a situation where the farmers have to suffer massive losses due to good production of food crops.

The Agriculture Ministry has decided to put the ICAR-NIAP on the job which worked for last four years and developed capacity to roll out the system as and when asked by the Ministry. They have completed the research in coordination with 14 State Agricultural Universities (SAU). First advisory should be given at the time of sowing and second advisory at the time of harvesting (whether to sell or hold for few months). Implementing this mechanism in all States, it will give crop-specific advisories considering local situation.

scattered production, dominancy of small and marginal farmers, etc. Obtaining marketing information for various crops from different locations requires huge number of personnel and other related aspects which are inadequate right now. So, public investment for the development of infrastructure under MIS can be increased for implementation.

Conclusion

The study shows that agricultural market intelligence system (AMIS) in India is inadequate and imperfect in nature. Agricultural business more or less operates with imperfect knowledge causing deprivation of income of the producer. In this background, the paper attempts to deliver some useful information on marketing intelligence, particularly, agricultural marketing intelligence. An entrepreneur may obtain this service on any crop on which he/she has planned for investment for the development of his business. In spite of this shortfall, effective AMIS can act as an effective component for delivering market intelligence to help reduce risk in decision making. DEMIC under Government of India has been used to deliver price forecast of selected agricultural crops based on different econometric models, so that farmers may take appropriate decision on production and marketing. Empirical study on the performance of DEMIC shows that it has, so far, published 42 reports covering 20 crops for the farmers. Market forecasting service on different crops like red gram, chilli, turmeric, sorghum, ground nut, cotton, etc. has created demand among the farmer-producers. Considering the efficiency of the scheme, it is suggested that Central Government and State Government jointly may establish Agricultural Market Intelligence Centres (AMIC) all over the country to provide timely market information including price forecasting to the farmers. This effort, in turn, will help development and growth of agri-entrepreneurship also in India.

Specific suggestions

The study raises some important institutional aspects on the improvement of the service of agricultural marketing intelligence in India, which are as follows:

Improvement of farmer-oriented agricultural marketing system including establishment of regulated market and modern infrastructural facilities; arrangements for guaranteed pricing mechanism for farmer-producers; establishment of marketing intelligence service-centres all over India; development of new forecasting models for location-specific and crop-specific purposes; increase in the number of experts and functionaries in marketing

Farmers' majority of whom are small and marginal farmers are the key producers. Continuous supply of quality produce can be ensured only when the farmers will get satisfactory price. But agriculture by its nature is a risky business and farmers run their business with imperfect knowledge in respect of market (price) and others. They expect a profitable return which they cannot predict before cultivation starts. Provision of adequate service on AMI is a useful tool which can help take appropriate decision on production and marketing to ensure income of farms and reduce risk therein.

In view of above, the paper has tried to trace out/highlight the existing system, status, function and impact of marketing intelligence generated from the institutional efforts. The knowledge of AMI is scale neutral and can act as an important component in supply chain (SC) and value chain (VC) management of any agri-produce or agri-enterprise. An entrepreneur may gather information on the marketing aspects of any crops on which he/she has planned for investment.

References

Acharya, S.S. and Agarwal, N. L. (2017). Agricultural marketing in India (Book), Oxford & IBH, New Delhi.

Blumberg, R. and B. and Atre, S. (2004). The Problem with Unstructured Data. Published in

Blumberg, R., and Atre, S. (2003). The problem with unstructured data. Dm Review, 13(42-49), 62.

Centre for Indian Agricultural Marketing Intelligence (CIAMI) (2016). Retrieved from https://www.msamb.com

Chand, R. (2016). e-Platform for national agricultural market. Economic and Political Weekly, 51(28), 15-18.

Chand, R. (2017). NITI Ayog, Policy Paper 1/2017, Govt. of India. Doubling Farmers' Income –Rationale, Strategy, Prospects and Action Plan.

DM Review in February (2003). Retrieved fromhttps://eecs.ceas.uc.edu.

http://macp.gov.in accessed on 4th January 2019

http://mospi.nic.in accessed on 4th January 2019

http://shodhganga.inflibnet.ac.in accessed on 4th January 2019

Kandpal, K. (2016). Awareness and Use of Agricultural Market Intelligence, Agropedia, Retrieved from http://agropedia.iitk.ac.in

Kumar, P., Joshi, P.K. and Mittal, S. (2016). Demand Vs. Supply of Food Grains in India – Futuristic Projection. Proceeding of Indian National Science Congress, 82, No. 5, December, 2016, pp-1559-1586.

Ramalingareddy, V. J. and Ramakrishna, G. (2018). ICAR Network Project On Market Intelligence - A Study On Price Behaviour, Market Infrastructure and Farmers' Awareness on APMC Act in Telangana, (Book) , Published by PJTSAU, Hyderabad.

Ramkishen, Y. (2007). New Perspectives on Rural & Agricultural Marketing, 7th Edition, Jaico

Saxena, R., Pabithra, S. and Paul, R. (2018). Network Project on Market Intelligence, Retrieved from www.ncap.res.in
www. indiastat.com accessed on 4th January 2019
www.freepressjournal.in accessed on 4th January 2019
www.hindustantimes.com accessed on 4th January 2019
Zakaku, A. (2015). Market Research as An Important Factor For the Development of Agriculture, Slovakia Academic Publishers, Retrieved from www. researchgate.net
Zakaku, A. (2015). Market Research as An Important Factor For the Development of Agriculture, Slovakia Academic Publishers, Retrieved from www. researchgate.net

16

A Study on Farmers' Awareness of Crop Insurance in West Bengal Policy Prescriptions and Entrepreneurial Pathways

Rupam Mukherjee and Debabrata Mukhopadhyay

Abstract

Agricultural development in India provides support to a large section of farmers who operate on small holdings and have very limited risk bearing capacity. Farmers are often exposed to natural vagaries, which adversely affect their agricultural production and farm income. Moreover, there is huge financial exclusion in rural sector of the nation. If there is a crop failure, farmers are crushed under the burden of debt. Farmers seek to avoid risk in terms of various managerial and institutional mechanisms. But it is widely believed that 'Crop Insurance' is the only institutional mechanism available against production risk in farming. Unfortunately, penetration of crop insurance schemes in India has been low in terms of the area of land insured and the number of farmers covered. There are the problems of low risk awareness and lack of insurance culture among the farmers. In this backdrop, the paper documents the findings of a survey of 140 farmers, which was taken up in some selected villages of North 24 Parganas district of West Bengal. The study shows that likelihood of this awareness increases with increase in landholding size, education level, borrowing history and social participation of the farmers, whereas it decreases with the non-farm income and livestock of the farmers. The author proposes measures to promote and spread awareness of crop insurance among the farmers as a risk mitigation tool in farming, which will increase farm production and stabilize the fluctuation in farm income. The study provides

Introduction

Planning for agricultural development in India has been important not simply for agriculture's contribution to the growth of the larger economy but because agriculture provides the basic sustenance of a large section of farmers who operate on small holdings and limited risk bearing capacity associated with farming. Almost 85% of all operational holdings in the nation are small and marginal in nature (Indian Rural Development Report, 2013). Quite often these small farmers experience price, production, technology as well as resource risks which make their income highly unstable.

With the commercialization of agriculture, farmers have to depend more on cash income not only for cultivation but also for self-consumption. More dependence on monetized inputs such as high yielding varieties of seeds, chemical fertilizers, pesticides etc. for cultivation has increased the farmers' borrowing propensity. But there is huge financial exclusion in rural sector of the nation. Due to the paucity of institutional sources of credit, farmers have to borrow from moneylenders and input suppliers, who lend money at exorbitantly high rates of interest and also in hard terms and conditions. If there is a crop failure, farmers are crushed under the burden of debt. The extreme manifestation of this debt crisis has ultimately resulted in unending chain of suicides of farmers in recent times in different parts of the nation. Moreover, the events like global warming, fluctuation in monsoon rainfall due to climate change and emergence of new breeds of pests and crop diseases are also playing havoc with the fortunes of the farmers.

Farmers seek to avoid risk through various managerial and institutional mechanisms. They may diversify their crops, favor traditional farming technique by restricting the use of modern and costly inputs, enter into sharecropping arrangements etc. In India, for a section of farming community, Minimum Support Prices for certain crops provide a means of their income stability. But for most of the crops and in many states, Minimum Support Price has not been implemented. Recently, mechanisms like 'contract farming', 'future trading' etc. have been introduced and they are expected to provide some risk cover against price fluctuation. But it is widely believed that 'Crop Insurance' is the only institutional mechanism available against production risk in farming.

Crop insurance provides financial support to the farmers in the event of failure of any of the crops covered under the insurance contract as a result of adverse weather conditions, pests and diseases. It also encourages the farmers to adopt the dignity of farmers. Moreover, the liability of the Government to bear the cost of relief measures to the farmers following crop failure is reduced to some extent as through crop insurance the farmers themselves contribute to their relief.

Crop insurance policy will stabilize farm income, reduce rural poverty and ensure financial inclusion of small and marginal farmers in the nation. For the last few decades Indian agriculture is suffering from a crisis due to its low productivity. Growth of this sector is essential not only to meet the challenge of food and nutritional security of growing population of the nation but also to tackle food price led inflation and the growing problem of rural-urban disparity in income and wealth. Effective implementation of crop insurance policy has the potential to promote growth of agricultural output and thereby accelerate the overall growth rate of the economy.

As per Government of India records, there were four crop insurance schemes operating in India till 2016– Comprehensive Crop Insurance Scheme, National Agriculture Insurance Scheme, Modified National Agriculture Insurance Scheme and Weather Based Crop Insurance Scheme. But the penetration of agricultural insurance was low and stagnant in terms of area insured and farmers covered. In India, total area covered under insurance in 2016-17 amounts to about 30% coverage of gross cropped area, less than half of what USA (89% coverage) and China has achieved (69% coverage).Only 19% of the farmers of the nation are insured till recently. Realizing the limitations of the existing system of crop insurance, the Government of India launched a new crop insurance scheme, Pradhan Mantri Fasal BimaYojana (PMFBY) from Kharif 2016.

Apart from the problem of adverse selection and moral hazard that can creep in crop insurance market due to asymmetric information between the insured farmers and insurance company, there are the problems of low risk awareness and lack of insurance culture among the farming community.

The World Bank Report (2010) on 'Government Support to Agricultural Insurance – Challenges and Options for Developing countries' has mentioned three important problems associated with crop insurance programmes. The first one is the problem of low risk awareness of the farmers. The report has found that although the farmers are very aware of their production risks, they often exhibit 'cognitive failure' in the sense they underestimate the likelihood or severity of catastrophic events. Secondly, the report has identified the problem of lack of insurance culture among the farmers. In developing nations like India, crop pays only when infrequent events occur – as a privilege of the rich. Thirdly, according to the report, the regulatory frameworks governing insurance markets in many low and middle income nations tend to be underdeveloped. As a result, regulatory overlay can in some cases inhibit increased penetration of insurance, including crop insurance.

Different studies have been conducted to assess the perception and awareness of the farmers about the crop insurance schemes in the nation. One such work has been done by Sundar and Ramakrishnan (2013). The study was conducted in Kunichampet village, Puducherry District, India and after interviewing 140 respondents through convenience sampling, it was found that farmers' awareness level about crop insurance was low. Most of the farmers were not willing to pay for crop insurance because of their unstable income, high premium rate, no or low compensation, problems with distribution channel and lack of financial knowledge.

The survey work done by Suresh Kumar, K.Palanisami, C.R.Ranganathan and R.Venkataram (2010) in Tamil Nadu reveals that factors such as gross cropped area, income other than agricultural sources, presence of risk in farming, number of workers in the farm family, satisfaction with the premium rate and the affordability of the insurance premium significantly and positively influence the adoption of insurance and premium paid by the farmers.

Another study on farmers' perception and awareness of crop insurance was conducted in North Eastern parts of Karnataka by Goudappa, Reddy and Chandrashekhar(2012). The study revealed that although National Agriculture Insurance Scheme(NAIS) crop insurance scheme is operating since 2002-03 in the study area, majority of the respondents are not aware of the implementing agency and who pays the compensations. Almost all respondents are in the wrong perception that banks will pay compensation and are the implementing agency. More than three- fourth of the insurance beneficiaries mentioned that bank compulsion was the motivation for opting for insurance. Further more than 80% of respondents are not aware of the extent of coverage premium paid, last date, procedure for insuring crops, method of loss determination and compensation worked out by agriculture insurance company. Respondent farmers were asked for their suggestions in improving existing scheme. They mentioned the need for quick settlement of claims. NAIS in operation needs to be continued with modification and simplification of modalities of indemnity, loss assessment, settlement of compensation and disbursement procedure.

of the study were that gender, education, and income of the household were the main determinants of awareness.

The study of Singh, Mishra and Ahmad (2017) examined the influence of the respondents' socio- economic characteristics on their adoption of crop insurance schemes in East Champaran and Sheohar districts of Bihar. A Discriminant analysis based on standardized canonical coefficient and correlation matrix identified that educational level, farm size, satisfaction level, awareness and access to source of credit were positive discriminators while negative coefficients were obtained for age, income level and number of earning members.

But there is almost no empirical study to identify the factors affecting the awareness and perception about crop insurance in the North 24 Parganas district of West Bengal. In this backdrop, this paper has documented the report of a survey, which was taken up during December 2016 to January 2017 in some selected villages of North 24 Parganas district of West Bengal to understand farmers' perception about crop insurance as a risk mitigation tool in farming.

The survey was conducted to fulfill following important objectives –

- To understand the awareness and perception of farmers about crop insurance as a risk mitigation tool in farming;
- To examine how the awareness of crop insurance is influenced by (a) non-farm income (b) size of landholdings (c) education level (d) livestock (e) borrowing history (f) social participation of the respondent farmers;
- To suggest measures to increase the awareness of farmers about crop insurance on the basis of feedback received from respondent farmers.

The plan of the paper is as follows – Section I introduces the paper by highlighting the motivation of the study, a brief review of literature and objectives of the study. Section II provides the sources of data and research methodology used in the study. Section III makes an empirical analysis of data, while Section IV concludes the study.

Data & Methodology

The study was conducted in Beraberia and Mathura village of Amdanga Block and Gokna and Ramchandrapur village of Baduria Block of North 24 Parganas district of West Bengal. North 24 Parganas district is located in southern side district of the state. Geographically, the district lies at 22° 71 N latitude, 88° 71 E longitude and 13m altitude. The district encompasses a geographical area of 4094 sq. km and is bounded by Nadia on North, Bangladesh (Khulna Division) on North and East, South 24 Parganas in South and Kolkata, Howrah and Hoogly on West. The climate of the district is tropical, like rest of the Gangetic West Bengal. The actual rainfall in the district was 1592 mm in the year 2016-17 (District Statistical Handbook, North 24 Parganas District, Government of West Bengal, 2017).

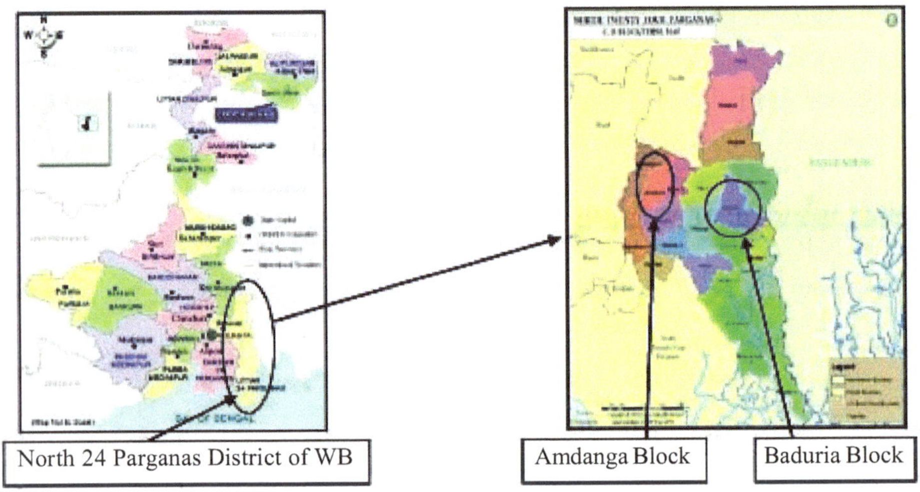

Source: www.mapsindia.com

The district ranks third in the state in literacy rate. The sex ratio of the district is 955 females for every 1000 males. The major religions in the district are Hinduism (73.46%) and Muslim (25.82%). Agriculture is the backbone of the economy. According to 2011 Census, the cultivable land in total geographical area of the district is about 67.18% and net sown area is 60.04%. The distribution of operational land holding is bottom heavy where small and marginal farmers dominate significantly. Major field crops of the district are rice (aus, aman&boro), jute, oilseeds, wheat and potato. Among vegetables, brinjal, cabbage, cauliflower, tomato, chilly, spinach and lady's-finger are important. Mango, banana, papaya, jackfruit and guava are the major fruits produced in the district.

Both secondary and primary data were used for this study. A formal survey was undertaken during January 2018 to April 2018, through interviews of selected farmers from the four villages under the study area using a pre-tested semi-

A systematic, multistage stratified sampling design was adopted for the study. In the first stage, two out of twenty two blocks of the district were selected purposively (namely, Amdanga Block and Baduria Block) based on the number of inhabitant farming households. Then in the second stage, two villages from each block were selected (namely, Beraberia and Mathura village of Amdanga Block and Gokna and Ramchandrapur village of Baduria Block) purposively having resemblance with the socio-economic characteristics of the selected blocks. Then in the last stage, 140 farming households were selected using random number table to size of farming households in the selected villages. Yamane's (1967) sample size determination formula was used to calculate the desired sample size (n) where,

$$n = N/[1 + N. (e)^2]$$

Where

n = sample size

N = population size (the total number of farming households in the selected villages)

e = level of precision (the acceptable sampling error)

In this study, N = 1346, e = 8% and thus n = 139.998 ≈ 140

Both descriptive and econometric methods are used to analyze the data. Descriptive data analysis is exploratory in nature in terms of charts and diagrams. In case of econometric analysis, a Logistic regression model is used to estimate how the likelihood of crop insurance awareness among farmers is affected by different socio-economic factors considered for the study. In Logistic regression model the estimation is made in terms of maximum likelihood method. The study tries to estimate the co-efficients of the following equation-

$$Yi = \log (p / 1\text{-}p) = \alpha + \beta_1 X_{1i} + \beta_2 X_{2i} + \beta_3 X_{3i} + \beta_4 X_{4i} + \beta_5 X_{5i} + \beta_6 X_{6i} + ui$$

Where, Yi = Awareness of the i-*th* farmer about crop insurance, is the response variable Yi = 0 if the farmer is not aware about crop insurance& Yi = 1 if the farmer is aware

A farmer is considered aware about crop insurance if,

(a) he/she has heard about crop insurance and its benefits and actually has purchased it, **or**

In the following table we have explained the exploratory variables used in the study.

Table 1: Summary of the explanatory variables considered in the study

Name of the variable	Type	Notation	Measurement	Expected influence oninsurance awareness
Non-farm income	Dummy	X1	1 = if Yes , 0 = otherwise	±
Land holding size of thefarmer	Dummy	X2	1 = if more than 2 ha, 0 =otherwise	±
Education level	Dummy	X3	1 = if more than primarylevel, 0 = otherwise	+
Livestock	Dummy	X4	1 = Yes, 0 = other wise	-
Borrowing history of thefarmer	Dummy	X5	1 = if taken loan, 0 =otherwise	+
Social participation offarmer	Dummy	X6	1 = if Yes, 0 = otherwise	+

Note:± affecting either positively or negatively
Source: Own survey (2018)

$\beta_1, \beta_2, \ldots\ldots\ldots, \beta_6$ are the co-efficients of the six explanatory variables considered in the study.

The goodness of fit of the model is checked in terms of Hosmer-Lemeshow test. The problem of multicollinearity, if any, among the explanatory variables is checked in terms of Variance Inflation Factor. In this study the statistical software SPSS is used for computation.

Empirical Analysis

In the descriptive part of the analysis, at first the demographic profile of the respondents are discussed. Among the 140 farmers interviewed, 30% were female and the rest of the 70% were male. If one considers the educational attainment of the respondent farmers, then most of them (54%) have studied only up to primary level. About 37% of the farmers extended their studies beyond primary level up to secondary level. Only 9% of the respondents have studied beyond secondary level of education (Figure 1).

The land distribution pattern in the area of study is bottom heavy. The average size of operational landholdings is very small. Small and marginal farmers, having

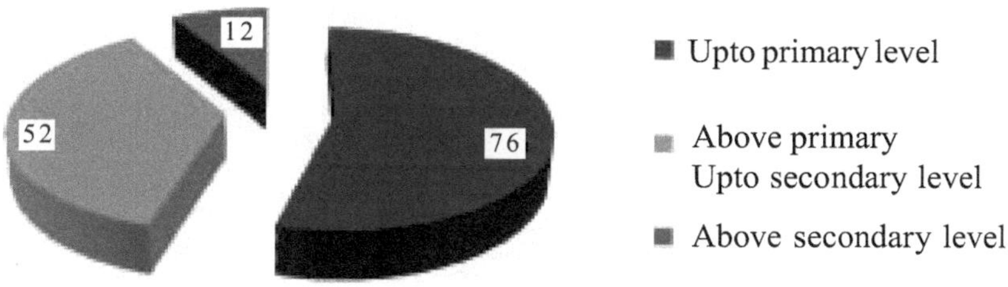

Fig. 1: Education level of respondent farmers
Source: Author's

landholding size less than or equal to 2 hectares of land predominate. This type of land distribution pattern is very much similar to land distribution pattern of the entire state as well (Figure 2). About 77% of the operational landholdings in the area of study are small and marginal in nature. Such a low size of land does not fetch adequate revenue to run the family. Moreover with commercialization of agriculture and increasing cost of inputs, farming is becoming a losing proposition for many farmers. They are too poor to combat with any risk associated with farming due adverse weather condition or pest attack. As a result livestock and non-farm sources of income have emerged as their complementary but sustainable rural livelihood strategy (Figure 3).

The figure shows that 76% of the respondents have either livestock or any other non-farm sources of income, whereas 11% of the respondents have both

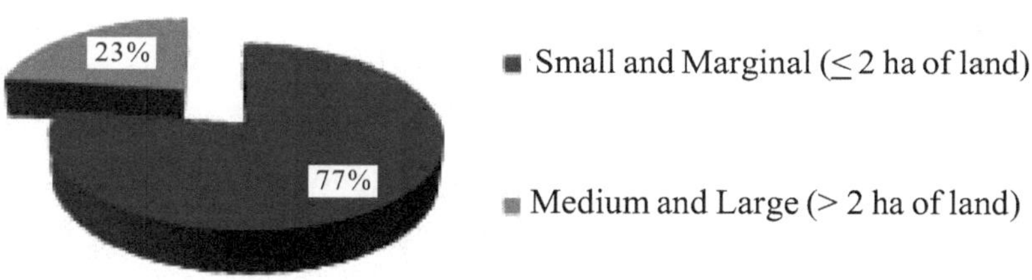

Fig. 2: Landholding pattern in the area of study
Source: Author's

livestock and non-farm sources of income. This means 87% of the respondents have livestock or any other source of non-farm income or both as risk mitigation strategy for farming. Only 13% of the respondents bank on farming activity for their livelihood.

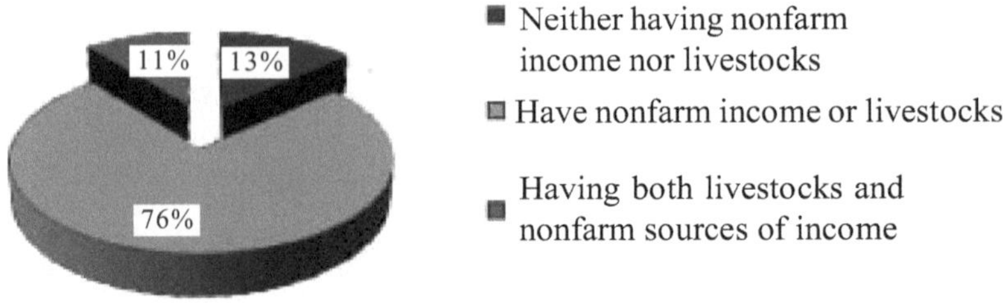

Fig. 3: Source of Risk mitigation for farmers
Source: Author's

organizations, like farmers' association, self-help groups, local clubs, local political party offices, co-operative credit societies etc. Social participation improves social cohesion.

The respondent farmers cultivate paddy and banana in Kharif season and cultivate potato, onion, and different vegetables like brinjal, chilly, tomato, cauliflower, cabbage, spinach and lady's- finger in Rabi season. About 51.43% of the respondents have reported that they cultivate different livestock products, mainly cows, goats and poultry products. Most of the respondent farmers reported that following are the important problems associated with farming:-

- Declining fertility of land due to multiple cropping and excessive use of chemical fertilizers
- Fluctuation in the price of output in the market
- Rising cost of inputs, particularly the cost of fertilizers, pesticides, irrigation and agricultural labour
- Not getting the correct price of output due to the existence of a long chain of middlemen between farmers and final consumers
- Uncertainty of monsoon, particularly in case of rice production in kharif season.

About 32% of the respondent farmers have reported that they have suffered from crop failure within the last five years and mentioned two important causes for crop failure –

- Rainfall fluctuation in case of rice production
- Crop disease in case of production of potato and brinjal

sources within last three years. But, importantly non-institutional sources of credit dominate (67%) where farmers have taken loan from money lenders, input suppliers or even from friends and relatives. Only 33% of loan credit is from institutional sources (commercial banks or co-operative banks etc.)(Figure 4).

Among the farmers having borrowing history, 70.31% are small and marginal farmers and remaining are medium and large farmers. The sources of credit for different categories of farmers are shown in Figure 5.

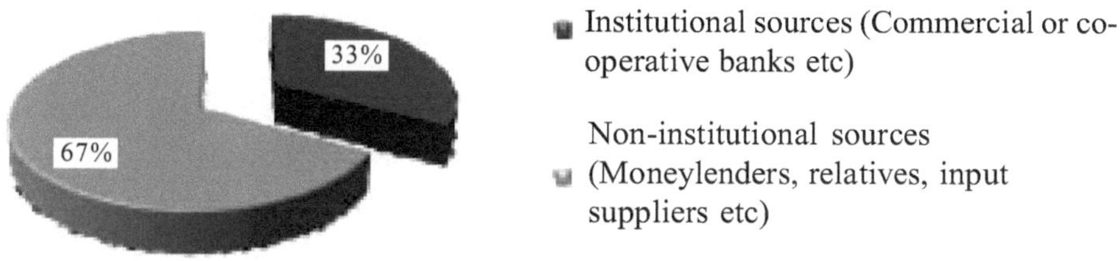

Fig. 4: Source of Borrowing
Source: Author's

In the next section, through the following tables based on the survey, one can understand the socio-economic profile and the level of crop insurance awareness among the respondent farmers in the area of study. Table 2 shows how crop insurance awareness and non-farm income of the respondent farmers are related to each other. Since non-farm income is a risk mitigation strategy in the area of

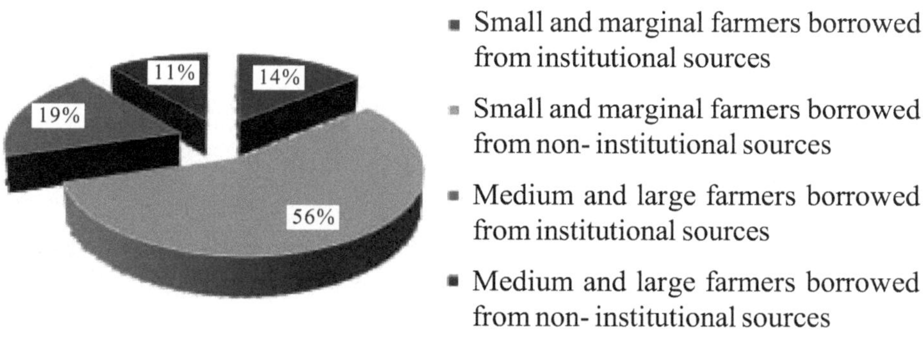

Fig. 5: Borrowing history of the farmers
Source: Author's

Table 2: Relation between Crop Insurance Awareness and Non-farm Income of the respondent farmers

Insurance Awareness	Non-farm income		Total
	No	Yes	
No	38	50	88
Yes	34	18	52
Total	72 (51.43%)	68 (48.57%)	140 (100%)

Source : Author's calculation

Table 3 shows the relation of crop insurance awareness with the size of landholdings. As the table shows, small and marginal farmers are less aware about crop insurance policy than medium and large farmers. About 71.3% of the small and marginal farmers are not aware about crop insurance, whereas 65.63% of the medium and large farmers are aware about crop insurance policy. This may be due to the fact that large farmers produce more and therefore invest more money for cultivation. Therefore the financial risk associated with farming will be more for them as compared to a small and marginal farmer. As a result, they are more aware about crop insurance as the risk mitigation tool in farming.

Table 3: Relation between Crop Insurance Awareness and Landholding size of the respondent farmers

Insurance Awareness	Landholding size		Total
	Less than or equal to 2 ha	More than 2 ha	
No	77	11	88
Yes	31	21	52
Total	108 (77.14%)	32 (22.86%)	140 (100%)

Source: Author's calculation

Table 4 shows the relationship between crop insurance awareness and education level of the farmers. Education improves reasoning ability of the farmers and also increases the financial literacy. Increased education enables farmer to develop the knowledge, understanding, capacities and confidence needed to adequately appraise and understand the policies they require. So it is expected that increase in educational attainment will increase crop insurance awareness of the farmers. As the table shows, 89.5% of the farmers who have studied

Table 4: Relation between Crop Insurance Awareness and Education Level of the respondent farmers

Insurance Awareness	Education level		Total
	Upto primary level	More than primary level	
No	68	20	88
Yes	8	44	52
Total	76 (54.28%)	64 (45.72%)	140 (100%)

Source: Author's calculation

Table 5 shows the relation between livestock and crop insurance awareness among farmers. Since farmers in the area of study perceive livestock as a risk mitigation strategy for farming, it is expected that farmers having livestock resources will be less aware about crop insurance. As the table shows, 72.2% of the respondent farmers who have livestock resources are not aware about crop insurance policy.

Table 5: Relation between Crop Insurance Awareness and Livestock of the respondent farmers

Insurance Awareness	Livestock		Total
	No	Yes	
No	36	52	88
Yes	32	20	52
Total	68 (48.57%)	72 (51.43%)	140 (100%)

Source: Author's calculation

Table 6 depicts the relationship between crop insurance awareness and borrowing history of the respondent farmers. In India, crop insurance schemes are mandatory for farmers who are taking short-term crop loan (loanee farmers) from financial institutions like commercial banks, co-operative banks, regional rural banks, etc. But it is voluntary for all other farmers (non-loanee farmers). The premium amount is deducted from the loan amount for loanee farmers and claim, if any, is adjusted against the loan amount. The non-loanee farmers pay premium from their pocket and receive the claim amount if crop loss is recognized. So insurance awareness will be more for that farmer having borrowing history from financial institutions. As the table shows, 71.87% of the respondent farmers who have borrowing history are well aware of crop insurance schemes. Quite strikingly, 92% of the respondents who do not have borrowing

Table 6: Relation between Crop Insurance Awareness and Borrowing History of the respondent farmers

Insurance Awareness	Borrowing history		Total
	No	Yes	
No	70	18	88
Yes	06	46	52
Total	76 (54.29%)	64 (45.71%)	140 (100%)

Source: Author's calculation

Table 7 shows the relationship between crop insurance awareness and social participation of farmers. Social participation increases awareness. As the table shows, 79.24% of the farmers who participate in social organizations are aware about crop insurance. Again, 88.5% of the farmers who do not participate in social organizations are unaware about crop insurance products.

Table 7: Relation between Crop Insurance Awareness and Social Participation of the respondent farmers

Insurance Awareness	Social participation		Total
	No	Yes	
No	77	11	88
Yes	10	42	52
Total	87 (62.14%)	53 (37.86%)	140 (100%)

Source : Author's calculation

In this survey, among the 140 farmers interviewed it is quite interesting to observe that only 52 farmers (37.14%) are aware about the crop insurance scheme and its benefits, which is unexpectedly low. Moreover, only 21 out of those 52 farmers have actually purchased crop insurance which is only 15% of the total respondent farmers in the area of study. Moreover, 9 out of 21 farmers who bought crop insurance have landholding size above 2ha., indicating the fact that they are medium and large farmers. All the 12 small and marginal farmers who bought crop insurance, had taken short term crop loan from commercial banks and they had to purchase crop insurance as loan conditionality. This signifies the lack of insurance culture in the area of study (Figure 6).

The respondent farmers informed that they came to know about crop insurance from fellow farmers, television, different hoarding and banners of the insurance

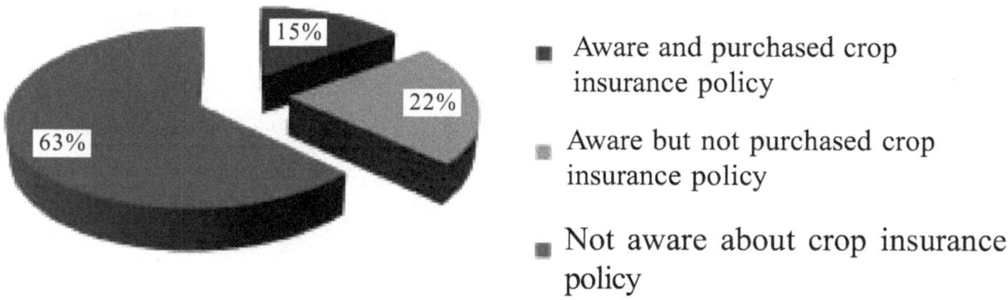

Fig. 6: Awareness about Crop Insurance for the Respondent farmers
Source: Author's

Most of the respondent farmers have reported that they prefer Kisan-Sabha, television, film show in the village for dissemination about benefits of crop insurance or the rural agent of the insurance company at the village level. Additionally, information at the doorstep should be an ideal source from which they would like to get information regarding crop insurance.

When the farmers, who are aware but have not purchased crop insurance yet, are asked about the reason for not availing crop insurance, they mentioned the following important factors –

- Lack of premium paying capacity, particularly for small farmers
- Not satisfied with the crops covered under the present crop insurance scheme
- Inadequate publicity of the scheme
- Many of them do not understand the difference between investing money in banks and investing money in crop insurance
- Many of them do not have the faith in insurance companies in getting the money at the time when they need it badly during catastrophes
- Many farmers think that the documentation procedure in banks to open an account to avail the benefit of crop insurance is very complex.
- Non-farm sources of income and livestock resources help them to mitigate financial loss and risk that may arise due to crop failure

After explaining to the non-awarded farmers the possible benefits of crop insurance in farming, about 28% of the farmers have expressed that they would

When the respondent farmers were asked about their opinion about crop insurance scheme, about 35% of them think that the current scheme has benefited mostly the large farmers, about 17% of them opines that the current scheme has benefited mostly the small and marginal farmers. About 48% of the respondent farmers reported that they have no idea in this regard.

The respondent farmers have given following suggestions for improvement of working as well as greater penetration of current crop insurance scheme –

- To include more crops under its ambit, particularly the vegetables like cabbage, cauliflower, spinach etc., which is grown by most of the small and marginal farmers in the area of study
- To reduce the rate of insurance premium such that marginal and small farmers can afford it or increase subsidy given by the government of the payable premium
- To raise the indemnity level in case of crop failure
- To conduct cutting experiments to assess the indemnity payments in the presence of villagers to ensure transparency in loss assessment of farmers
- To settle claims as fast as possible in case of calamities
- In addition, it is suggested that loss assessment should be made not on the basis of area approach but on the basis of individual approach. Insurance agents should reach to the doorsteps of the farmers at regular intervals such that the awareness of crop insurance among the farmers rises over time and they can understand clearly the possible benefits of such insurance schemes and can also contact those agents frequently for any query.

To initiate the econometric study in terms of logistic regression, the first step is to check whether there exists any multicollinearity among the explanatory variables considered in the study in terms of Variance Inflation Factor (VIF). Table 8 shows that mean VIF is 1.57, which is even less than 2. This implies that there exists no problem of multicollinearity among the explanatory variables in the study. So logistic regression can be performed. The result of the Logistic regression in terms of the statistical software package SPSS is shown in Table 9. At first, if model summary is considered, then both Cox and Snell R Squared and Nagelkerke R Square are called Pseudo R Square, which shows the variation of explained variable by the explanatory variables considered in the model.

Table 8: VIF Statistics

Variables	VIF	1/VIF
Non-farm income	1.42	0.704
Landholding Size	1.20	0.837
Education Level	1.28	0.780
Livestock	1.49	0.671
Borrowing History	2.06	0.485
Social Participation	1.96	0.509
Mean VIF = 1.57		

Source: Author's Calculation

The Hosmer – Lemeshow test shows how well the data fits the model. In this case the Chi-square significance value is 0.836 and one can conclude that the model is a good fit.

Next, one can consider the classification table, which is also called the confusion matrix. In this matrix, in case of crop insurance awareness, 83 cases are predicted as negative (No) which are observed as negative (No) as well. They are called True Negative (TN). Similarly, 46 cases are predicted as positive (Yes) which are observed positive as well. They are called True Positive (TP). There are 5 cases which are predicted as negative but observed as positive. They are called False Positive (FP). Lastly, there are 6 cases which are predicted as negative but observed as positive. They are called False Negative (FN).

Accuracy is one of the most commonly used measure for classification performance and it is defined as a ratio between correctly classified samples to the total number of samples.

i.e., Accuracy = (TP + TN) / (TP + TN + FP + FN) = (46+83) / (46+83+5+6) = 129 / 140 = 92.1

The complement of accuracy matrix is the Error rate or Misclassification rate.

i.e., Error rate = 1 – Accuracy rate = 1 – 92.1 = 7.9. Two other concepts are important in this connection. The first concept is Sensitivity or True positive rate or sometimes called the Hit rate of a classifier. This can be defined as the positive correctly classified samples to total number of positive samples.

Table 9: Summary Result of Logistic Regression

Model Summary

Step	-2 Log Likelihood	Cox & Snell R Square	Nagelkerke R Square
1	48.13*	0.623	0.850

**Estimation terminated at iteration number 7 because parameter estimates changed by less than 0.001*

Hosmer and Lemeshow Test

Step	Chi-square	df	sig
1	4.229	8	0.836

Classification Table

Observed		Predicted		
		Insurance Awareness		Percentage Correct
		No	Yes	
Insurance Awareness	No	83	5	94.3
	Yes	6	46	88.5
Overall percentage				92.1

Cut off point is 0.5 by default

Variables in the Equation

	Coefficient (β)	Standard Error	Wald	Sig.	Exp (β)
Non-farm income	-2.050	1.088	3.547	0.060	0.129
Landholding Size	1.575	1.008	2.439	0.118	4.829
Education Level	2.421	0.683	12.582	0.000	11.260
Livestock	-2.226	1.129	3.889	0.049	0.108
Borrowing History	2.371	0.622	14.513	0.000	10.707
Social Participation	2.068	0.824	6.307	0.012	7.911
Constant	-4.923	1.808	7.409	0.006	0.007

Source: Author's Calculation by SPSS

So sensitivity of a classifier can be defined as:

Sensitivity = TP / (TP + FN) = 46 / (46 + 6) = 46 / 52 = 88.5

The second concept is the concept of Specificity of a classifier. Specificity or True negative rate or inverse recall is expressed as the ratio of correctly specified i.e., Specificity = TN / (FP + TN) = 83 / (5 + 83) = 83 / 88 = 94.3

Finally one can consider the values of the coefficients of the explanatory variables in logistic regression. As the Table 9 shows, except for landholding size, all other explanatory variables provide statistically significant effect on likelihood of crop insurance awareness. The Wald statistic is defined as:

Wald stat = $(\text{Coefficient} / \text{Standard Error})^2$

The last column of the last table shows the odds ratio.

Let us consider the effect of each explanatory variable in the model one by one on the likelihood of crop insurance awareness. The first explanatory variable is non-farm income of the farmer. As the table shows, since the coefficient of non-farm income is negative, this signifies that the likelihood of crop insurance awareness falls with the non-farm income. In terms of odds ratio, it can be interpreted as the farmers having non-farm income is 0.129 times more likely to be aware about crop insurance than of those farmers having no non-farm income. This result is significant at 10% level. This result is justified in the sense that in the area of study, non-farm income is one of the risk mitigation strategies in farming, particularly for small and marginal farmers. So, farmers having higher non-farm income are less aware about crop insurance policy.

With the rise in landholding size, the likelihood of crop insurance awareness rises as the coefficient of this explanatory variable is positive. But the effect of landholding size on insurance awareness is not statistically significant.

Increase in educational attainment increases the likelihood of insurance awareness. The farmers who have studied more than primary level are 11.26 times more likely to be aware about crop insurance than the farmers who have studied only up to primary level. This result is significant at 1% level. The reason is quite clear. Education improves reasoning ability of the farmers and also increases the financial literacy. Increased education enables farmer to develop the knowledge, understanding, capacities and confidence needed to adequately appraise and understand the policies they require. So it is expected that increase in educational attainment will increase crop insurance awareness of the farmers.

The likelihood of crop insurance awareness falls with the livestock resources of the farmers. As the table shows, farmers having livestock resources are only 0.108 times more likely to be aware about crop insurance than those farmers compared to those farmers who do not have livestock resources and therefore aware about crop insurance policies.

The likelihood of crop insurance awareness rises for those farmers having borrowing history from financial institutions like commercial banks, co-operative banks, Regional Rural banks etc. More specifically, the farmers having such a borrowing history are 10.707 times more likely to be aware about crop insurance than the farmers having no such borrowing history. This result is significant at 1% level. The interpretation is quite obvious. In India, crop insurance schemes are mandatory for farmers who are taking short-term crop loan (loanee farmers) from financial institutions like commercial banks, co-operative banks, regional rural banks etc. But it is voluntary for all other farmers (non-loanee farmers). The premium amount is deducted from the loan amount for loanee farmers and claim, if any, is adjusted against the loan amount. The non-loanee farmers, pay premium from their pocket, and receive the claim amount if crop loss is recognized. So, insurance awareness will be more for those farmers having borrowing history from financial institutions.

Lastly, the likelihood of crop insurance awareness increases with increase in social participation of the respondent farmer. More specifically, as the table shows, the farmers who participate in social organizations are 7.911 times more likely to be aware about crop insurance than those farmers who are not social. This result is significant at 5% level. Social participation increases the knowledge base of the farmers and also increases the chance of being informed about different social and government policies when farmers meet in social gatherings.

Conclusion

The present study unearths some of the important challenges for the government and crop insurance providers in the nation. Firstly, there is lack of insurance culture and awareness among farmers. Thus the main challenge is how to improve the awareness about crop insurance among farmers by conducting crop insurance awareness generation programmes. Secondly, to increase the penetration of crop insurance in the nation the government can motivate the private crop insurance companies to enter the market. This challenge becomes very pertinent as all over the world; the share of private crop insurance business is very limited compared to government run multi-peril crop insurance schemes. Actually, crop insurance policy has some typical and unique problems compared to other life or health insurance products. The crop loss due to natural calamities correlated to other geographical areas as well. Moreover, continuous monitoring is vital for the successful implementation of the programme. Operation of crop insurance policy requires trained manpower and robust infrastructure for acquiring data to calculate accurate premiums, administering the contracts, rapid assessment of losses in case of natural calamity, conducting claims adjustment and to address the problem of asymmetric information. Since administrative costs constitute part of premium, the more the administrative cost the more will be the premium rates. This problem becomes more critical in case of developing nations due to the predominance of low income and small landholding farmers. The smaller the policy (farm), the higher the administrative costs. The third challenge is how to include non-loanee farmers in crop insurance scheme. Fourthly, there are also problems of inclusion of more crops under the ambit of the existing crop insurance policy and lastly, how the poor farmers can afford to insurance premium, which relates to the question of premium subsidy by the government and obviously this question links with the present fiscal situation of the government. The present study provides valuable inputs to the government and private insurance companies (which is recently taking off in the nation) regarding how to improve awareness about crop insurance in terms of proper policy designing, not only to stabilize the income of small and marginal farmers and augment output production to counter the problem of agrarian distress, but also to reduce unending chain of farmers' suicide in different parts of the nation as witnessed in recent times.

References

Alagh Y.K. (2004), "Agricultural Policy in an open economy" in India's economic and social development : National and International perspective, International Conference in honour of Professor C.H.Hanumantha Rao, 16-17 November, Hyderabad Administrative Staff College of India and Centre for Economic and Social Studies.

All India Debt and Investment Survey, National Sample Survey Organization Report (various issues).

Annual Report (2013-14), Department of Agriculture and Cooperation, Government of India, , pp-89-90.

Bhalla G.S. and Singh G. (1997), "Recent developments in Indian agriculture: A state level analysis", Economic and Political Weekly,13.

Binswanger H.P. (1980), "Attitude towards Risk:Experimental Measurement in Rural India", American Agricultural Economics Association, August.

Birthal P.S. and Negi D.S. (2012), "Livestock for Higher, Sustainable and Inclusive Agricultural Growth",Economic and Political Weekly 47 (26 & 27), pp-89-99.

Central Statistical Organization Report, 2013, 2014, 2015.

Centre for Monitoring Indian Economy Private Limited (CMIE), Economic Intelligence Service, Agriculture, June 2010 Central Rice Research Institute Report, 2011.

Department of Agriculture and Cooperation, Government of India, Report of the Committee to Review the Implementation of Crop Insurance schemes in India, 2013-14, pp-40-41,93.

Dev S. M. and Rao N.C. (2010), "Agricultural Price Policy, Farm Profitability and Food Security", Economic and Political Weekly,45 (26&27), p-174-182.

Directorate of Economics and Statistics, Government of India, 2010. Economic Survey, Government of India, 2013-2014.

Ghosh N. and Yadav S.S.(2008), "Problems and Prospects of Crop Insurance : Reviewing Agricultural Risk and NAIS in India", Report to Institute of Economic Growth, University of Delhi Enclave, 30th September.

Goswami B.N., Venugopal V.,Sengupta D.,Madhusudan M.S., Price K.X.(2006), "Increasing trend of extreme rain events over India in a warming environment", Science 314 , pp-1442-1445.

Goudappa S.B., Reddy B.S., Chandrashekhar S.M.(2012), "Farmers Perception and Awareness about Crop Insurance in Karnataka",Indian Research Journal of Extension Education, Special Issue, Vol. II, pp-218-222.

Gulati A. and Narayanan S.(2003), "The subsidy syndrome in Indian agriculture", New Delhi, Oxford University Press.

Gulati A., Bathla S., (2002), 'Capital Formation in Indian Agriculture: Trends, Composition and Implications for Growth', National Bank for Agriculture and Rural Development, Mumbai, Occasional paper series-24.

Hardekar.J.B., R.B.M, Huirne and J.R. Anderson (1997) 'Coping with Risk in Agriculture',CAB International, New York.

Hazell P.B.R.(1988), "Risk and Uncertainty in Domestic Production and Prices", in J.W. Mellor and R.Ahmed edited book Agricultural Price Policy for Developing Countries, Oxford University Press, pp-96-102.

Indian Council of Agricultural Research Report 2011.

Indian Rural Development Report (2012-13), Orient Black Swan International Rice Research Institute Report 2007.

Jeromi P.D.(2007), "Farmers' Indebtedness and Suicides- Impact of Agricultural Trade Liberalization in Kerala",Economic and Political Weekly , August 4, 2007.

Kannan E., Sundaram S., (2011), 'Analysis of Trends in India's Agricultural Growth', Working paper 276, The Institute for Social and Economic Change (ISEC), Bangalore.

Kumar A., Singh K.M., Sinha S.,(2010), "Institutional Credit to Agriculture Sector in India :Status, Performance and Determinants", Agricultural Economics Research Review, Vol.23, pp 253-264.

Kumar D.S., Palanisami K., Ranganathan C.R., Venkatram R. (2010), "Farmers' Perception and Awareness towards Crop Insurance as a tool for Risk Management in Tamil Nadu" Indian Council of Agricultural Research, Centre for Agricultural and Rural Development Studies (CARDS), May, National Agricultural Innovation Project No. 40013101, Component IV.

Mahul O. and Stutley C.J. (2010), "Government Support to Agricultural Insurance: Challenges and Options for Developing countries", The World Bank, Washington, D.C.

Meterological Department of Government of India (various Reports)Ministry of Agriculture, Government of India, Reports (2012),2016.

Misra, V.N.(1998). 'Economic Reforms, Terms of Trade, Aggregate Supply and Private Investment in Agriculture Indian Experience', Economic and Political Weekly, August 1.

Mukherjee D. and Sarkar N. (2001), "Has there been an acceleration in the growth of agriculture

National Sample Survey Organization Report 2011.

Newbery D.M. and Stiglitz J.E.(1984), "The Theory of Commodity Price Stabilization : A study in the Economics of Risk", Oxford Economic Papers, New Series,November, Vol. 36, No. 3, pp- 336-358.

Newbery D.M.(1991), "Agricultural Institutions for Insurance and Stabilization",The Economic Theory of Agrarian Institutions, December, Oxford University Press.

Raju, S.S., Chand R., (2008), "A Study on the Performance of National Agricultural Insurance scheme and Suggestions to Make it More Effective"; Agricultural Economics Research Review, Vol.21, pp11-19.

Raju, S.S., Chand R., (2008), "Agricultural Insurance in India: Problems and Prospects", NCAP Working Paper No. 8, Indian Council of Agricultural Research, March.

Ramaswami B., Ravi S., Chopra S.D. (2004), "State of Indian farmer: A Millennium study", Risk Management, Department of Agriculture and Cooperation, Ministry of Agriculture, Government of India, Vol.-22, Academic Foundation, New Delhi.

Rath N., (1989) 'Agricultural Growth and Investment in India', Journal of Indian School of Political Economy, Vol.1, No.1, January – June.

Sharma V.P. and Thaker H. (2010), "Fertilizer subsidy in India: Who are the Beneficiaries?",Economic and Political Weekly, Vol XIV, No. 12, March 10.

Singh G. (2010), "Crop Insurance in India", Working Paper No. 2010-06-01, Research and Publication wing, Indian Institute of Management, Ahmadabad, June.

Singh S. (2004), "Crop Insurance in India – A Brief Review", Journal of Indian Social and Agricultural Statistics,57 (Special Volume), pp- 217-225.

Singh S., Vyas V.S. (2006) 'Crop Insurance in India: scope for improvement', Special Article, Economic and Political Weekly, November 4.

Sinha S (2004), 'Agriculture Insurance in India: Scope for participation of private insurers', Economic and Political Weekly, June 19.

Sinha S. (2007), 'Agriculture Insurance in India', Centre for Insurance and Risk Management, Working paper Series, June.

Sundar J. and Ramakrishnan L. (2013), "A study on Farmers' Awareness, Perception and willing to join and pay for Crop Insurance", International Journal of Business and Management Invention, Vol.2, Issue 1, January, pp-48-54.

Vaidyanathan A. (2006), "Farmers' Suicides and the Agrarian Crisis", Economic and Political Weekly, September 23, pp-4009-4013.

Vyas V.S., Singh S.(2005), 'Agricultural Crop Insurance: Performance and Needed Reforms', A Report submitted to Agriculture Insurance Company of India.

www.aicofindia.com www.cmie.com www.indiastat.com

17

Market Performance and Organic Farming: A Matrix of Caselets

Joydip Dasgupta

Abstract

Entrepreneurs take responsibility of their 'business' tad differently than their counterpart, the traditional businessman. A businessman walks on the pre-defined route whereas the entrepreneur creates his own alley-way, which if successful, becomes the rulebook for that trade. Lately, ecological issues have taken centre-stage as climatic changes have endangered the sustainable growth of the business. A new breed of entrepreneurs, alias ecopreneurs, functions in this 'new' space and endeavour to frame an innovative business landscape. Ecopreneurs possess singular focus on the safe-keep of the ecology. But in order to sustain the efforts of businesses in ecology, it is imperative that they remain economically viable too. Thus, ecopreneurial process is not only about fulfilling the business' responsibility towards ecology, but also about the marketability of the product or service. In order to evaluate the ecopreneurial process, organic farming is considered as a case. In this paper, selected organic farms are analysed in an environment - market continuum, developed particularly for this study which is in tandem with the works of Schaltegger (2002) and Blake and Mouton (1964).The study reveals inadequacy of market performance of the individual and farm level ecopreneurs in the state of West Bengal, in spite of their strong inclination towards care for the environment.

Keywords: Ecopreneurship, Business Ecology, Organic Farming

Introduction

Entrepreneurs take responsibility of their 'business' tad differently than their counterpart, the businessman. A businessman walks on the pre-defined route whereas the entrepreneur creates his own alley-way, which if successful, becomes the rulebook for that trade. The entrepreneur depends on innovation and uses a creative approach in his method of trade. He offers such products, services or processes which create an 'era' in that particular trade. On the other hand, the main objective of a businessman is to generate revenue by employing the human, financial, and other resources. In an attempt to be creative as well as sustainable in his endeavour, the entrepreneur has to look into newer avenues of the ever-changing society in order to find spaces where he can leave a mark.

In recent years ecological issues have taken centre-stage as climatic changes have endangered the sustainable growth of the business. Food safety[1] - a vital aspect of the welfare economy – is interrelated to the way food is produced/ processed. Large-scale, highly industrialized agriculture is considered as the conventional system of farming and is imperative to meet the growing needs of the population. There is an alternative way which advocates major shifts toward a more ecologically sustainable agriculture(Beus and Dunlap, 2010). This alternative way is termed organic farming[2] alias sustainable agriculture, regenerative agriculture or low-input agriculture which minimizes health-hazards. The specific features of this alternative way of agriculture are lower nitrogen application (which reduces nitrate concentrations in foods), avoidance of pesticides in the agriculture process (which ensures no pesticide residues in foods) and abstinence from use of chemical fertilizers (to ensure low concentrations of chemical residues). It is important to realize that theoretically, organic agro-products are costlier because the entrepreneurs in an attempt to internalise negative externalities end up raising private costs. Lately, a new breed of the entrepreneurs, alias ecopreneurs, has evolved who perceives the presence of an entrepreneurial opportunity in the frailty of the human environment and translates that into the business model. This paper attempts an assessment of the role of the ecopreneur in the domain of organic farming. The modified framework originally developed by Schaltegger (2002) is used in our study to assess the performance of certain selected organic farming enterprises and their market performance in the state of West Bengal.

Review of Literature

and deals with uncertainty (uninsurable risk) in order to reap financial benefit. In 1928, Joseph Schumpeter advanced the foremost theory of entrepreneurship; anyone seeking profits must innovate. The primary function of the entrepreneur is to convert an innovation into a successful business. It is the essential driver that enables him to withstand the competitive business environment. Subsequently the notion of 'creative destruction'[3] is introduced into the literature by Schumpeter as a technique of innovation. Israel Krizner differs significantly and highlights on 'opportunity' as the main facet in the realisation of entrepreneurial process. He showcases his argument on 'alertness' of the entrepreneur which is a mental state essential for early detection of profit opportunity.

In addition to the fundamental studies of Knight, Schumpeter and Krizner, there are several studies on the various functional aspects of entrepreneurship. While the study of Bennett (1991) pivots on entrepreneurship as start-up business, the studies made by Kyrö (2001) and Timmons (1986) consider the issue of striving for growth. Researches of Schumpeter (1934), Staber (1997), and Wiklund (1999) raise the issue of linkage of innovativeness and creation of competitive advantage as the most significant aspect of entrepreneurial endeavour.

Unsustainable use of environmental resources in the production process creates negative externality which generates disequilibrium in the market. This disruption in the market creates an entrepreneurial opportunity which the 'alert' entrepreneur can exploit in order to create a niche in the market and generate supernormal profit[4]. The 'alert' entrepreneur, also known as eco- entrepreneur/ ecopreneur/ green entrepreneur and sustainopreneur, interprets the issue of environmental degradation as an entrepreneurial opportunity. Bennett (1991), Berle (1991) and Blue (1990) initiated academic research on the issue of entrepreneurship and ecology. The common parlance of the research works of Anderson and Leal (1997), Andersen (1998), Decker et al. (1998), Isaak (1998), Keogh and Polonsky (1998), and Kyrö (2001) is the spill-over effect of the subject into the general terms of environmental economics and is inclined on environmental issues.

Melay and Kraus (2012) in a thought-provoking study argues that there is strong regional bias due to the origin of the articles as a substantial number of research work originates in only four countries (USA, UK, Canada, and Germany). It is evident from existing literature that though various authors have used various terms, viz. 'environmental entrepreneur', 'green entrepreneur,' 'eco-resources in order to create a niche in the market. The ecopreneurs create eco-entities which produce goods and services that are beneficial for the human environment. Ecopreneurs are anxious about the environment and are faithful towards 'sustainable' growth of the business. But for this they need to do their businesses for a substantially long period of time which is referred to as a sustainable business. For a sustainable business, foremost criterion is mitigating the uncertainty of net cash flows[5] which pivots on marketability.

Kotchen (2009) reflects on this aspect, market viability, to lessen the uncertainty in generation of cash flow for a sustainable eco-entity. Market for a particular product often does not pre-exist. Thus, the ecopreneur is often required to create market. Tenability of the ecopreneur depends on how successfully he bridges the gap between environmental consciousness and market success.

Schaper (2002) opines that in addition to government legislations and regulations, support agencies have to play an important role in making this entrepreneurial activity a successful one. Pivoting on several case studies, Kainrath (2009) infers three facets of ecopreneurship as the key to success; Eco – innovation, Eco – commitment, Eco – opportunity. Holger (2006) highlights that the success of the ecopreneur is a function of competitive advantage, which is linked to the entrepreneurial spirit. He probes on the much-debated question of environmental values and economic success.

Isaak (2002) introduces the concept of 'green-green' business and defines ecopreneur as one who radically transforms the economic sector in which he or she operates through his innovative green-green business. A significant departure is observed in the studies of Pastakia (1998, 2002) where the author interprets ecopreneurship as a social movement. The author considers entrepreneurial endeavour as environmental grass-root movement and emphasizes on 'individual initiative' as an instrument of change.

Certain common issues that are generated from the above-mentioned literature are as follows. To begin with, ecopreneurship embodies entrepreneurial endeavours with strong ecological focus. Second, the ecopreneur is an 'alert' entrepreneur, high on entrepreneurial spirit, who comprehends entrepreneurial opportunity in the environmental dilapidation that continually dampens human environment. Third, supportive role of the government along with facilitative role of the industry agencies acts as a catalyst for the growth of ecopreneurs. The Schaltegger (2002) framework is an appropriate model for assessing an ecopreneurial endeavour on the basis of the first two aspects.

Objective of the Study

The broad objective of the study is to make an assessment of selected ecopreneurs. Specifically, this paper tries to map this heterogeneous mix of ecopreneurs operating in the arena of organic farming with respect to their societal impact and commercial success, using a framework specifically designed for the purpose.

Research Methodology

Qualitative research is defined as research that utilizes results from open-ended interviewing to explore and understand the attitudes, opinions and feelings of individuals or a group of individuals (Wolcott, 1990). Pranati Datta (2004) opines that perception study of individual observation brings much more valid understandings about social processes than technically sound questionnaires, which are generally done in quantitative study. Perception study seems to be adequate for analyzing qualitative aspects like environmental consciousness of entrepreneurial endeavours. This study takes an explanatory approach and aims at capturing the perception of environmental consciousness of the entrepreneurial endeavours. This perception-based study is developed using responses to open-ended questions about the extent of environmental contributions of the ecopreneur and the commercial market success achieved by each respondent/set of respondents. To substantiate the secondary data-based learning, this study uses primary surveys of entrepreneurs from different parts of West Bengal.

It is imperative that the success of the entrepreneur depends not only on his focus on the environment but also on how well he is able to influence the market with his eco–friendly product, service and/or process. This is measured in terms of the market performance. The notion of market performance depends not only on how deep he can penetrate in the market but also on how long he is able to stay in business. In order to investigate how well the process of ecopreneurship is realised, the framework suggested by Schaltegger (2002) is relevant and matches our query of assessing the effectivity of the selected entrepreneurial endeavours. Taking queue from the study of Schaltegger (2002) we propose to position our chosen entrepreneurial endeavours in the environment–market continuum[6] in the light of two particular aspects; environmental focus (vertical axis) and market performance (horizontal axis). Accordingly, nine bubbles representing nine configured positions may be fitted in the environment – market matrix (Figure 1), which are given as follows:

iii. Entrepreneurs who have less influence on the market but have significant environmental focus. (Alternative Actors)

iv. Entrepreneurs who are able to penetrate the market moderately but have very less environmental focus.

v. Entrepreneurs with moderate market performance along with moderate environmental focus.

vi. Entrepreneurs with moderate market performance but high environmental focus. (Bioneers)

vii. Entrepreneurs who have penetrated the market significantly but have very low environmental focus.

viii. Entrepreneurs with high market performance along with moderate environmental focus. (Ecopreneurs)

ix. Entrepreneurs with high market performance along with high environmental focus.

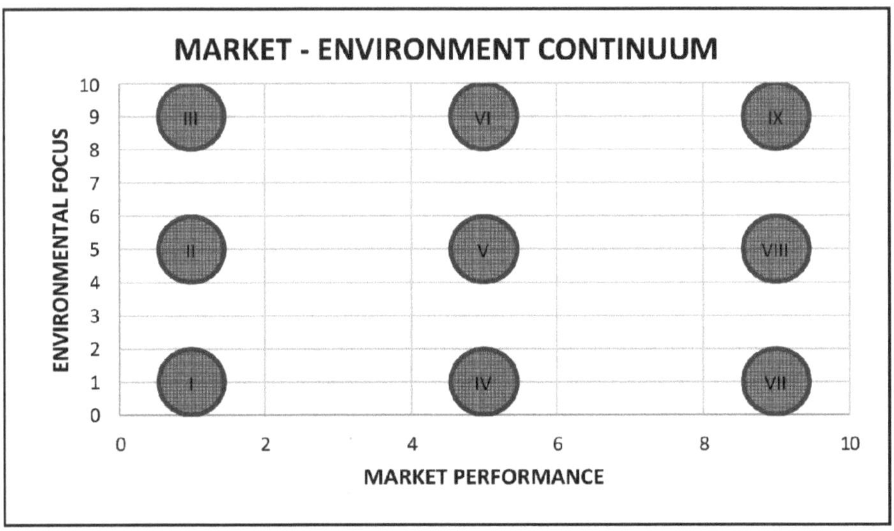

Fig. 1: The Environment – Market Continuum
Source: Author

In our model high environmental focus is represented by III, VI and IX which have strong environmental focus. Schaltegger (2002) refers to III as alternative duty and environmental management (whose environmental goals are supplementary to core business goals ie, moderate environmental focus V and VIII). We submit here in line with the definition of ecopreneur proposed by Pastakia (1998), that the ecopreneur is more focused on the environment and the market performance is not the primary agenda. Only in case of VII the entrepreneur takes mass marketing drive while keeping the environmental protection role as a trustee.

The Findings

A survey of thirty-five respondents has been conducted in the state of West Bengal which is clubbed into 16 homogeneous clusters. Figure 2 is a pictorial representation of the clusters. The respondents were heterogeneous in the sense that some were individual eco-based entrepreneurs, some others operated in partnerships or cooperatives and some respondents were managers of non-governmental organizations (NGOs). However, their common thread was strong environment-friendly agri-activities in the commonly used terminology of 'organic farming'. The respondents were chosen on the basis of information regarding their eco-conscious attitude for their farming system. For this purpose, advice provided by members of 'Jouthya Samabay'[7] has been considered. Questions are focused mainly regarding the nature of fertiliser, manure and pesticides used by the self-claimed eco-conscious farmers. Some questions are associated with the personal lifestyle of the farmers. Some of the respondents are organic agri- operators and some others are consultants and play advisory roles. However, each enterprise cluster filled in one questionnaire for this study.

Since all the respondents are directly or indirectly associated with organic/natural/pure farming and are self-claimed proponents of the grass-root environment movement, it may be reasonably assumed that they are all at the higher end of the Y axis, representing high level of environmental focus. But the degree of environmental contribution is found to be varying amongst the respondents. While some vehemently objected the use of chemicals in agro – farming, others used chemicals in dire cases[8] and differed with the opinion expressed by environmental experts, assurance agencies and media in this regard. The responses from the entrepreneurs regarding their environment-related activities and market performance are gathered on a scale of 00 to 09 based on open ended questions. Each of the 16 clusters (some are individual respondents, some others are groups as explained in Figure 2) has been allotted a combined average score for their market performance (as an indicator of

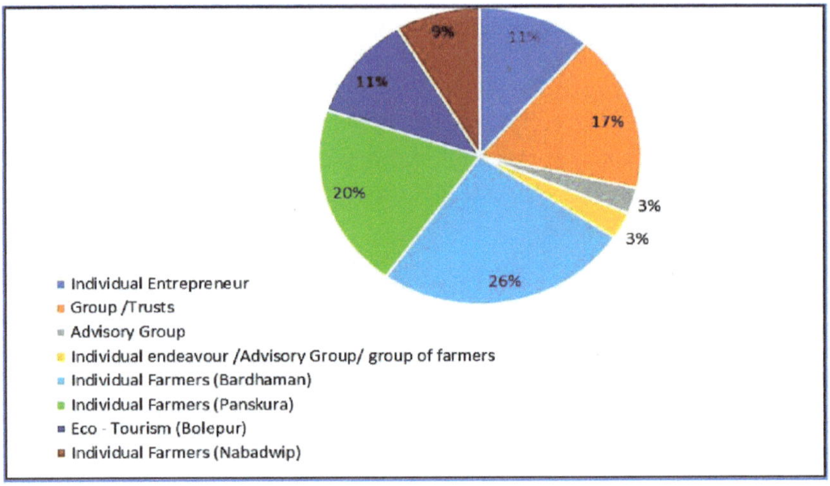

Fig. 2: The Respondents
Source: Author

One particular ecopreneurial endeavour (Respondent K) has obtained a perfect score of environmental focus as well as market performance. It is considered as the frame of reference because of its successful business model which has helped the respondent sustain in the competitive environment alongside maintaining its environmental concerns.

Respondent I, one of the entrepreneurial endeavours under study, is a non-government development organization working in fourteen (14) districts of West Bengal and other states. Its major concern is to address the issue of food and livelihood security of the rural poor through sustainable management of natural resources. They focus primarily on ecologically appropriate farming practices that have been able to reach out to almost eight thousand farmers in the state of West Bengal. Following their responses They are allotted highest score (09) as regards their environmental focus. As such they are not organic farmers neither do they have direct linkage with the market for organically produced agro – products. But they have seriously performed the organically produced agro – products trade and has substantial indirect influence on the market, more in the form of B2B model. They have very recently taken up marketing of two organically produced agro – products from the district of Malda[9] , though their direct market performance is observed to be 01 in our model) is low.

Respondent A[10] is a grass-root entrepreneurial endeavour in the districts of penetration. Thus, on the basis of their response they are ranked very highly (09) as regards their environmental focus but ranked moderately (04) as regards their market penetration.

Some farmers (ten [10] in number) residing mainly in the village of Debibarpur, district of Bardhaman were also interviewed about their concern for the environment[11]. For simplicity and for convenience of our academic pursuit, the farmers of this region are clustered (Respondent M). Analysis reveals that their concerns for environment are not uniform and are biased as regards the agricultural produce that they set aside for their household consumption. In case of emergency they use chemicals indiscreetly (may be a dash less than the absolute commercial agro – producer).The individual farmers considered as ecopreneurs for this cluster scored more than the mid-value (five [05]) as regards their environmental focus but have very little contribution to the market as produce is not supplied to the market. Thus, they are ranked zero as to their market performance.

Three entrepreneurial endeavours (D in the sample) selected in Bolepur, are considered in the study because of their eco – centric commitment towards the community they cater to. All three of them clustered as one, practice organic production in their holdings. All three respondents of these cluster exhibited significant environmental consciousness and thus score six (06) as regards their environmental focus but has almost zero market performance. The point of argument is that their core business activity is the eco–tourist centers and merely for that purpose, organic farming is being carried out which puts a serious question mark on their eco – commitment. The only contribution they offer to the market is organic agri – produce for their guests of the eco – tourist centre they run. A score of one (01) is allotted as regards the market performance of these ecopreneurial endeavours.

Seven (07) individual agro – producers (respondent O) of the village of Dharanda and Janabarh in the District of Purba-Medinipur were interviewed. It is observed that the farmers have a less than moderate commitment towards human environment and their preference for not using chemical fertilizer and pesticides is only superfluous. Almost all of them point that insufficient and irregular supply of organic manure and organic fertilizers along with issue of productivity enforce them to use chemical fertilizers and manures. It is also observed that the larger the area under cultivation the lower is the environmental focus and vice versa. These agro – farmers have significant market penetration, especially, for their

Some other ecopreneurial endeavours (Respondents B, C, D, E, F, G, H, J and Respondent L) which work at individual level are also positioned in our environmental focus – market performance continuum on the basis of perception developed during the course of the survey. They report high environment score but low market success.

Respondent P comprises of three agro – farmers around the town of Nabadwip who practice agro – farming as they are desirous of offering chemical-free agricultural produce to their family God. They have no commercial agenda and hence get a score of 0 on market success and high score of 7 on environment.

The result of the survey is represented in the position matrix (Table 1) and a pictorial representation of the position matrix is shown in Figure 3 (Environment –Market Continuum).

Table 1: Position Matrix of the Ecopreneurial Endeavours

Sl.No.	Entrepreneurship	Score	
		Market	Environment
1.	Respondent A	4	9
2.	Respondent B	2.5	7.5
3.	Respondent C	3	7
4.	Respondent D	1	6
5.	Respondent E	3	8
6.	Respondent F	2	7
7.	Respondent G	2	8
8.	Respondent H	2	6
9.	Respondent I	1	9
10.	Respondent J	1	8
11.	Respondent K	**9**	**9**
12.	Respondent L	2	7.5
13.	Respondent M	0	6
14.	Respondent N	0.5	6
15.	Respondent O	7	4
16.	Respondent P	0	7

Source: Author's Own

Note: Scores on environmental focus and market performance is allotted to each group/ individual endeavour considering the ecopreneurial endeavour of K (Sl. no. 11) as the frame of reference

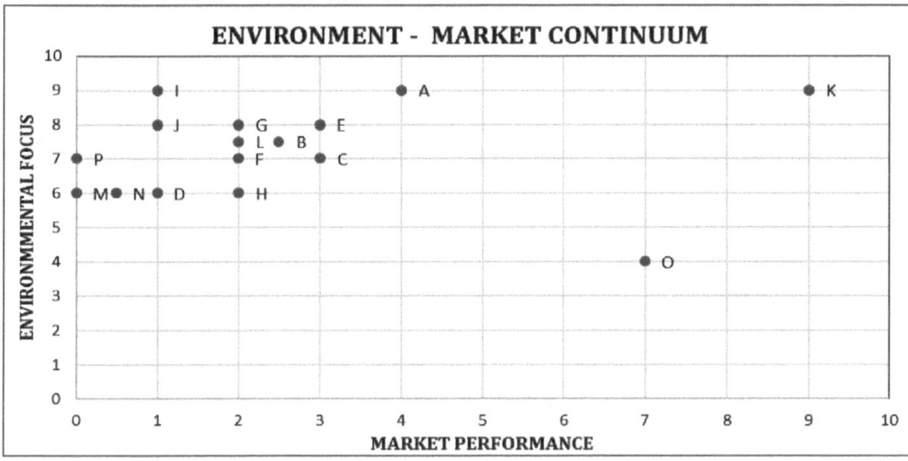

Fig. 3: The Environment – Market Continuum
Source: Author

Findings

From the survey it is observed that all the respondents rank highly on the index of eco- consciousness. In this respect the only exception is respondent O (cluster of agro-farmers of villages in and around Panskura, West Bengal). Responses on the interview with the agro- farmers (respondents O) suggest that in order to sustain in the business and in response to the market demand on value-for-money and conventionally accepted colour of the products, they compromise with their eco – consciousness.

In this case, our study suggests that market performance and eco-friendliness are inversely related with each other.

The ecopreneur, in order to have a long term societal impact, has to depend not only on his focus on the environment but also on the market performance (tradability of his eco – friendly product and/or service). Our study suggests that the ecopreneurs who are focussed on environmentally friendliness of the product and/or service and process are low on market performance, except for the respondent K which has achieved success on both parameters. Thus, ecopreneurs are advised to create a successful business model in order to sustain in the business and create positive vive for the society.

Conclusion

innovations. These initiatives include a challenge on behalf of the eco – conscious producers to internalise, minimise or neutralise the negative environmental externalities associated with a conventional production process. An analogy is derived in the comment made by Paul Brooks in respect to Rachael Carson's *Silent Spring* where 'individual initiative' and 'courage' is underscored in order to make the world (human environment) a better place to live in. Significantly, Pastakia (2002) made subtle modifications to his earlier opinion of who an ecopreneur is and writes; 'the definition of ecopreneurs has been broadened to include those ongoing enterprises that have succeeded in bringing about change'. Thus, the author embraces the element of 'success' as a yardstick for realisation of the ecopreneurial process. It is imperative that in order to ensure a long-term impact on society, which is the primary intent of these 'change agents', the ecopreneurial endeavours have to sustain in business as long as possible. Thus, long term sustenance is the key to what Pastakia states as 'successes'.

On drawing analogy with the Schaltegger framework and integrating Pastakia's opinion, we find that respondent K is an 'ecoprenuer', respondent O belongs to the 'environmental management' category and respondent A is a 'Bioneer' while Respondents B, E and C are progressing into 'Bioneers'

In this light, our paper investigates the market performance of the some ecopreneurial endeavours which are eco-initiatives either at individual level or at farm level. The ecopreneurial endeavours are chosen to include only those who have robust eco – consciousness/eco - commitment and for that purpose enterprises associated with the process of organic farming are chosen. The study reveals that high 'market performance' is not evident amongst all the ecopreneurial endeavours except the self-claimed organic farmers of the village of Dharinda, Panskura (O) and its surrounding who have achieved commercial success but are low on their environmental contribution. But the other respondents who are strong in their environmental focus have not achieved much on their market success score.

The author posits that marketability, the efforts of 'Jouthya Samabay' are noteworthy. They are not only assisting with the marketing of the organically produced agro – products but also organising camps and talks of several environmental experts to raise awareness. Their efforts act as an outreach programme for individual initiatives at grass-root level as the crusade of individuals, who are working relentlessly for the resurrection of forgotten folk rice varieties of Bengal that are brought to the notice of the consumer.

West Bengal, is in nascent stage as regards their market success and still remains a social movement at grass-root level. This is in conformity with the definition of the ecopreneur as stated by Pastakia in 1998 but severely fall short of the 'success' which Pastakia included in his definition of the ecopreneur in 2002. The learnings from this study lead the authors to suggest that the lacunae in success of organic production lies in its market performance. Hence the desired focus of potential agri- entrepreneurs is to strike a balance between the responsibilities towards environmental and commercial success which is not necessarily a downward sloping curve.

References

Agriculture, Profitability and Climate Change: Can Accounting Help Identify Best Farming Practices? Empirical Case Study in Spain. (n.d.). Retrieved January 9, 2019, from https://www.scirp.org/journal/PaperInformation.aspx?PaperID=74607

Alam, M. S., & Mohiuddin, G. (2014). Chronological Development of Entrepreneurship Concept – A Critical Evaluation. American Journal of Economics, 4(2), 130–135.

Allah, M. A., & Nakhaie, H. (n.d.). Entrepreneurship and risk – taking. 3.

Anderson, A. R. (1998). Cultivating the Garden of Eden: environmental entrepreneuring. Journal of Organizational Change Management, 11(2), 135–144. https://doi.org/10.1108/09534819810212124

Ardichvili, A., Cardozo, R., & Ray, S. (2003). A theory of entrepreneurial opportunity identification and development. Journal of Business Venturing, 18(1), 105–123. https://doi.org/10.1016/S0883- 9026(01)00068-4

Beus, C. E., & Dunlap, R. E. (2010). Conventional versus Alternative Agriculture: The Paradigmatic Roots of the Debate*. Rural Sociology, 55(4), 590–616. https://doi.org/10.1111/j.1549-0831.1990.tb00699.x

Brooke, G. T. F. (2010). Uncertainty, Profit and Entrepreneurial Action: Frank Knight's Contribution Reconsidered. Journal of the History of Economic Thought, 32(02), 221–235. https://doi.org/10.1017/S1053837210000179

Croitoru, A. (2012). Schumpeter, J.A., 1934 (2008), The Theory of Economic Development: An Inquiry into Profits, Capital, Credit, Interest and the Business Cycle, translated from the German by Redvers Opie, New Brunswick (U.S.A) and London (U.K.): Transaction Publishers.3(2), 12.

Crosson, P. (1989). What is alternative agriculture? American Journal of Alternative Agriculture, 4(1), 28–32. https://doi.org/10.1017/S0889189300002599

Datta, P. (2004). Push-Pull Factors of Undocumented Migration from Bangladesh to West Bengal: A Perception Study. The Qualitative Report, 9(2), 335–358.

Davidsson, P. (2004). A general theory of entrepreneurship: The individual-opportunity nexus. International Small Business Journal, 22, 206–209.

Death of a Small Planet. (n.d.). Retrieved November 9, 2018, from http://dwardmac.pitzer.edu/Anarchist_Archives/bookchin/planet/planet.html

Decker, R. L., Lorentz, R. D., Hostager, T. J., & Neil, T. C. (1998). Seeing environmental opportunities: effects of intrapreneurial ability, efficacy, motivation and desirability. Journal

Dejardin, M., Nizet, J., & Dam, D. V. (2015). Entrepreneurial functions by organic farmers. Retrieved from https://www.elgaronline.com/view/9781849808231.00027.xml

Douglas Keogh, P., & Polonsky, M. (1998). Environmental Commitment: A Basis for Environmental Entrepreneurship? Journal of Organizational Change Management, 11, 38–49. https://doi.org/10.1108/09534819810369563

E. Beus, C., & Dunlap, R. (1990). Conventional Versus Alternative Agriculture: The Paradigmatic Roots of the Debate. Rural Sociology, 55, 590–616. https://doi.org/10.1111/j.1549-0831.1990.tb00699.x

Eckhardt, J., & A Shane, S. (2003). Opportunities and Entrepreneurship. Journal of Management. Journal of Management, 29, 333–349. https://doi.org/10.1016/S0149-2063(02)00225-8

Entrepreneurship alsökonomischer Prozeß - Perspektivenzur Förderungunternehmerischen Handelns | Springer. (n.d.). Retrieved January 18, 2019, from https://www.springer.com/de/book/9783824466276

Farinelli, F., Bottini, M., &Akkoyunlu, S. (2011). Green entrepreneurship: the missing link towards a greener economy. 8(3), 7.

Frese, M., & M. Gielnik, M. (2014). The Psychology of Entrepreneurship. Annual Review of Organizational Psychology and Organizational Behavior, 1, 413–438. https://doi.org/10.1146/annurev-orgpsych-031413- 091326

Gedik, ª., Miman, M., &Kesici, M. S. (2015). Characteristics and Attitudes of Entrepreneurs Towards Entrepreneurship. Procedia - Social and Behavioral Sciences, 195, 1087–1096. https://doi.org/10.1016/j.sbspro.2015.06.153

Gibbs, D. (2006). Sustainability Entrepreneurs, Ecopreneurs and the Development of a Sustainable Economy. Greener Management International, (55), 63–78.

Gupta, A. K., & Prakash, A. (n.d.). On Internalization of Externalities. 26.

Introduction to the Methods Used to Study Perception - The Mind Project. (n.d.). Retrieved January 14, 2019, from http://www.mind.ilstu.edu/curriculum/perception_intro/intro_to_methods_short.php

Isaak, R. (2002). The Making of the Ecopreneur. Greener Management International, 2002(38), 81–91. https://doi.org/10.9774/GLEAF.3062.2002.su.00009

Kainrath, D. (2009). Ecopreneurship in Theory and Practice: A Proposed Emerging Framework for Ecopreneurship. Retrieved from http://urn.kb.se/resolve?urn=urn:nbn:se:umu:diva-30102

Kirzner, Entrepreneurship & the Market Approach to Development - Online Library of Liberty. (n.d.). Retrieved November 1, 2018, from http://oll.libertyfund.org/pages/kirzner-entrepreneurship-the-market- approach-to-development

Kirzner, I. M. (1960). The economic point of view. Ludwig von Mises Institute.

Klein, P. G. (2008). Opportunity discovery, entrepreneurial action, and economic organization. Strategic Entrepreneurship Journal, 2(3), 175–190. https://doi.org/10.1002/sej.50

Klein, P. G. (2010). The capitalist and the entrepreneur: essays on organizations and markets. Auburn, Ala: Ludwig von Mises Inst.

Knight, F. H. (n.d.). Risk, Uncertainty, and Profit. 445.

Kotchen, M. J. (n.d.). Voluntary Provision of Public Goods for Bads: A Theory of Environmental Offsets (SSRN Scholarly Paper No. ID 1375992). Retrieved from Social Science Research Network website: https://papers.ssrn.com/abstract=1375992

Kotchen, M. J. (2009). Some microeconomics of eco-entrepreneurship. In Advances in the Study of Entrepreneurship, Innovation & Economic Growth: Vol.20. Frontiers in Eco-

Kyrö, P. (2015). Handbook of Entrepreneurship and Sustainable Development Research. https://doi.org/10.4337/9781849808248

Laino, A. (2012). The Externality (SSRN Scholarly Paper No. ID 2042626). Retrieved from Social Science Research Network website: https://papers.ssrn.com/abstract=2042626

Lenox, M., & York, J. (2012). Environmental Entrepreneurship. The Oxford Handbook of Business and the Natural Environment. https://doi.org/10.1093/oxfordhb/9780199584451.003.0004

Lytle, M. H. (2007). The gentle subversive: Rachel Carson, Silent spring, and the rise of the environmental movement. New York: Oxford University Press.

Making Ecopreneurs: Developing Sustainable Entrepreneurship (2nd ed.). (2012). International Journal of Entrepreneurial Behavior& Research, 18(3), 383–386. https://doi.org/10.1108/13552551211228052

Melay, I., & Kraus, S. (2012). Green entrepreneurship: Definitions of related concepts. Int. J. Strateg.

Manag, 12, 1-12.

Micro-ecopreneurs and the UK food industry: short-term fad or sustainable reality? | Industrial and Commercial Training | Vol 45, No 6. (n.d.). Retrieved December 1, 2018, from https://www.emeraldinsight.com/doi/abs/10.1108/ICT-02-2013-0004

Nemes, N. (n.d.). Comparative Analysis of Organic and Non-Organic Farming Systems: A Critical Assessment Of Farm Profitability. 39.

Nicholas Georgescu-Roegen. (2018). In Wikipedia. Retrieved from https:/en.wikipedia. org/ w/ index.php? title=Nicholas_Georgescu-Roegen&oldid=865851391

Pastakia, A. (1998). Grassroots ecopreneurs: change agents for a sustainable society. Journal of Organizational Change Management, 11(2), 157–173. https://doi.org/10.1108/09534819810212142

Pastakia, A. (2002). Assessing Ecopreneurship in the Context of a Developing Country The case of. India, Greener Management International, 108.

Perception Study – NEVIR Pedia. (n.d.). Retrieved January 14, 2019, from http://www.nevirpedia.nl/manual/ir- programme/perception-study

Petrariu, I. R., Bumbac, R., &Ciobanu, R. (n.d.). Innovation: a path to competitiveness and economic growth.

The case of CEE countries. 12.

Reingold, E. M., & Merikle, P. M. (1988). Using direct and indirect measures to study perception without awareness. Perception & Psychophysics, 44(6), 563–575. https://doi.org/10.3758/BF03207490

Reviews. (2004). International Small Business Journal, 22(2), 206–216. https://doi.org/10.1177/0266242604043697

Ricketts, M., & Kirzner, I. M. (1992a). Kirzner's Theory of Entrepreneurship-A Critique. In B. J. Caldwell & S. Boehm (Eds.), Austrian Economics: Tensions and New Directions (pp. 67–102). https://doi.org/10.1007/978-94-011-2186-6_3

Ricketts, M., & Kirzner, I. M. (1992b). Kirzner's Theory Of Entrepreneurship-A Critique. In B. J. Caldwell &

S. Boehm (Eds.), Austrian Economics: Tensions and New Directions (pp. 67–102). https://doi.org/10.1007/978-94-011-2186-6_3

Risk, Uncertainty, and Profit. (n.d.). Retrieved January 18, 2019, from Econlib website: https://www.econlib.org/library/Knight/knRUP.html

Schaltegger, S. (2002b). A Framework for Ecopreneurship Leading Bioneers and Environmental Managers to Ecopreneurship.

Schaper, M. (2002). Introduction: The Essence of Ecopreneurship. Greener Management International, 2002(38), 26–30. https://doi.org/10.9774/GLEAF.3062.2002.su.00004

Schaper, M. (2016). Making Ecopreneurs: Developing Sustainable Entrepreneurship. CRC Press.

Shane, S., & Venkataraman, S. (2000). The Promise of Entrepreneurship as a Field of Research. The Academy of Management Review, 25(1), 217–226. https://doi.org/10.2307/259271

Short, J. C., Ketchen, D. J., Shook, C. L., & Ireland, R. D. (2010). The Concept of "Opportunity" in Entrepreneurship Research: Past Accomplishments and Future Challenges. Journal of Management, 36(1), 40–65. https://doi.org/10.1177/0149206309342746

Œledzik, K. (2013a). Schumpeter's View on Innovation and Entrepreneurship. SSRN Electronic Journal. https://doi.org/10.2139/ssrn.2257783

Œledzik, K. (2013b). Schumpeter's View on Innovation and Entrepreneurship. SSRN Electronic Journal. https://doi.org/10.2139/ssrn.2257783

Œledzik, K. (2013c). Schumpeter's View on Innovation and Entrepreneurship. SSRN Electronic Journal. https://doi.org/10.2139/ssrn.2257783

Taylor, D. W., & Walley, E. E. (Liz). (2004). The green entrepreneur: Opportunist, Maverick or Visionary? International Journal of Entrepreneurship and Small Business, 1(1–2), 56–69. https://doi.org/10.1504/IJESB.2004.005377

Ucbasaran, D., Westhead, P., & Wright, M. (2008). Opportunity Identification and Pursuit: Does an Entrepreneur's Human Capital Matter? Small Business Economics, 30(2), 153–173.

University of National and World Economy, &Gevrenova, T. (2015). Nature and characteristics of green entrepreneurship. Trakia Journal of Science, 13(Suppl.2), 321–323. https://doi.org/ 10.15547/tjs.2015.s.02.068

Wagener, S., Gorgievski, M., &Rijsdijk, S. (2010). Businessman or host? Individual differences between entrepreneurs and small business owners in the hospitality industry. The Service Industries Journal, 30(9), 1513–1527. https://doi.org/10.1080/02642060802624324

Wagner, M. (2009). Eco-entrepreneurship: An empirical perspective based on survey data. In G. D. Libecap (Ed.), Advances in the Study of Entrepreneurship, Innovation & Economic Growth (Vol. 20, pp. 127– 152). https://doi.org/10.1108/S1048-4736(2009)0000020009

Wasdani, K. P., & Mathew, M. (2014). Potential for opportunity recognition: differentiating entrepreneurs. International Journal of Entrepreneurship and Small Business, 23(3), 336. https://doi.org/10.1504/IJESB.2014.065526

Wiklund, J., & Shepherd, D. (2003). Knowledge-based resources, entrepreneurial orientation, and the performance of small and medium-sized businesses. Strategic Management Journal, 24(13), 1307–1314. https://doi.org/10.1002/smj.360

Wiklund, J., & Shepherd, D. (2005a). Entrepreneurial orientation and small business performance: a configurational approach. Journal of Business Venturing, 20(1), 71–91. https://doi.org/10.1016/j.jbusvent.2004.01.001

Wiklund, J., & Shepherd, D. (2005b). Entrepreneurial orientation and small business performance: a configurational approach. Journal of Business Venturing, 20(1), 71–91. https://doi.org/10.1016/j.jbusvent.2004.01.001

WOLCOTT, H. F. (1990). MAKING A STUDY "MORE ETHNOGRAPHIC." Journal of Contemporary Ethnography, 19(1), 44–72. https://doi.org/10.1177/089124190019001003

Endnotes

[1]Food safety is a scientific discipline describing handling, preparation, and storage of food in ways that prevent food-borne illness. [https://en.wikipedia.org/wiki/Food_safety]

[2]Organic Farming is a sustainable method which depends upon natural way of farming and using techniques like crop rotation, vermi-composting, bio-fertilizers, crop management, animal manure, off-farm organic waste, crop residues etc., instead of synthetic chemicals, which allows soil to stay alive and food to besafe. [https://medcraveonline.com/MOJFPT/MOJFPT-04- 00092.pdf]

[3]The term 'creative destruction', was first used by Joseph Schumpeter in his book titled Capitalism, Socialism and Democracy (1942) to define the process of disintegration that brings about revolutionary changes in the economic structure from within and in the process creates a new system. [https://www.investopedia.com/terms/c/creativedestruction.asp].

[4]Normal profit is the factor payment for 'organization'. It is also considered as a return for bearing risk of operation. But 'above normal profit' is the return generated for bearing 'uncertainty'. This argument is forwarded in an earlier section of this paper and follows discussion on risk and uncertainty by Frank knight in 1921.

[5]Net cash flows – excess of cash inflows over cash outflow – is the main objective of operations of a business. Though 'profit/loss' – income over expenditure (or vice versa) – is frequently used as parameter of wellbeing of business net cash flow generation is considered as the true reflection of wellbeing of the business from the perspective of the internal stakeholders of the business.

[6]The framework developed has analogy to the Blake and Mouton managerial grid. [http:// www. dcookacademic.com/uploads/1/0/8/8/10887248/blake_mouton_ managerial_ grid.pdf]

[7]'JouthyaSamabay" is an entrepreneurial endeavour of a group of people who are occupationally engaged otherwise and has embarked upon the task of raising consciousness of consumers regarding food safety and in the process, are developing themselves as a marketing service for organically produced food products in Kolkata. They have recently started a retail outlet of organically produced and processed food products and some other related items at Mandirtala, Howrah.

[8]They (Madan Maity, KhokanBera and Shanti Prasad Ghosh and others) opined that there is no escaping the attacks of 'majra' and 'golpachak' (pests) and then certain pesticides like 'Hamla', 'Bilbo' and 'ContafPlus' has to be applied to save the produce.

[9]This information is collected through discussion with one member of 'JouthyaSamabay".

[10]One of the leading ecopreneurs of this endeavour is Chinmoy whose personal environmental consciousness in purported in the entrepreneurship.

[11]This feed was collected from one member of 'JouthyaSamabay" as they collected some Organic products from the area for sale in and around Kolkata.

FSC
www.fsc.org
MIX
Papier | Fördert gute Waldnutzung
FSC® C083411

Kolibri 360 GmbH
Ferdinand-Jühlke-Straße 7
99095 Erfurt, Deutschland
produktsicherheit@kolibri360.de